T0246395

'Across Europe, the period of fascist dictat
emergence of brave networks of resistanc
illuminates the stories of Irish involvement
racy. The bravery of Samuel Beckett is here,
more forgotten men and women. How many of us knew the name of
Maureen Patricia O'Sullivan? This book is a reminder that at times
service involves more than fighting, as we meet people in every aspect
of the resistance movements who played their part. A triumph.'

Donal Fallon, author

'An eye-opening account of how ordinary people caught up in
extraordinary situations helped to fight the Nazis, despite Irish
neutrality. From helping fugitives to breaking codes, from gathering intelligence to sabotage, from active service with the resistance
to propaganda, the sheer range of activities is astonishing. Some of
those who resisted are well known, but most are not; their courage
has been recognised at last in this ground-breaking book.'

David McCullagh, broadcaster and historian

'This is a truly important and groundbreaking book, which brings
together the extraordinary stories of more than 50 individuals who
were involved with the Resistance to Fascist regimes during World
War II. Some are already known, like Delia Murphy and Samuel
Beckett, while others well deserve to have their often dramatic and
heroic lives brought to light – such as Catherine Crean, who died at
Ravensbrück concentration camp, or the indomitable Kerrywoman
Janie McCarthy – who served in five Resistance movements – or the
Cork nursing nun Sr Katherine McCarthy. Men, of course, were
active in the Resistance networks but it is often the women's lives
which emerge so strikingly – especially in cases like that of Mary
Herbert, who gave birth to a baby while acting valiantly as a courier
in France.

Our view of history constantly evolves and acquires fresh
reassessments, and *The Irish in the Resistance* brings a vital new
perspective to the history of Ireland during a period which has
shaped so much of modern consciousness. Clodagh Finn and John
Morgan write with knowledge and authority, their work backed by
meticulous research, unearthing some archive material previously
unknown. And there is a compelling feeling for the humanity of
these remembered lives: here the poignant personal stories inter-
twine with the great drama of European history.'

Mary Kenny, author and journalist

THE
IRISH
—— IN THE ——
RESISTANCE

Clodagh Finn is a journalist and author of *Through Her Eyes: A History of Ireland in 21 Women* and *A Time to Risk All*, a biography of Mary Elmes, the 'Irish Oskar Schindler'.

In 2022, she collaborated with the Lord Mayor of Dublin, Alison Gilliland, to write *Her Keys to the City*, highlighting the overlooked contributions of 80 women who shaped Dublin.

She writes 'An Irishwoman's Diary' in the *Irish Examiner* and has worked as a sub-editor and feature writer for several newspapers, and as a freelance writer and editor in Paris. She has a degree in French and Archaeology from University College Dublin and is particularly interested in writing about overlooked people from history.

John Morgan is a lawyer who has a longstanding interest in the history of World War II, particularly in relation to Allied Resistance and escape lines. John is a Trustee of the Escape Lines Memorial Society (UK) and co-founder of the Basque Pyrenees Freedom Trails' Association (Basque Country/Spain).

THE
IRISH
— IN THE —
RESISTANCE

THE UNTOLD STORIES OF THE ORDINARY
HEROES WHO RESISTED HITLER

CLODAGH FINN AND JOHN MORGAN

Gill Books

Gill Books
Hume Avenue
Park West
Dublin 12
www.gillbooks.ie

Gill Books is an imprint of M.H. Gill and Co.

978 07171 9135 2

Designed by Marsha Swan
Edited by Noel O'Regan
Proofread by Sally Vince
Printed and bound in Great Britain by Clays Ltd,
Elcograf S.p.A.
This book is typeset in Sabon.

*The paper used in this book comes from the wood
pulp of sustainably managed forests.*

A CIP catalogue record for this book is available
from the British Library.

5 4 3 2 1

MIX
Paper | Supporting
responsible forestry
FSC
www.fsc.org   FSC® C018072

To Peter and Eileen, with love,
and for two exceptional Toms
(Finn and Kennedy)

Denmark
Monica de Wichfield

United Kingdom

Netherlands

Rubel Ross

Agnes Bernelle

London

Germany

Belgium
Brussels

Robert Armstrong

Catherine Crean

Bill Magrath

Janie McCarthy

Mary Cummins and
Mary O'Shaughnessy

Fr Kenneth Monaghan

Paris

Margaret Kelly

Samuel Beckett

France

Switzerland

Maureen 'Paddy' O'Sullivan

Clermont-Ferrand

Italy
Vatican City

Turin

Bordeaux

Mary Herbert

Brian Rafferty

John Keany

Delia Murphy Kiernan

Pyrenees

Spain
Madrid

Contents

INTRODUCTION

The Dawn of the Resistance

From a Spark to a Flame

On 18 June 1940, General Charles de Gaulle stepped in front of a microphone at the BBC in London and delivered a rousing speech, urging the French to resist Nazi forces. 'Whatever happens, the flame of French Resistance must not and will not be extinguished,' the self-appointed leader of the French in exile said.

His rallying call would later be credited with providing the spark that ignited a resistance movement not only in France but anywhere the Third Reich had boots on the ground. Few heard his speech, but news of it spread. People responded in myriad ways, depending on their circumstances.

Among them, some 50-plus Irish men and women would, over the course of the war, risk their lives to resist Nazi occupation. For the most part, they were ordinary people – governesses, teachers, gardeners, housewives, priests and nuns – who found themselves in an extraordinary situation and took incalculable risks to help another human being in difficulty.

Some took up arms; others gathered intelligence, sheltered fugitives, hid Jews, carried messages, committed acts of sabotage or parachuted behind enemy lines. Some of them even died for the Resistance.

Yet, few are remembered, with the exception of writer and playwright Samuel Beckett, who famously returned to France from a holiday in Ireland the day after war was declared on 3 September 1939. 'You simply couldn't stand by with your arms folded,' he said. His work as a translator and intelligence-gatherer who went to the 'edge of daring' for the Gloria SMH resistance network is well known. When the network was blown in 1943, he narrowly escaped arrest and fled to the south of France where he, again, joined a resistance cell.

The heroic work of many others, though, has passed under the radar. Ordinary heroes such as Janie McCarthy, a teacher from Killarney, Co. Kerry, who joined at least five different networks during the war. She was introduced to the Resistance by her friend and student Elisabeth Barbier, one of the relatively few French people to hear General de Gaulle's broadcast live. Barbier was so inspired by his passionate words that she resolved, there and then, 'to do something', even though scoliosis often confined her to a *chaise longue*. She enlisted Janie McCarthy's help, which explains how a teacher in Paris came to join one of the earliest resistance networks to establish contact with London.

General de Gaulle's spirited message gave hope at a time when morale was at an all-time low. The lightning assault by German troops on north-west Europe had been rapid and devastating. The impenetrable fortifications of the Maginot Line, built in north-eastern France after World War I to prevent just such an attack, proved useless. Instead, the Germans pushed through the tough, forested terrain of the Ardennes.

Denmark, Norway, Belgium, Luxembourg and the Netherlands had all fallen. If the extraordinary evacuation of Dunkirk in northern France had not taken place a few weeks earlier, some 330,000 Allied French, Belgian and English troops might have been lost too. On 10 June, the French government fled Paris and, four days later, the Germans entered the city unopposed.

Demoralisation was complete. Although not for General de Gaulle, a junior French government minister and general who evacuated to England in early June 1940 to garner British support. While he acknowledged that the French had been subdued by superior German mechanical, ground and air forces, he refused to consider defeat. 'Believe me,' he said in his broadcast speech, 'I speak to you with full knowledge of the facts and tell you that nothing is lost for France... Has the last word been said? Must hope disappear? Is defeat final? No!'

He broadcast again on 22 June 1940, the day the Franco–German Armistice was signed. Under its terms, France was divided into two zones: the German-occupied zone, which included Paris to the north and the country's entire Atlantic coast, and the so-called 'free zone' to the south, governed out of Vichy by Marshal Philippe Pétain's puppet administration.

That message was a lot more widely received. It was clear that de Gaulle's appeal was slowly beginning to yield results, even if the early acts of resistance in the summer of 1940 were sporadic and unorganised. In some cases, they were little more than acts of defiance, but they boosted morale nonetheless.

Cinema audiences in Paris cheered when the Allies appeared on news reels. In Fontainebleau, outside Paris, people gathered openly to listen to daily 'Free French' broadcasts from the banned BBC. In Belgium, a young girl cut 'V' for victory shapes out of newspapers and scattered them around Brussels. In Denmark, a woman refused to let a German officer on a train light her cigarette.

Elsewhere, the action was less tentative. Someone with a pocket knife slashed a tyre on a Gestapo military vehicle. Another cut a telephone cable.

Those individual and often spontaneous acts gradually coalesced into more organised action. Groups began to form. Networks were set up, with broadly similar aims. Countering German propaganda was vital to give hope to a population under occupation. Clandestine leaflets, tracts and newspapers were published and distributed.

Intelligence-gathering was key. In the early days, pigeons were used to transmit information back to London on German installations and movements – some birds were so effective that they were decorated afterwards. Later, wireless radios became more common. Sabotage formed an important part of resistance work too; any activity that might throw a spanner into the German war machine was an act of resistance. Hiding and helping Jews and other fugitives also formed a central plank of many resistance networks.

In 1940, British Prime Minister Winston Churchill set up the Special Operations Executive (SOE), a secret organisation designed to 'set Europe ablaze'. He sent thousands of agents into countries all over occupied Europe to give resistance groups support, weapons and training. In turn, those agents – at least seven Irish people among them – bolstered the numbers in the Resistance, which, by 1943, had developed into a strong and widespread mass movement.

The French Resistance, perhaps the one most prominent in public consciousness, was complex and elaborate. It had two distinct entities; *réseaux*, or networks, which had links with Allied intelligence groups, and *mouvements*, formed and run solely by the French. In 1943, many groups unified under the National Resistance Council in an attempt to co-ordinate their efforts.

Many other countries had well-developed resistance networks too, although they are less well known. The formation and structure of those networks looked different in each place, but the central aim was always the same – to undermine the Nazis.

In all cases, the Resistance drew members from all strata of society, but it is estimated that only a small percentage of the general population, between one and three per cent, got involved. And only about a tenth of those were women, although that might be underestimated because women's contributions were not always recognised. It is striking, then, that more than half of the Irish people involved in resisting the Nazis were women.

That bias towards women is evident in *The Irish in the Resistance*; partly because it reflected the reality on the ground and partly because we have chosen to tell unknown or lesser-known stories, which very often are those of women.

For the most part, the Irish were involved in two main resistance activities: the slow, plodding – and extremely dangerous – job of gathering intelligence, and the equally risky undertaking of helping Allied soldiers escape.

Some of them sought out the Resistance, anxious to play a part in the defeat of the invading force. Others found themselves drawn into illicit activity by accident, or, like with Janie McCarthy, as a consequence of who they knew.

Another woman with the surname McCarthy also got involved from the very start, simply because she saw the need for it. Katherine Anne McCarthy, a nursing sister from Cork, joined one of the earliest and largest resistance networks, Musée de l'Homme, because she saw that wounded soldiers, once well, had to be ferried to safety. It is estimated that she helped up to 200 soldiers before she was arrested in the summer of 1941. The story of her torture, trial, death sentence (later commuted) and lengthy imprisonment in Ravensbrück provides a chilling reminder of the fate awaiting resisters who were caught.

In Italy, Monsignor Hugh O'Flaherty's work in founding the Rome Escape Line, which helped save up to 6,500 people, has been told on screen, in fiction and non-fiction. Here, the focus is on Delia Murphy Kiernan, who used her position as the Irish ambassador's wife to 'risk her neck', as she put it, to help Allied soldiers escape.

In Paris, Sligo-born Fr Kenneth Monaghan used his position as a Passionist priest at St Joseph's church on Avenue Hoche, near the Arc de Triomphe, to spirit fugitives and evaders out of Paris. Elsewhere in Paris, Dublin-born Margaret Kelly, founder of her own famous dance troupe, hid her Jewish husband in the city, right under the noses of the Nazis.

German citizens also worked to defeat Hitler. Berlin-born Agnes Bernelle used her native language to broadcast black propaganda from London to misinform German troops and send secret messages to the Resistance. Not far away, in Bletchley Park, Rubel Ross, of London and Wicklow, joined the team of codebreakers who were undermining the enemy by working to unravel the Enigma code. She was so horrified when she heard Hitler speak in Munich in 1936 that she volunteered to join the Auxiliary Territorial Service (ATS) as soon as she could after war broke out.

Special agents Maureen Patricia O'Sullivan, Captain (Capt.) Brian Rafferty and Capt. John Keany parachuted behind enemy lines to help the Resistance in the fight against Nazi occupation, while Mary Herbert sailed into France, under cover of night, to work as a courier.

Robert Armstrong lost his own brother in World War I, so it was easy to see why he took a job to honour the war's innumerable dead as head-gardener at a military cemetery in France. While tending the graves of dead soldiers, he also took it upon himself to help living ones – even going so far as to take the coat off his own back to give it to an American airman on the run.

Monica de Wichfeld, who spent her childhood in Fermanagh, actively sought out the Resistance. When she returned to an occupied Denmark, she found the atmosphere deeply shocking and wanted to be in what she called 'the real world', fighting. She went on to lead a resistance network before her arrest.

In Belgium, Irish governess Catherine Crean helped Allied airmen escape. She too was arrested and sent to the unspeakably brutal concentration camp for women at Ravensbrück. Four other Irish women were also held there, arrested for helping Allied soldiers escape. They were Mary Cummins, Mary O'Shaughnessy, Agnes Flanagan and Sr Katherine, or Kate, McCarthy.

There were many others who risked their lives to help strangers. Sometimes an act of humanity as banal as giving food to a hungry man was enough to upend your life, as

Bridget Bolger from Wexford found to her cost when she fed an Allied airman.

Una Haldene from Tyrone helped servicemen escape from Italy. She was aware of the dangers involved not only for herself but for the many other women willing to help when they could. 'The boys have found second mothers in the women who feed, wash for them and even nurse them through serious illnesses, risking their lives every minute of the day and night in doing so,' she wrote in her diary in 1943.

There were many more whose selfless acts of courage have been forgotten.

What follows, then, is an account of those neglected Irish men and women who endured the tensions and dangers of undercover resistance work in cities and villages across occupied Europe: hunched over illicit radios in attics; braving check-points carrying documents and messages; planning attacks on Nazi installations and rail lines; sheltering Jews and evaders, and smuggling them over treacherous mountain paths and other frontiers to freedom.

TAKING A STAND

I

Janie McCarthy's Indomitable Spirit

'HER PLACE SEEMS TO HAVE BEEN A RENDEZ-VOUS FOR
HELPERS AND A CENTER TO ESTABLISH CONTACTS EVERY
TIME THE ORGANISATION WAS BROKEN.'
                    AMERICAN INTELLIGENCE DOCUMENT

Paris, Spring 1943: Janie McCarthy was on the move again. Down five flights of stairs, out on to the rue Sainte-Anne, then right towards the metro. She was on her way to see two downed Allied airmen hiding in the north-west of the city. The stations were full of German soldiers, but she had already passed among them with an escaped pilot pretending that he couldn't speak, or hear. That ploy had worked more than once, in fact, but she wouldn't need it this time. She was alone, bringing food, news – and much-needed good cheer.

Light relief was welcome. The waiting had been torturous for American radio operator Sergeant (Sgt) Iva Lee Fegette (24) and his fellow fugitive Technical Sergeant (TSgt) William Whitman (22) since their aircraft crash-landed in a muddy field at Provins, some 76km east of Paris, in early December. They had been told to be patient, but three weeks had since gone by without any further word from the Resistance. When Janie McCarthy finally visited, it gave them hope, even when she informed them that conditions were not yet right for the airmen's journey south. From there, they hoped to be guided over the Pyrenees on an escape line – or freedom trail – taking them into neutral Spain.

Janie McCarthy would return to see them several times and try to raise their spirits. As Sgt Fegette said of her later, '[Ms McCarthy] kept us laughing all [the] time'.

It is very unlikely that they told Janie any details of their ill-fated mission. It was better to say as little as possible. But we can keep pace alongside Sgt Fegette and TSgt Whitman throughout their dangerous journey because of the detailed accounts they gave after the war. It is instructive to do so because it also gives us an insight into how Janie McCarthy, an English teacher from Killarney, Co. Kerry, operated within a clandestine network that was only as strong as its weakest member.

——— ———

The two men, members of the 303rd Bomber Group, had set off from Molesworth base in England on 12 December 1942 at 10.30 a.m. They were on a mission to attack the airfield at Romilly-sur-Seine in north-central France, but before they reached their target, around noon, German fighters knocked out two of the engines of their B-17 Wulfe Hound.

The aircraft lost altitude quickly. The crew followed procedure during the descent, releasing its bomb load to lighten the aircraft, destroying maps, equipment and other incriminating papers. They must have been thinking the worst, but the pilot's forced landing was textbook perfect. All ten crew crawled out uninjured as a French family waving a white flag ran towards them. Sgt Therrien, a French speaker, asked which direction they should take. Any direction but north, they were told. They took cover in nearby woods and decided their best chance of survival was to split up into pairs and start walking.

They had no idea where they were, so set off with little more than hope and a regulation emergency 'aids box'. It was packed with Horlicks tablets, chocolate, water purifier tablets, matches, a water bottle and an all-important compass. The kit also included a welcome supply of chewing gum: 'Takes your mind off things,' Sgt Fegette commented later.

The mind of the fugitive could settle on any number of terrifying things, but fear of capture must have been foremost in their thoughts that December day. As they made their way through a forest, the first people they encountered were woodcutters. They attempted to communicate through sign language, but to no avail. The evaders were put out by that, concerned the men might be supporters of the Germans. However, the woodcutters did not betray them; they had simply turned a blind eye.

Turning a blind eye was in itself a brave act because anything that might be construed as helping an Allied airmen could lead to arrest, torture, imprisonment and even death. Ordinary civilians had been sent to prison camps just for giving food or clothes to a fugitive soldier. Yet, on their six-month journey from that forest in occupied France to eventual safety in the UK, via Gibraltar, these two airmen met close to 100 people. All of them took enormous risks to help them.

Many were not even members of any organised resistance network, but ordinary people prepared to give an American a barn to sleep in, civilian clothes, cigarettes, a bath or some food. After a few days – and a near-encounter with a lorry full of Germans – the two men randomly met a man who, as they put it, 'arranged the rest of their journey'. He was obviously in the Resistance or in touch with one of its networks. He made a telephone call to Paris and, shortly afterwards, the airmen were driven to a castle in the north of France where they were holed up for 54 days.

They arrived in Paris on 15 February 1943 – and into the care of Janie McCarthy and other members of Comet, a resistance network dedicated to helping aviators find a path out of France and into neutral Spain.

Janie McCarthy was born on 19 January 1885 to Margaret and Michael McCarthy, a shopkeeper on High Street and later New Street (Lower), Killarney. She went to school at the local Mercy Convent and was in her early twenties when her elder brother Joseph emigrated to New York in 1908. She didn't follow him but, unusually for the time, instead struck out for Vannes in Brittany in northern France.

She worked there as an *au pair* for the Meslier family, but also taught English. By 1911, she was advertising conversational lessons at moderate prices in the local papers. She had posts in a number of local schools and was clearly a gifted teacher. Less than a decade later, she was named *Officier d'Académie*, as part of the prestigious *Palmes académiques*, a national order given for distinguished service to education. This was unusual for a non-French person.

News of the award made the papers in France and at home. In February 1920, the *Cork Examiner* ran a photograph of her under the caption, 'Talented Killarney Lady'. 'She is Professor of English,' the article read, 'and the first lady in the United Kingdom to receive this distinction.'

This young woman was already making a name for herself.

Three years later, she moved to Paris where she enrolled in the Sorbonne to study language and French civilisation. Given her academic credentials, it was not surprising that she would pursue further education. She rented a *chambre de bonne*, or maid's room, at 64 rue Sainte-Anne, which put her at the centre of everything. The Opera House, the *Comédie Française* (the French national theatre), the Tuileries Gardens and the Louvre museum were all within walking distance.

In the years that followed, she built up a wide network of connections through her teaching and taught the 'sons and daughters of princes and kings of royal households of places as far away as Indo-China,' one newspaper noted.

Her presence at the heart of Paris, coupled with her wide-ranging contacts, help to explain how she came into contact with resistance activity so early in the war. There were just three degrees of separation between Janie McCarthy and the man who established the Saint Jacques resistance network. She and Elisabeth Barbier were friends; Elisabeth knew Michel Louett, who in turn knew network founder Capt. Maurice Declos.

At first, Janie McCarthy might have thought the war was not going to last long. Paris, and France as a whole, settled into an uneasy normality during the so-called Phoney war (*la drôle de guerre*), from September 1939 to May 1940. There were little more than skirmishes between troops who, for the most part, stayed behind their respective defence lines. In May, however, any hope of a short war was shattered when German troops swept through the low countries. Millions of refugees from Belgium, the Netherlands and Luxembourg poured into Paris. Many took shelter in the Gare Montparnasse train station, a short walk across the River Seine from Janie McCarthy's flat.

Drue Tartière, who would later work with Janie McCarthy in the Comet resistance network, worked near the station. She described the scene in detail: 'The large, gray, dismal railroad station was a mass of misery. I saw grandmothers holding dead babies in their arms, women with parts of their faces shot away, and insane women who had lost their children, their husbands, and all reason for living. Some of these Belgian peasants would suddenly remember the many things they had been forced to leave undone on their property, the cattle untended, the dogs unfed, and then they would let out screams of rage and despair, which resounded through the big bare station.'

After the fall of France in June 1940, Parisians themselves flooded into the station in an unprecedented mass exodus from the city. Tartière was among them: 'I noticed that as far as the eye could see the streets around the station were one mass of people with their belongings, trying to get on trains going anywhere out of Paris. The day was stifling, and there were panic, misery, and anxiety wherever one looked. On the road out of the city people were pushing baby carriages or pulling small carts, others were on loaded bicycles, and some were walking, carrying their children and their valises. Some were moving their families and possessions in wagons drawn by oxen. Farther on, we saw dead bodies on the side of the road, French men, women, and children who had been machine-gunned by German Stukas [dive bombers]. Cars were lying in ditches, overturned, and men and women stood near them, weeping.'

Janie McCarthy decided to stay in Paris, even as many other Irish people joined the mass evacuation south. Ireland's diplomatic representatives, Con Cremin and Seán Murphy, shut up the Irish legation office at the rue de Villejust in Paris and, with their secretary Ina Foley, travelled towards Tours. They were joined by Fr Travers, rector of the Irish College in Paris. He later returned to Paris and, with a janitor, kept a wartime vigil at the college, successfully batting off attempts to have the building requisitioned.

When Murphy returned to Paris briefly in late August 1940, he described a city that had a 'very empty air'. The population had dropped to just 1.4 million, according to a census taken on 12 August, down from 2.8 million in 1936. There was a heavy German presence, though: several first-class hotels had been requisitioned – from the Continental to the Ritz – and there were large numbers of German soldiers and officers on the Champs-Élysées.

The Irish legation, however, was just as they had left it, with a tricolour flying outside, as Murphy explained in a confidential report addressed to Joseph P. Walshe, secretary of the Department of External Affairs in Dublin, dated 27 August 1940.

He went on to say that several Irish people had requested advice or Irish papers to avoid any difficulties with the German authorities.

It's not clear if many, or indeed any, of those managed to secure an Irish passport before the Germans began an internment campaign a few weeks later. In September, more than 100

Irish holders of British passports were interned at a military barracks in Saint Denis, a suburb north of Paris. Several Irish people were also held at a military fort in Besançon in the east of France. Helene Lee-Lynch, a 67-year-old English teacher from Whitegate in Cork, was among them. She had been in France for more than 40 years and, like many of the 2,000 or so Irish people in France, still had a British passport. While most others were released quickly, news of Miss Lee-Lynch's detention in September 1940 did not reach her family until the following August, according to a report in the *Irish Press*. They made immediate, and ultimately successful, calls on the Irish legation in France to have her released.

So, for Janie McCarthy, her Irish passport was a blessing. Not only did it protect her from detention, but it also left her free to visit the barracks weekly and bring food and clothes to internees. Those mercy missions were not an organised act of resistance, but they were an early indication that she was planning to play an active role as the war unfolded.

Meanwhile, the nascent resistance movement began to slowly take shape. The Saint Jacques network – named after the founder's alias – started the tentative process of sounding out people who would be prepared to help and, if the circumstances demanded it, join in the fighting.

They set out a clear vision of the mission ahead. One of its primary aims was to gather as much information as possible on enemy activity and on the willingness of the local population to resist in the strategically important area from the Cherbourg peninsula in Normandy to the Belgian border.

There was also a need to organise anti-enemy propaganda as the Germans were masters at putting their own spin on events. The network would need writers, artists and printers to publish pamphlets and newspapers, and courageous volunteers to distribute them. Later, they would enlist photographers and engravers to make fake identity papers.

It also needed saboteurs who would secretly damage or interfere with as many enemy military posts and as much equipment as they could. Those working in German factories would later be instructed in how to put machinery out of commission or damage products.

For now, though, the focus was on intelligence-gathering. The new *résistantes*, Mme Barbier and Janie McCarthy, were joined by two others – Danish citizen Natacha Boeg and Frenchman Jean Albert-Sorel – as they embarked on their first mission: to gather and collate information on the movements of enemy troops.

Janie McCarthy was tasked with gathering as much intelligence on enemy rail traffic as possible, so she travelled north by train, two or three times a week, to collect information on troop movements and enemy installations.

She made an unlikely *résistante*. One surviving photograph, taken in 1920, shows a young woman half-smiling at the camera. She's wearing a stylish blouse with a statement collar and her hair is neatly pinned up at the ears in a kind of faux bob.

There is no known photo of her during the war years, but we have this pen-picture from bombardier lieutenant Sidney Casden, whom she helped in 1943: She is 'about forty-five years old, with greying hair. She is plump and teaches English'. She might not have considered that description a compliment, but it highlights Janie's hidden strength – she was an inconspicuous middle-aged woman in the thick of a war being fought mostly by young men.

——— ———

The first significant outward demonstration against the German occupiers in Paris took place on 11 November 1940 when some 500 students marched along the Champs-Élysées. They held French flags aloft and some carried two fishing rods, chanting 'Long live... *deux gaules*', which literally meant 'two fishing rods' but was pronounced the same way as de Gaulle, the French leader in exile.

The Germans violently broke up the protest. There were several arrests and some were imprisoned and beaten. The vast majority were released shortly afterwards, but the demonstration would later be seen as an important step in galvanising the Resistance.

Janie McCarthy settled into a difficult winter. Christmas 1940 was one without cheer. German troops bought everything they could to send home – children's toys, perfume, jewellery and clothes. Not that the ordinary civilians would have been able to afford such luxuries, but they hadn't yet settled into living under occupation. The black market, which many would come to rely on for daily food essentials, was not yet firmly established and the Resistance was still in its infancy.

The Saint Jacques network, however, was active from the start. Janie continued to give English lessons in her small apartment and, at regular intervals, she gathered intelligence on German troop installations in northern France. Mme Barbier centralised all the information and gave it to Michel

Louett who, in turn, passed it on to codemaker Charles Deguy to code for transmission.

In January 1941, a radio operator and transmitter were parachuted into France to facilitate better contact with London. The Saint Jacques network sent information on a vast array of subjects: railway traffic, flight paths, politics, port information, even consular love affairs.

Mme Barbier involved herself ever more deeply in all aspects of resistance work. She was seen as the 'linchpin' in the growing organisation. Her efforts, though, did not go unnoticed. She received two visits from the Gestapo at her home on the rue Vaneau. They did not arrest her, but their presence made her wary and more cautious. Even so, the network was completely caught off guard when it was smashed, without warning, in August 1941. The Germans arrested codemaker Charles Deguy. He was jailed and later shot in August 1942. Michel Louett managed to escape and took refuge in Mme Barbier's apartment, despite the fact that the Gestapo were already suspicious of her. It was time to regroup.

Plans to set up a new network may well have been hatched in Janie McCarthy's small fifth-floor flat, as it seems to have been a focal point whenever a network was compromised. As an American military intelligence document noted: 'Her place seems to have been a rendez-vous for helpers and a center to establish contacts every time the organisation was broken.'

After a gap of several months, Janie reappears as a documented member of two different groups: Vaneau, which was set up by Mme Barbier and most likely named after her street, and Comet. The Comet Line was one of the biggest escape organisations in Europe, involving a large network of volunteers who guided shot-down airmen from Brussels through France and over the Pyrenees into neutral Spain.

Janie joined Comet in October 1942. For the next year, her focus was almost entirely on helping airmen to get out of occupied Paris. Or to help them find a temporary safe haven within the city.

The experience of the two young sergeants who crash-landed near Paris and eventually came under Janie's watchful eye casts a revealing light on how nerve-racking it was to duck and dodge the occupying force on a daily basis – and just how dangerous it was to be one of the people helping them do that. They were lodged by various members of the network; a night here and two nights there, before having to move on yet again.

On one occasion Janie McCarthy called to collect them from a safe house and bring them to another, the home of Elisabeth Barbier. On another occasion, the two men stayed at an apartment directly across the road from the German Air Ministry.

There were high-risk trips out into the city too. The two airmen were guided to a department store in Paris where they had their photograph taken for false identity papers. They had to pretend they were deaf and mute. The ruse is mentioned so often in escape reports, it's a wonder the Germans did not become wise to it. But they did not. The photographs arrived three days later, but it was still difficult to get train tickets to go south.

The hiding continued. And the watching, as Janie and members of her network waited for the right circumstances to help the men make the next step in their journey to safety. By the end of 1942 there were concerns that the Comet network had been compromised. As Fegette recalls: 'Madame [probably Barbier] knew that the [organisation] had been broken to some extent. She knew someone was in touch with Germans – she didn't know what to do with us.'

It was decided the two men would go to the American Hospital in Neuilly in the western suburbs of Paris. They ventured out into the city, one walking several feet behind the other. They walked for an hour and a half through Paris, but lost their way. They started back towards the Champs-Élysées to get their bearings, but as they were passing the Rond-Point on the famous avenue someone lobbed a hand grenade into a restaurant full of Germans. Chaos ensued and the whole area was cordoned off. Yet, the two men managed to walk away and eventually find their way to a safe house near the hospital.

Travelling was out of the question now, so they waited – yet again. Janie McCarthy made frequent visits and helped to boost the men's flagging morale.

Eventually, five months after being shot down in France, the two men travelled by train to the edge of the Pyrenees where they made contact with a guide. They made their way across the mountains in rain and cloud, following the lights in the distance that brought them into Spain. They arrived on 3 May 1943. Sgt Fegette was charted as the ninety-fourth evader on the Comet escape line and Whitman the ninety-fifth. Less than three weeks later, they made it to Gibraltar and, on 25 May 1943, they were safely back in Britain.

The many airmen Janie McCarthy helped during the war had experiences similar to that one, even if they never shared the details with her. She knew to keep conversation light or say nothing at all as she guided them through occupied Paris en route to one of the escape lines that ran from Belgium, through France, all the way into Spain.

Even by French standards, Janie McCarthy's resistance record is impressive. For obvious reasons, a large amount of her secret work went unrecorded, yet it is striking how often her name appears in surviving post-war documents.

For instance, Royal Canadian Air Force sergeant Clarence Howard Witheridge mentioned that Janie and her fellow agent Lucienne Bodin collected him from the train in Paris in October 1943. They went to Lucienne Bodin's apartment on the rue des Petits-Champs, where she and her husband Jean sheltered dozens of airmen.

Janie McCarthy's flat was just a stone's throw away and there is little doubt that she would have sheltered American and British airmen if her lodgings had allowed it. Her room under the eaves of number 64 rue Sainte-Anne was just about big enough to allow one-to-one private English lessons. Although she regularly fed evading airmen, it was not large enough to house them – though there is a reference to her harbouring a soldier on one occasion.

In any case, there was no question of her commitment, as her neighbour Lucienne attested. She said Janie was 'very devoted to the aviators' and spoiled them a lot.

British bomber command navigator, Gordon Mellor, describes meeting an English teacher with a strong Irish accent when he was sheltered in Robert and Germaine Aylé's flat in Paris. She appeared unperturbed by the presence of Mellor and he took part in the English lesson that the woman – most likely Janie – went on to give the couple.

Janie herself mentioned Robert Aylé in her post-war deposition. Both she and Aylé went to pick up two Americans and bring them back to his flat. She also described making trips to Perreux in the Loire in central France and Vernon in Normandy to collect five aviators. On another occasion, she said she brought two aviators, Lt Frank R Perrica from Baltimore and Savafore Tafoya from Los Angeles, to Elisabeth Barbier's flat.

In turn, the aviators name her in their escape reports. Sgts Whitman and Fegette – who memorably said she kept them laughing all the time – mentioned her visits. Sgt Cecil Spence and Sidney Devers said she put them in touch with the organisation, while Sgt Allan Robinson said Janie visited him while he was staying with Elisabeth Barbier. Sidney Casden and Andrew Hathaway also singled out Janie; she was the one who brought them to Marie-Thérèse Labadie who sheltered them.

Marie Thérèse also confirmed that Janie, or 'Miss Mack' as she was known, was involved in helping airmen. She said Janie looked after 'supplies, conveying, interpreting and liaising'.

Another airman, Frank Bulfield, spoke of her work too, suggesting that she held a central role in ensuring that aviators were who they said they were. In his post-war deposition, he said she was 'called in to question aviators for identification by radio from London'.

'Her modus operandi was simple,' the *Evening Echo* newspaper noted after the war. 'She simply enrolled refugees as members of her classes, or as professors and members of Prof McCarthy's staff.'

Another newspaper noted that she lost only one person, a French medical student, during the course of the war.

But the Gestapo were never far away. In January of 1943, Andrée de Jongh the leader of the Comet Line was arrested.

There were further arrests later in the year, including that of Janie's friend, Robert Aylé.

At the start of January, Janie McCarthy was on her way to have dinner with Elisabeth Barbier in her home on the rue Vaneau when a student called to her flat unexpectedly. It not only delayed her, but saved her from arrest and deportation.

The Germans had arrived at Elisabeth Barbier's house a short time earlier, accusing her of being part of an escape line. Some members of the network had been betrayed by a Belgian guide. Elisabeth, however, was not going to give anything away and when the telephone rang, she refused to answer it. One of the Germans slapped her, but she still refused. Instead, he picked it up and said: 'I am the doctor. Elisabeth is sick. You must come.'

At that, Elisabeth started to scream, alerting the caller who immediately hung up. The German, then furious, 'beat the living daylights' out of her, as she described it later.

Elisabeth, her maid and her mother, Camille Foucher Estmaur, were all arrested. Elisabeth was put in solitary confinement in Fresnes, a jail just south of Paris where resistance fighters and Allied secret agents were detained and sometimes executed. After four months, she was moved to a shared cell. She endured 25 hard interrogations, but later said that she didn't give away a single name or address.

Her maid was released after six months, but Elisabeth and her mother were sent to Ravensbrück, Hitler's notorious concentration camp for women.

It was a terrible blow for the network, but a particularly devastating one for Janie McCarthy. She might have stopped her activity then, after the capture of her close friend, but she continued to work to help airmen escape from Paris with a number of different organisations, including the Shelburn Line. It brought evaders to the Brittany coast to be picked up by the Royal Navy's 15th Motor Gun Boat Flotilla.

However, it wasn't long before that network was compromised too. On 21 November 1943, days after she had completed a similar mission, three of Janie's fellow Shelburn members met at a café near the Gare d'Austerlitz train station where they were planning to help two American pilots, Fred Huntzinger and Benjamin Zum, escape towards Spain.

The Gestapo was waiting to intercept them. The two Americans and three *résistantes* were arrested: Janie's neighbour Lucienne Bodin, Suzanne Bosnière and Marie Betbeder-Matibet. Janie knew Marie Betbeder-Matibet. They had much in common. They were both teachers – Marie was French but taught English – and both had visited Saint Denis to bring aid to those interned.

They were all jailed in Fresnes and later sent to Ravensbrück where Marie died in 1944. Lucienne's husband Jean was also arrested, but both of them survived.

Shaken by the events, Janie McCarthy left her flat on the rue Sainte-Anne and went into hiding. She rented a room at the Pension Port Royal on the other side of the river in the 5th arrondissement. In late November, she sent a telegram to her sister in Killarney. It read: 'Well but anxious about you all.'

Sometime later, she moved back into her own flat and continued her work, moving through Paris quietly and inconspicuously.

It's not known how many Allied soldiers Janie helped but, during the course of the war, she was a member of at least five different resistance organisations. She narrowly escaped arrest on more than one occasion and went into hiding after fellow resistance members, many of them close friends, were arrested in 1943. Yet, she continued her clandestine work until France was liberated.

It says something about Janie McCarthy that she was still in Paris at all. She might have returned to Ireland when war broke out in September 1939, but she made a very deliberate decision to stay. She 'destroyed' – that was the word she used afterwards – her British passport, so that she could qualify for an Irish one. This was a woman taking steps to identify herself as a neutral citizen so that she could stay put in her adopted city. By then, Janie had already spent nearly three decades in France. It was home.

When the war was over, she continued to teach English in her garret flat in central Paris.

Her steadfast work and unflinching commitment were recognised in three countries after the war. She received a Resistance Medal and Croix de Guerre for bravery from France, a Tedder certificate for helping British service personnel and an American Medal of Freedom. Notably, though, she did not receive any financial compensation.

In Ireland, her clandestine wartime activities were well known as she proudly wore her medals on trips home to Killarney. She was celebrated in the local press too. In 1954, *The Kerryman* ran a feature honouring those who had 'left Kerry and achieved distinction'. Janie was the only woman in a list of over 100 men.

The article included an interesting detail that doesn't appear elsewhere. It said she also helped to hide Frenchmen who were trying to escape forced labour and deportation to Germany under an obligatory work law that came into effect in 1943. It says she helped them go to England or to join the *Maquis* (literally 'scrubby underbrush'), the underground army that hid and trained guerrilla resistance fighters in the French countryside.

The write-up, which described the dangers she took and the awards she received, went on to describe Janie as 'modest and retiring'. Whatever about the former, she was certainly not retiring. She was outgoing, gregarious and fun. That was how friends described her on her annual trips home.

One of them, Phil O'Connell, told writer Breda Joy in 2016 that her aunt Sally and Janie were good friends. They often shared a cigarette, nightcap and a chat. 'One time, I recall Janie bringing Annie a roll of the best French material to have a costume made. I can see Janie now, hair in a bun, smart French costume (suit) and of course all of her medals on a ribbon, and speaking both in French and in English.'

Another Kerrywoman, Sheila Mulcahy, got to know Janie very well, too, when she studied in France in the late 1940s and 1950s. She paints a picture of a kind, generous, energetic woman who went out of her way to help others. Once, when Sheila was cash-strapped, Janie gave her some French francs which were hidden in a book on a shelf. Her appearance might have been unremarkable, she said, but her personality was anything but. 'Talk about animation. She was a very outgoing person and good fun and great company.'

Sheila also gave this tantalising description of Janie's tiny, top-floor flat that witnessed so much activity during the war:

'One room was her sitting room and her bedroom; a small kitchenette adjoined it. She would have visitors – mostly young women who had been her pupils and who were quite glamorous Parisian women. They would be whispering in the kitchenette. I suspected that it was about their romances.'

Janie McCarthy continued to teach English in that flat into her seventies and even in the last year of her life when she was ill. She was still giving lessons, from her bed, right up to being hospitalised in November 1964. She died a month later, on 20 December. When she was buried at the cemetery in Levallois-Perret, her friend Louise Schilman remarked that she saw 30 men weeping over her grave. A sight to behold for a woman who never had a boyfriend, she added.

That grave remained in place for a decade but when the lease on the plot expired, her remains were exhumed and transferred to a communal grave. When, in 2021, Killarney tour guide and genealogist Mary G. O'Sullivan retraced the *ossuaire* (ossuary) that contains her remains, along with hundreds of others, she was horrified. 'She was courageous and patriotic, and her spirit inspired others. It is a tragedy that she lies in a paupers' grave,' she said. It was a point made a few years earlier by writer Isadore Ryan.

If the last trace of her has been erased at a French cemetery, her memory has been honoured and revived in her place of birth. In 2022, Killarney's Mayor Marie Moloney unveiled a commemorative plaque on Mission Road to a woman she described as a 'true heroine'.

2

Cat and Mouse Games

'YOU SIMPLY COULDN'T STAND BY WITH YOUR ARMS FOLDED.'
SAMUEL BECKETT

Paris, 16 August 1942: Despite the danger, Samuel Beckett and his partner Suzanne Deschevaux-Dumesnil set out across the city to warn a fellow resistance member that their network had been infiltrated. They went into Suzanne Roussel's apartment block, but as they began to climb the stairs Beckett became 'obsessed with a premonition of danger', as he later put it. The feeling that something was terribly wrong became so acute that the couple turned back

Suzanne Deschevaux-Dumesnil returned to the apartment later that day – alone. She took the precaution of calling to the concierge's office to make sure that everything was as it should be. The building's caretaker told her nothing was amiss and that the woman she sought, Suzanne (aka 'Hélène') Roussel, was at home on her own. Reassured, she made her way up the same stairs she had attempted that morning and knocked on the door.

The Gestapo answered. They had been waiting for Roussel and, at first, they thought the *résistante* herself had walked right into their trap. Suzanne managed to convince them otherwise, saying she was simply visiting to feed the cat while her friend was away.

In fact, both Suzannes were members of the Gloria SMH resistance cell, although the Gestapo had no inkling of Beckett's partner's involvement. That, however, did not stop them taking her away for interrogation. She stuck to her story and they seemed to accept it, although they insisted on searching the flat she shared with Beckett at 6 rue des Favorites in the 15th arrondissement. Luckily, by then Samuel Beckett, alias 'Samson', had already packed up whatever belongings he could and destroyed all incriminating documents.

Beckett escaped arrest by a hair's breadth thanks to a telegram Mania Péron had sent a few hours earlier to say her husband Alfred Péron had been arrested. Madame Péron asked Beckett if there was anything he could do 'to correct the mistake'. It was her coded way of warning them to get to safety. The couple tried to alert other members, such as Roussel, which led to Suzanne's arrest. Thanks to her quick-thinking cover story, she was later released. However, Paris was no longer safe. It was time to go into hiding.

——— ——

Earlier that year, in January, senior Nazi and German government officials had gathered on the shores of Lake Wannsee in Germany to hammer out the so-called Final Solution, a repugnant agreement designed to commit genocide on all Jewish people. SS General Reinhard Heydrich, head of the German secret police, said that Europe would be 'combed from east to west' to systematically exterminate all Jewish people. They planned to round up and kill some 11 million Jews, including 4,000 from Ireland. The Wannsee Conference, as it became known, set a target of some 165,000 Jewish people in occupied France and 700,000 people in the unoccupied (or Vichy) zone.

The general public, including those in the Resistance, were not aware of the conference, but it was evident to everyone that mass deportations were gathering pace throughout the year. Just weeks before Beckett's network was rumbled, the biggest roundup of Jewish people during the entire war took place in Paris. On 16 and 17 July, French police, acting on orders from their German occupiers, arrested some 13,000 Jewish people, including thousands of children. Half of them were immediately interned at Drancy, a transit camp in northern Paris, before being sent to their deaths at Auschwitz and other concentration camps. Thousands more were held in appalling conditions at an indoor cycling track, the Vélodrome d'Hiver, a few kilometres from Beckett's flat. Later, they too were sent by cattle wagon to be murdered in the Nazi's extermination camps. There were very few survivors.

Samuel Beckett was already keenly aware of the dangers facing Jewish people. His friend, Paul Léon, the translator and scholar who rescued James Joyce's papers after the writer and his family fled their Parisian flat, had been arrested the previous year. When, in August 1941, Beckett bumped into him still walking openly in Paris, he was alarmed, and told him to leave the city at once. Léon explained that his son was due to finish his *baccalauréat* exam the next day, 21 August. By a cruel twist of fate, that was the very day Paul Léon was arrested and interned at Drancy holding camp. Almost without exception, those held there were sent to Auschwitz concentration camp.

Concerned about his welfare, Beckett gave his own rations to Léon's wife, Lucie. 'Sam Beckett used to bring me his bread ration and also his cigarette ration, so I could get them through to the camp. I will never forget this great kindness on his part,' she later said. 'At that time he was probably in almost as much trouble as we were, and he certainly needed those rations himself.'

Beckett would have known what Paul Léon was experiencing because he wrote several letters to his wife, describing the lack of food, sleeping on wooden planks – 'I regret not being plumper' – and the humiliation of having a registration number as if he were a convict.

'My dearest, dearest Lucie,' he wrote on 9 October 1941, 'Please forgive me, my love, for my complaints, my sadness, my lack of refinement – my only excuse is that I am diminished morally, physically, and in every other way too... I have very little hope but I am praying.'

Beckett had been horrified by that year's anti-Jewish legislation, which had stripped many of his friends of their citizenship and so many other rights. His abhorrence of the Nazi regime pre-dated the war. He had witnessed the rise of Third Reich ideology in Berlin and his German diaries from 1936 to 1937 show that he had no stomach for it. During his time there, he referred to people being 'appallingly Nazi' and wrote that Hitler's hateful ideology would 'start the vomit moving upwards'.

The arrest and detention of his friend Paul Léon had been the final push towards action. He joined Gloria SMH, a network specialising in intelligence, in late 1941. The network's own records date his involvement from September 1941, but he said himself that he joined in November.

Now the arrest of Alfred Péron in August 1942, another good friend of long standing, sent Beckett and Suzanne into hiding. The two men met in 1926 when Péron took up an exchange lecturer post at Trinity College Dublin. He taught Beckett French. They met again in Paris where they resumed their friendship, became tennis partners and co-workers.

Péron introduced Beckett to SMH and came to his flat regularly, bringing intelligence gathered from a range of different sources. Had he been stopped, Péron had the perfect cover story because it was entirely true: he was helping the Irish author to translate his novel, *Murphy*.

Beckett later described his resistance work collating, translating and typing information: 'Information came in from all over France about the German military movements, about movements of troops, their position, everything that concerned the occupying forces. They would bring this information to me on various scraps of paper... It was a huge group. It was the boy scouts! They brought it all to me. I would type it all out clean. Put it in order and type it out, on one sheet of paper as far as was possible. Then I would bring it to a Greek who was part of the group. He lived in what is now the Avenue René Coty, I think. And he would take photographs. And my sheets would be reduced to the size of a match-box... Probably unreadable but it could be magnified. And then he would give them to Madame Picabia, the [former] wife of [Francis] Picabia, the painter. She was a very respectable old lady; nothing could be less like a Resistance agent. And she could get over to the other zone, the so-called unoccupied zone, without any difficulty. And so it was sent back to England.'

Madame Picabia was a woman in her sixties and mother to Jeannine Picabia (aka Gloria). Jeannine set up Gloria SMH in 1941, with Jacques Legrand (aka SMH, the initials of His Majesty's Service in reverse). By the time Beckett joined, the organisation was already working directly with the SOE. That meant it was co-ordinated from London and, in theory at least, had more resources at its disposal.

While Jeannine Picabia was a key member of the network, her mother was also deeply involved. She sheltered fugitives and was a regular courier. Beckett passed on the miniaturised film to her, which she hid in a shopping bag, or her underwear, and travelled into the unoccupied zone to hand it over for delivery to London. If stopped, she was ready to play the peasant woman going about her daily business.

By then, resistance networks had combined resourcefulness with ingenuity to cover up a vast array of clandestine activities. For instance, it was common for resisters to write messages on a thin slip of paper, or a cigarette paper, wrap it tightly around a needle and insert it into a cigarette.

Beckett, like many others, would have been familiar with the *boîte aux lettres* system of securely passing on information or objects. A *boîte aux lettres vivante* was, literally, a living postbox; a trusted intermediary, or 'cut-out' in spy lingo, who facilitated the passing of information between agents. The more common *boîte aux lettres mortes*, or dead-drop, was an agreed place where resisters could leave messages or objects. It might be a hole in a tree, or a locker in a station, or a crumpled cigarette pack left in a particular place.

No matter what role a person had in the Resistance, it was highly dangerous work. And it was important. Opinions vary, but it has been estimated that the work done by the hundreds of thousands of people who resisted Nazi oppression around the world shortened the war by several months.

Samuel Beckett played down both his own importance – his rank was that of second-lieutenant – and the risks involved. It is difficult to assess the value of the intelligence he collated, but there is no doubting the ever-present threat of arrest and imprisonment.

'The danger,' author James Knowlson explained, 'arose at three separate stages: the original delivery to him of the scraps of paper which could have caused a lot of suspicious traffic to his flat; the physical presence of clandestine material there, while he was processing it; and, finally and the most dangerous of all… the transportation of the sheets of paper of typed information to his own contact.'

Beckett and Suzanne shared those hazardous runs, taking highly sensitive information to a man they knew only as 'Jimmy the Greek'. Had they been stopped and the incriminating papers discovered at any stage on the relatively short journey across Paris from their apartment on rue des Favorites to Avenue du Parc de Montsouris (now Avenue René Coty), they risked arrest, deportation and death. And as historian David Murphy observed: 'The military value of the paperwork [Beckett] was carrying would have been obvious to even the dullest policeman.'

The fact that neither he nor Suzanne knew their contact's real name – André (Hadji) Lazaro – was not at all unusual as it was a way of protecting the network. Gloria SMH had about 80 members, but few of them were known to each other. Most groups were organised in small secure cells so that agents would not be able to betray the entire organisation if arrested.

Those safeguards and cautious working methods went only so far, however, in part because the German side was equally adept at dirty tricks. Beckett's network was infiltrated by a Roman Catholic priest, Robert Alesch, who earned himself a reputation as an anti-Nazi preacher in his parish to the south-east of Paris. In reality, he was working with the Abwehr, the German military intelligence service, and succeeded in inveigling himself into Gloria SMH with a daring, but plausible, plan to spring one of its members from prison.

London agreed to fund the escape, paying a hefty sum that would have paid the wages of a skilled worker for a year. Alesch is thought to have kept the money, but there is no doubt that he betrayed several members of the network, prompting many arrests and forcing others to go into hiding.

Samuel Beckett and Suzanne Deschevaux-Dumesnil were now on the run, with few possessions and no money.

They turned to their friend, American artist Mary Reynolds. She had helped them two years before when they joined the mass exodus leaving Paris after the Germans occupied the city in June 1940. She had helped them rent a house where they spent a relatively pleasant three months at Arcachon, a town on the Atlantic coast not far from Bordeaux. Beckett played endless chess with Reynolds's husband, artist Marcel Duchamp, before returning to Paris that September.

Two years on, however, their situation was much more precarious – and dangerous. For one thing, they were fugitives. Anybody caught helping them ran the risk of arrest and deportation. Even so, Mary Reynolds agreed to let them stay in her Paris apartment for one night. They spent the next few weeks going from one friend's house to another, or staying, under assumed names, in small hotels.

Beckett grew a moustache, but he was not really suited to a life of subterfuge. At least that is what Suzanne claimed years later, recounting how the couple had to flee a hotel shortly after they had checked in because, without thinking, Beckett had signed his real name on the guest register.

After leaving that hotel suddenly, they spent another tense ten days with fellow writer Nathalie Sarraute and her husband Raymond who were staying at a house outside Paris. It was safer there, but the house was small and crowded and the facilities were rather basic. There are various accounts of the discord between Beckett and Nathalie; she said he was not sufficiently grateful and he reputedly said that she was sharp, although he did appear to get on very well with Raymond.

Whatever the truth of it, the strain was understandable. Beckett and Suzanne were living on their nerves trying to figure out the next step, while the Sarrautes were running an enormous risk. In any event, the couple couldn't stay there indefinitely. That was clear. They decided that the best option was to cross into the unoccupied zone and hide out there.

The Sarrautes had contacts in another resistance network. False papers were arranged and the couple made contact with smugglers – or *passeurs* – who agreed to bring them secretly over the demarcation line, the border separating the occupied north from the unoccupied south. It was a measure of the strength of the Resistance, and the contact that Beckett and Suzanne had with it, that they were hidden safely for about six weeks before escaping to the south.

Beckett later told Professor Laurence Harvey, a friend and an authority on his work, about the crossing: 'I can remember waiting in a barn (there were 10 of us) until it got dark, then being led by a *passeur* over streams; we could see a German sentinel in the moonlight. Then I remember passing a French post on the other side of the line. The Germans were on the road; so we went across the fields. Some of the girls were taken over in the boot of a car.'

Through friends of Suzanne's, they eventually found a safe refuge in Roussillon, a village not far from Avignon. The Germans had not yet invaded the free zone – that would happen a few months later in November in response to the Allied landings in North Africa – but even when they did, the village remained relatively safe. It wasn't easy to get to, and suitable accommodation was scarce.

In an attempt to get his papers in order, Beckett contacted diplomatic representatives at the Irish legation in Vichy. The office, like all other diplomatic interests, had followed the French government to Vichy after the Germans occupied Paris. The Irish legation wasn't always able to do very much within this oppressive regime, but Samuel Beckett was infuriated by the reception he received. The representative he met 'was extremely unsympathetic and unhelpful', he said.

That unnamed person advised him to go to the local police station and admit travelling illegally into the free zone. He did so and was later fined for the violation, but at least he secured a provisional pass that allowed him to travel.

In Roussillon, they were faced, yet again, with the problem that dogged them all through the war – a dire lack of money. At various stages, Beckett had difficulty getting his hands on the monthly income of £20 from his father's estate. At the start of the war, his brother Frank in Dublin, paid it into the French bank, La Société Générale, but as the conflict went on, he had to find other ways of transferring the money.

Financial aid from the Irish Department of External Affairs was restricted and available to only a few. The authorities in Dublin kept a tight control on the purse strings, imposing monthly limits of £25 for a married couple, £15 for a single person and £5 for a child. With rising wartime inflation, the allowance for a single person in today's terms was worth about €750 at first, but less than €500 two years later.

'It is certain that the Department expects us to live on our *patrimoine* [heritage],' Beckett wrote in a strongly worded letter to Con Cremin in late 1942, calling for the ceiling to be lifted. During his time in hiding, he sent several letters to the legation, complaining about restrictions on his movements and being subjected to 'innumerable petty vexations', including regular identity checks.

He complained that he had complied with all the regulations and that his only lapse, crossing the demarcation line illegally, had been excused after paying a fine, yet the authorities were constantly prying into his identity. For instance, he wrote of the authorities in Roussillon, 'They can't believe that I can be called Samuel and am not a Jew.'

When the harassment continued, he appealed to the legation in June 1943 to intervene on his behalf: 'Would a Swiss citizen be baited in this manner, or a Swede? Or is an Irishman less entitled than they to the common courtesies and privileges extended to non-belligerents?'

He received a prompt response from Seán Murphy, who was surprised to hear that he had been subjected to periodic examinations by the local police authorities. Murphy said he had, once again, asked the Ministry of Foreign Affairs to request 'that the state of affairs which has persisted to date should be altered'.

Murphy was sympathetic to Beckett, saying that his treatment seemed to 'go beyond what would be either reasonable or necessary'. He promised to take further action and he asked Beckett to tell him of any further incidents.

——— ———

In the meantime, Beckett and Suzanne had both found work and settled into some kind of daily rhythm. She gave music lessons while he worked on the Aude family farm. He was paid in produce – meat, milk, eggs, vegetables and fruit. He didn't complain about the punishing nature of the manual labour, although he found the region's extreme weather – searing heat in summer, bitter cold in winter – particularly challenging.

After the war, the farmer's son, Fernand Aude, said he was impressed by Beckett's stamina when they worked together on the farm. He remembered that Beckett had got a nasty cut while pruning vines at one stage, but shrugged it off saying that it was due to his own carelessness.

There were some moments of joy too. Beckett had managed to bring some of his notebooks with him and started to work on his novel *Watt* again. There were long walks and some socialising. While the couple kept a low profile, they mixed with others in a similar position to them. Beckett had spotted another Irish name on the register of visas for foreigners at the Mayor's office; that of Anna O'Meara Beamish who, it turned out, would become a neighbour and friend.

Anna O'Meara de Vic Beamish, to give the woman her full name, was a Dublin-born novelist who moved to the region after being forced to give up her job teaching English in

Cannes. She was well known in the town; she cut an unusual figure by dressing in men's clothes, smoking a pipe and reading with the help of a monocle. She was well-liked, too. Suzanne and Beckett often visited her for tea or they met her in the café where they listened illicitly to the BBC to hear how the Allied forces were faring in North Africa.

Miss Beamish had two Airedale Terriers and walked them late at night. That was probably the source of the rumours that she was a British intelligence agent. There were stories that she used the cover of night to transmit radio messages from the fields in Roussillon to London. There is no evidence to back the claim, even if Miss Beamish was known to support Jewish refugees in the area.

One of those Jewish refugees, Marcel Lob, had helped Suzanne and Beckett settle in Roussillon when they first arrived. In March 1944, Lob was betrayed, arrested and sent to the notorious holding camp in Drancy. The couple did all they could to help his wife Yvonne petition for his release or, failing that, delay his deportation. They succeeded, for a time at least.

The incident may have influenced Beckett's decision to seek out the Resistance for a second time. This time, he joined the *Forces françaises de l'Intérieur* (French Forces of the Interior) in May 1944, a reorganised group that unified several paramilitary resistance units.

In Roussillon, the network made use of the topography to hide weapons and supplies in the network of caves set into the region's ochre cliffs. At the start of the war, it hadn't engaged in fighting or sabotage, but that was changing as the Allies advanced. Beckett regularly joined the *maquis* – guerrilla fighters – on trips to pick up or drop off supplies. He was also given some rifle training and issued with a gun when the network dug hideouts on both sides of the *Route Nationale 100,* preparing to ambush retreating Germans.

They never came – at least not on Beckett's watch. While Samuel Beckett was prepared to bear arms for the Resistance, he said himself that he wasn't cut out for it. On one sortie, he was horrified when he saw the group slaughter a lamb for food. 'I was lily-livered,' he told his friend Laurence Harvey.

That was not the view of his comrades at Gloria SMH, however, or those who later recommended him for a Croix de Guerre (with silver-gilt star) for bravery. The citation for France's military honour read: 'A man of great courage, over two years he provided quality information to a large intelligence network. Carried out his task to the extreme limit of daring. Hunted by the Germans, he had to lead a difficult clandestine life from 1943.'

——— ———

In early 1945, some months after the liberation of Paris in August 1944, Beckett and Suzanne returned to the city and found, to their amazement, that their apartment was more or less intact. Beckett was anxious to return to Dublin because it had been six years since he had seen his mother or brother Frank.

Beckett set out for Dublin in April, travelling via England. He expected the journey to be straightforward but he was stopped by immigration officials still suspicious of anyone who had spent so much time in wartime France. They confiscated his Irish passport – and his manuscript of *Watt.* If he wanted them back, he would have to tell the British War Office what he had been doing in France during the war.

The details of that interview/interrogation, marked top secret, were not declassified until 2003. They make fascinating reading and give extra insights into Beckett's resistance work. For instance, during the interview he told H.W. Astor of MI5 about his premonition of danger on the staircase in Paris three years previously. On the strength of it, he and Suzanne turned back, narrowly escaping the Gestapo who were lying in wait.

Astor was keen to understand how the British-backed resistance cell had been infiltrated, but found that Beckett knew very little. He wrote: 'With regard to the arrests which took place in 1942, Beckett appeared rather vague, but was of the opinion that the difficulties began about May of that year, when one of the *passeurs* at Chalons (presumably Chevalier) was arrested. So far as Beckett is aware, Chevalier did not give away important information.'

He went on to explain that Beckett had scant knowledge of the running of the organisation and knew only a few of its members. With no appreciation that the man in front of him would go on to become one of the century's most important writers, he noted: 'Although Beckett appears fairly intelligent and well educated, he knew very little about the organisation of SMH/Gloria.'

H.W. Astor came to the conclusion that Samuel Beckett did not pose a security risk: 'So far as Beckett himself is concerned, he appeared helpful and created a favourable impression. I can see no reason to regard him with suspicion from a security point of view. He is anxious to visit his mother in Ireland as soon as possible, as he has heard that she is ill, but he is very anxious then to return to France, which he regards as his real home.'

That was a point that Beckett himself made several times. As he famously told the *New York Times* journalist Israel Shenker many years later: 'I preferred France in war to Ireland in peace.' He had moved there in 1936 because he wanted to get away from his job – teaching French at Trinity College, Dublin – and, more than that, Ireland itself. He didn't like the country: 'You know the kind of thing – theocracy, censorship of books,' he said.

Samuel Beckett left the British War Office and as he walked through a forlorn, bomb-ravaged city, 'a remarkable coincidence occurred', as James Knowlson put it. Making his way down Oxford Street, he bumped into the woman who gave his former network its name, Jeannine Picabia, aka Gloria. She and her mother, the indomitable elderly lady who had smuggled miniaturised film in her shopping basket, had made it through Spain to England.

Neither of them knew then exactly how many others had made it to safety. Suzanne 'Hélène' Roussell had been arrested shortly after Beckett and his partner Suzanne called to warn her. She survived the war, unlike so many others in Gloria SMH. Twelve of their members were shot and at least 80 others were deported.

Alfred Péron was one of the deportees, but Beckett did not yet know his good friend's fate. He would find out when he reached Dublin, just a few days later, that his friend had survived his time at Mauthausen in Austria, one of the Nazi's most brutal and severe concentration camps. Péron was alive when it was liberated by the Swiss Red Cross in 1945. The years of mistreatment, lack of food and hard labour took their toll, however, and Péron died on the journey back to Switzerland on 1 May 1945.

His dear friend Paul Léon also died, in Auschwitz-Birkenau on 5 April 1942. In one of his last letters to his wife, dated 22 March 1942, he wrote: 'We don't know what our fate is to be.'

In the last surviving letter, written four days later, on 26 March, he wrote: 'But the most important thing for me is to tell you that I love you as much as I did 20 years ago and that – if I don't get to see you again – it is you that I shall love forever.'

Marcel Lob, the Jewish man who had helped Beckett in Roussillon, survived thanks to the efforts of rail workers in Paris who delayed the trains scheduled to leave from Drancy en route to Auschwitz.

When Beckett arrived in Dublin he was shocked to see how his mother had aged. In turn, his family were taken aback by his gaunt, emaciated figure. After visiting family, friends and going to see a dentist – dental problems were a lifelong issue – he was anxious to get back to Paris.

Getting there, however, was not at all straightforward. And if he did make it to Paris, as a foreigner – even one who considered France his home – he risked losing his apartment. When he found out that the Irish Red Cross was setting up a hospital in Saint-Lô, a town in Normandy reduced to rubble by the Allies after the D-Day landings, he applied for the job of hospital quartermaster/interpreter.

The job might have been Beckett's ticket back to France, but he proved to be an able and committed member of the

Irish team, which included some 50 Irish doctors, nurses and staff who planned to build a hospital amid the ruins.

The German-occupied town had been so heavily bombarded in a single night during the Allied invasion of Normandy in June 1944 that virtually nothing remained. It was like an 'upturned dustbin', one observer said. Some 2,000 of the 2,600 buildings had been completely destroyed. Beckett noted the stark statistic in disbelief.

He arrived in the 'capital of ruins', as it became known, in heavy rain in August. The place was 'a sea of mud' with no accommodation of any kind. He was lodged temporarily with three men in a small room where he shared a bed with physician, Dr Alan Thompson, a friend from his schooldays at Portora Royal School in Enniskillen.

Soon work began on building wooden huts and an operating theatre to serve a population that had lost its only hospital in sustained aerial bombardment. In August 1945, the Irish Red Cross shipped six ambulances, a truck and a utility wagon, several hundred tons of food, hospital beds and tons of heavy equipment from Dublin to Cherbourg. Beckett, a fluent French speaker, was able to arrange to get the material to Saint-Lô, liaise with relevant authorities in France and keep track of the stock.

'It was my job to store the supplies and do the driving,' he said in 1989. 'I used to do a lot of driving, drive the ambulance and the truck. It was a big concern. We had about six ambulances and a truck. I used to drive up to Dieppe to get supplies and bring back nurses.'

Some of those nurses later described being terrified as Beckett drove at speed. His willingness to cover the 150 miles from the port to Saint-Lô 'as quickly as possible' was also mentioned by Dr Jim Gaffney, an Irish pathologist and member of the team. Though Dr Gaffney was not alone in remarking that Samuel Beckett was deeply conscientious about his work.

Perhaps the most telling anecdote from that time was told by Beckett himself to Lawrence Harvey. He recounted that, one night, he and a number of the team went to a party a distance from Saint-Lô. When their Red Cross van failed to start on the journey back, rather than stay overnight, Beckett set out on foot. He walked from 1am to 6am and reached the hospital in time to get the train he had planned to take to Paris. Two others had given in to exhaustion en route.

'Sheer obstinacy, an unwillingness to give up, was, he commented himself, a constant trait in his character,' Knowlson wrote.

That tenacity explains, perhaps, how he got through his days in the Resistance and in hiding. It would serve him again when he returned to Paris, a city on its knees, to begin an extraordinarily productive writing phase. He turned out six works between 1946 and 1950.

Like so many others, he spoke little about his close shave with the Gestapo, his work in the Resistance or his years in hiding in Roussillon. He seldom mentioned the honours bestowed on him by the French government: the Croix de Guerre and the Médaille de la Reconnaissance française. When he did eventually talk about the war years, he was very clear about his reasons for taking the action that he did.

'I was fighting against the Germans who were making life hell for my friends, and not for the French nation.'

ESCAPE LINES

3

A Kit Kat, a Mars Bar and an Orange

'EVERYTHING WAS EVER SO QUIET. THE AIRPLANE WAS
SLASHED TO PIECES AND WE WERE VERY LUCKY TO SURVIVE.'
BILL MAGRATH

Red Cross office, Paris, 1941: When RAF pilots Sgt Bill Magrath
and Sgt Oliver James heard the door locking behind them in
an upstairs room, they were certain their escape attempt had
come to an abrupt end. They had gone down a side street near
the Arc de Triomphe and seen a placard marked 'Red Cross'
in front of a building that looked like a warehouse. Having
already made it on foot from Rouen to Paris, a distance of
some 135km, it felt like a godsend. They didn't think twice
about venturing inside. The new arrivals caused a ripple of
excitement and when they asked for help, a man took charge.
He was sharp and business-like and asked them a series of
questions before leading them up a staircase. He showed them
into a room and then locked the door from the other side.

'Aw, we've lost,' Bill said to his companion, believing their
luck had finally run out.

———— ————

Sgt Bill Magrath, a 19 year old from Co. Fermanagh, had been unsettled from the moment he set off on a mission with the 82 Squadron more than a year and a half before, on 13 April 1940. When the squadron set out on a sunny morning from the Royal Air Force (RAF) at Watton in Norfolk, he had an overwhelming feeling that he was not coming back.

'When we set out on that raid – it seems like a funny thing to say now – but I knew I wasn't coming back,' he said later. That was why he tucked into his rations as soon as they were airborne, making short work of the Kit Kat, Mars bar and orange he had been given. 'I always worked on the principle that there was no guarantee of me enjoying this later, so I ate the lot immediately. At least I'd won that if nothing else.'

His gut instinct proved right. As the squadron approached its target, the aerodrome at Aalborg, in Denmark, they flew into 'a hornet's nest of 109s', to use Sgt Magrath's evocative phrase. Messerschmitt Bf 109s had superior firing power and were much faster than the 12 British Blenheim bombers flying in formation in a cloudless sky. The enemy planes opened fire, hitting the port engine, on the left of Magrath's plane. It caught fire, but the Blenheim still managed to shoot down a 109 and drop its bomb load on the target.

'It was the most frightening thing because I was looking down through this bomb sight and you could actually see the anti-aircraft going down the barrels of the gun – you could see the flame and the whole thing coming up at you,' Magrath recalled.

When they were hit again, the starboard engine caught fire. The heat and the fumes were overpowering. They made a forced descent in a fjord running west from Aalborg. It was about

14.00, five hours after take-off that morning. The mission was an unmitigated disaster: 11 of the 12 planes had been shot down. The twelfth had turned back earlier with engine trouble. Of the 33 men who set out that morning, 20 were dead.

In fact, the mission had been doomed from the start. The 82 Squadron had lost its experienced wing commander – Percy 'Paddy' Bernard, the earl of Bandon, in Cork, had been promoted – and the unit was being asked to go to the extreme limit of its flying and firing range. They were under pressure to succeed as the Germans had extended Aalborg's airspace in preparation for attacks on England.

The stakes were high which, in part, explains why the squadron continued on even after cloud cover disappeared.

'We gave the Germans all the time in the world to see where we were and where we were going,' Magrath said later.

All Bill Magrath remembers is coming to in the water. 'Everything was ever so quiet. The airplane was slashed to pieces and we were very lucky to survive. I drifted in and out of consciousness. Some people waded out from the island and brought us ashore. I was put at the bottom of the boat. I was still interested in [a female rescuer's] legs, so I knew I [was] going to live.'

After the crash-landings, all 13 survivors were arrested, Magrath among them. He had sustained serious injuries. His right arm and shoulder were badly broken. His right leg and hip sustained similar injuries and he was blind in one eye. He was taken to Aalborg hospital and later sent to a German prisoner-of-war hospital where he underwent an operation so specialised it would not have been available in the UK at the time.

That was cold comfort, though, because at one stage he was certain he was not going to make it. 'When I was in hospital, I was in a good deal of pain. I knew I could die if I wanted to. I had a choice: if I relaxed, I could die; if I wanted to keep fighting the pain, and fighting the pain, I might live.'

He chose to fight. And more than that, when he was physically able, he chose to try to escape.

——— ———

Escape attempts by prisoners of war (POWs) were intrinsically bound up with the Resistance movement – the former's chance of success was heavily dependent on the latter. For instance, one prisoner who had unscrewed a lavatory window on a train and jumped from it was entirely reliant on the good will of the people he met afterwards.

It was highly unlikely that an escaper would bump into an active resistance member straight off. More often than not, fugitives put their lives in the hands of people they encountered along the way; ordinary people who were willing to take enormous risks for strangers. Anyone found sheltering or helping an escaped Allied soldier risked arrest, torture, imprisonment, even death. Yet, many helped men – it was mostly men – on the run, giving them food, clothes or shelter.

Those 'little acts of courage', as Sgt Magrath once described them, were also little acts of resistance, even if informal ones.

Sympathetic helpers often knew, or had a way of contacting, resistance members. Helping Allied airmen get to safety was a central aim of many networks, particularly later in the war after America joined the conflict.

The man who jumped from the train was captured days later, but escape attempts were so common that the Germans took extraordinary measures to prevent them. When prisoners were being transported by train, their boots were often removed to discourage escape. In the Stalag Luft camps, where hundreds of airmen including Sgt Magrath and James were held, microphones were hidden in the Nissen huts to rumble any whispered plans to flee. At one point, the Germans even employed a seismologist to detect any prisoner tunnels under construction.

Even if a prisoner made it to freedom, luck played a huge role. In a sense, Bill Magrath's injuries worked in his favour because after spending more than a year in camps in Germany and what is now Poland, his name was put forward for a prison repatriation scheme. Allied and Axis forces had apparently agreed to exchange prisoners who were no longer fit for action.

On 28 September 1941, Bill Magrath was moved from Stalag Luft 1 near Barth in northern Germany – a camp where there was 'terrific morale', he said – to Stalag IXC in Bad Sulza in central Germany. All prisoners on the repatriation list were assembled there.

'The wounded men, about 100 altogether, were kept in a quarry for the five days during which we were at Stalag IXC,' Magrath later told British intelligence. 'The badly wounded slept in a disused factory and the others had to sleep outside. Most of us had only two blankets each and many had no greatcoat. In order to keep warm three of us used to huddle together at night in the open.'

They all left for Rouen in northern France at the beginning of October. The journey took two days, but it was comfortable and the prisoners ate well; they had been supplied with several hundred Red Cross food parcels.

Sgt James later described their journey to the town. 'Rigorous measures were taken to prevent contact with the French,' he wrote in a post-war debriefing report. 'The windows were shut and the blinds down and Feld Gendarmerie [German military police] were keeping back the crowds of women. On our way through Belgium [earlier] we threw Red Cross parcels out of the window, and the Belgians made whoopee all along the line.'

In Rouen, they were held at the Caserne Jeanne d'Arc, a barracks named after the town's most famous resident, the fifteenth-century symbol of freedom Joan of Arc. From there, they were taken to Heilag, a prison camp built on a racecourse on the outskirts of town. By then, Bill Magrath began to realise that the repatriation scheme was not going ahead, which meant he would be stuck in the camp indefinitely. He started to think seriously about making an escape.

Another prisoner, Sgt Oliver 'Ollie' James, a pilot with 83 Squadron from Salisbury in England, had exactly the same thought. They made an ideal team, as Magrath explained later: 'With his dash and my caution, we made a fairly good combination.'

James had been shot down near Morlaix in Brittany, France, on 22 March 1941. He was captured and taken to hospital where his left arm was amputated. Eight months later, now in Rouen, he felt strong enough to attempt an escape with the physical and mental strain that entailed.

On 14 November 1941, under cover of darkness, the two men with two others – Sgt Patterson and Sgt Maderson – cut their way through the barbed-wire fence with a pliers a French worker had left behind, perhaps deliberately. They crept past a Nissen hut full of Germans, so close they could hear them talking inside. Once outside the camp, they split up into groups of two to increase their chances. Magrath and James set off in grim weather, scavenging what they could from the fields, such as rutabaga or swede. The root vegetable became a wartime staple in France, a difficult reality for a nation which had dismissed it as animal fodder before severe food shortages changed their minds.

But in the cold of November, there were slim pickings for the two airmen. With little to eat and no idea of how they were going to get to Paris and the American embassy, they knew they were going to need help. After inadvertently going around in circles, they eventually reached Les Essarts, a village about 10km south of Rouen.

They thought their best bet would be to approach the local priest. 'He was a bit frightened, but awfully brave,' Sgt James said later. He took them to his house where they were revived with a hot meal and a hot bath. After that, the priest made the rounds of some trusted parishioners to secure civilian clothes for the two escapees.

He gave them some money and drilled them in the French they would need to buy two tickets to Paris at the local station. He assumed the role of the ticket man and they had to practise their set phrases on him. Sgt Magrath's schoolboy French, learned at Portora Royal School in Enniskillen, came in very useful, he said later. When he and his brother were pupils there, they were teased for their accents – they were known as Och Aye 1 and Och Aye 2 – but during the war his knowledge gained from his alma mater would get him out of a tight spot.

The journey to Paris went without a hitch, but they found themselves in a city under enemy occupation with no idea of where to go, or who to trust. There were severe food shortages, a curfew was in place and the atmosphere was tense and uncertain. One resident bemoaned the 'black boots stomping noisily along the stone pavements', an evocative description of a city under German occupation.

In the countryside, they had stuck out like 'sore thumbs', as they put it. Even in civilian clothes, an Allied soldier was conspicuous. The stride of their walk was different. So too was the way they held a cigarette. Or they might give themselves away simply by the manner in which they dug their hands deeply into their pockets. In Paris, all of that was less obvious. At least in a bustling metropolis, the two airmen blended in with the crowd. But they had another big problem. After buying a guide of the city, they made their way to the American embassy and found, to their horror, that it was closed. Like all other diplomatic missions, the embassy had been operating out of Vichy, the administrative capital of the free zone, since the Germans occupied the city in June 1940.

Then, as Magrath recounts, they did something totally reckless as curfew approached: 'We went up to this lady of the streets and said, "We are on the run, can you shelter us?" That was a hell of a risk to take. She turned up trumps. She took us home to the little flat she had. She gave us some ersatz coffee [a coffee substitute often made from acorns] and a slice of bread. We weren't in the passionate mood. We slept on the floor of her room. She took us to the cinema to watch a German war film telling us how well they were doing. We watched it with Germans sitting all around us, it gave us a very funny feeling.'

Sgt James gives such a different account of being sheltered that he must be referring to a second night they spent in Paris. According to his escape report, an elderly woman took them to her home where her son and daughter-in-law insisted the airmen take their bed.

In both cases, though, it shows how ordinary people were willing to help soldiers despite the danger.

The next day – or the one after that, if they spent two nights holed up in Parisian flats – they made their way to a church. Given their positive experience with the *curé* a few days before, they were hopeful of support, but they tried two churches without success. The priests did not want to get involved. 'They didn't betray us either,' Magrath said later, only too aware that was a distinct possibility.

The two men kept going and found themselves near the Arc de Triomphe, the famous monument at the western end of the Champs-Élysées dedicated to those who died for France.

Coming across a Red Cross office down a side street seemed like serendipity. The elderly woman at the reception desk put down her knitting, welcomed them in and led them into a big hall. Inside, several women were seated at a trestle table, knitting and packing parcels destined for POWs.

When a man led them into a room and locked the door from the outside, Magrath feared the worst. However, a short time later, another man they described as a monk entered the room.

Sgt Bill Magrath recalled that moment with particular clarity: 'He looked at the two of us and asked who we were. As soon as we spoke, he homed in on me and said, "You're Irish," and I said, "Yes."'

Then the interview proper began. 'Where are you from? Where did you go to school? Who did you know there?'

Sgt Bill Magrath began to give his answers, telling his rather gentle interrogator that he was from near Clones and had attended Portora Royal School in Enniskillen in Co. Fermanagh – coincidentally, Samuel Beckett attended the same school decades earlier. When quizzed further, Magrath gave the name of the headmaster, the names of others who had gone there and confirmed the presence of a monastery in the town.

If a discussion about the fabric of a town in Northern Ireland seemed surreal, it was one Irishman's way of establishing the bona fide credentials of another in an occupied city in wartime. The man asking the questions was not a monk, but Fr Kenneth Monaghan, a Passionist priest from Drumcliff in Co. Sligo who was now taking enormous risks to help Allied soldiers on the run at the nearby St Joseph's church.

First, he had to establish that these evaders who arrived in Paris in November 1941 were who they said they were. The impromptu verification process differed for each person but as a man who had himself spent time in a monastery outside Enniskillen, he knew exactly what to ask a person purporting to know the town.

Fr Monaghan was no stranger to war either. When he was ordained in 1929, his 'remarkable' career prior to his entry into the Passionist Order was reported in disbelieving prose in several newspapers. 'Priest's thrilling career' ran the headline in the *Frontier Sentinel* on 19 January 1929. It went on to sketch his 'adventurous military career' from his entry into the Royal Irish Regiment as a private at the outbreak of World

War I to his lucky escape from a death sentence in a Russian jail some years later.

The Catholic Standard gave this pithy summary: 'Bank clerk, soldier, German prisoner of war, Russian prisoner of war, then bank clerk again, and now Passionist priest.' Another still, the *Nottingham and Midland Catholic News*, described how Fr Kenneth, born Michael Joseph Monaghan in Sligo in 1893, had 'escaped Trotsky's vengeance'.

The newspaper neatly summed up Fr Kenneth's career like this:

'He served in France, and was taken prisoner at St. Quentin [in 1918]. After the War he volunteered for service with the [anti-Bolshevik] 'White Russians'. When his regiment mutinied, most of the Russian officers were murdered, and he was thrown in Moscow's criminal prison at Trotsky's command. Here, and suffering great hardships, he was sentenced to death with twelve other British officers.

'Had it not been for the heroic succour of the Anglican Chaplain of the English Church, the Rev. Mr. North and his wife, he would probably have starved in the prison, but ultimately in an exchange of prisoners, arranged by Sir James O'Grady, he was repatriated and returned to England via Finland. The next year he returned to his old post with a London [banking] firm, and later entered the Passionist Order at Enniskillen.'

Later, he was appointed chaplain to the British Expeditionary Forces and was due to go to Dunkirk, but was ordered back to St Joseph's in Paris. Another eventful chapter opened there because, as a British passport holder, he was arrested and detained briefly by the Gestapo at the start of the war.

If anybody knew of Sgt James and Sgt Magrath's plight, it was Fr Kenneth. Perhaps his own experience prompted him to take such risks to help fugitives at St Joseph's, the Irish church on the upmarket, tree-lined Ave Hoche off the Arc de Triomphe. His work during the war was arguably even more newsworthy than what went before but, for obvious reasons, Fr Kenneth never said a word about it. We know of him through the testimony of Magrath and others.

Once the priest had established the two escaping sergeants were genuine, Magrath says he set about helping them to secure false identity papers, travel permits and train tickets for the next leg of their dangerous journey.

We only have Sgt Magrath's brief account of this process, but behind those actions lay a complicated network of people working clandestinely at enormous personal risk. The journey to secure any of the documents necessary to escape was dangerous. We don't know whether Fr Kenneth personally secured the papers, or if somebody else went on his behalf.

In any case, it involved making contact with one of the many photographers, artists and printers secretly manufacturing false papers. It was a question of using whatever materials you could find to fashion a realistic-looking document.

One master of the craft, Jewish man Adolfo Kaminsky, created thousands of documents. He used a sewing machine to punch perforation holes in the official stamps. He made rubber stamps from discarded wood and found a way to reproduce watermarks and letterheads.

His most important discovery, he said later, came about because of his previous job as a dry cleaner. He had seen the power of lactic acid in removing stains. 'It was very important because that enabled us to use existing identity documents, existing papers that were real. And you could erase things from them without leaving any trace,' he explained in 2017.

The Germans, aware of the many excellent counterfeiters in operation, frequently changed the watermarks and stamps on travel passes and identity papers in an attempt to outwit them.

——— ——

Fr Kenneth also needed help from several others to smuggle airmen out of Paris. Among these helpers were two Irish women.

Lily Hannigan was from Dublin. She and her sister Agnes both worked as governesses in Paris. When the war broke out, Lily moved to Poigny-la-Forêt, south-west of Paris, where she worked for a well-to-do family, teaching their six sons.

She told an *Irish Independent* reporter in 1956 how she came into contact with the Resistance – or rather, how it came into contact with her:

'"It happened quite accidentally," she insists. An American plane came down in the garden of the house where she was governess to a family of six boys. The crew was unhurt, and she directed them to a hiding place in the forest nearby. By devious means, she got in touch with personnel who arranged for the Americans to be smuggled out.'

One of those people was Fr Kenneth. The sisters were parishioners at St Joseph's. Lily continued to attend mass there, regularly cycling the 120km round-trip from Poigny-la-Forêt to deliver messages from her local resistance network.

Lily was instrumental in saving 'many' other lives too. Her efforts were later recognised in the US. 'Lily, who is now

Mrs Patrick Collins and the mother of a bonny child, has a certificate of acknowledgment from President Eisenhower for her share in rescuing American parachutists,' the *Irish Independent* noted.

The name of another Irishwoman, 'Miss Fitzpatrick', has also been linked to Fr Kenneth Monaghan's resistance work.

That is interesting because an American intelligence document reveals that Miss Fitzpatrick was also a friend of Killarney-born *résistante* Janie McCarthy.

'She did not personally help aviators,' the document continues, 'but brought food and clothes and 1.000 frs... to an aviator who had been shot down near Le Perreux, in 1945. She does not remember the name. She also brought clothes (given by Mr Aubant) to Mr Kenneth Taylor, (1 Cours de France, Athis Mons, Seine et Oise) who helped lots of British and American personnel. The aviators were kept in a monastery at the same address.'

The document says she helped British aviators too, but does not give any detail.

It is not only possible, but likely, that other Irish people helped Fr Kenneth spirit fugitives, POWs and downed airmen out of Paris. Or, at least, they knew about it. Lily's sister Agnes told writer David O'Donoghue in 1993 that she knew of the priest's work, although she said it was a 'closely guarded secret'. She even claimed he had been sent to Paris by British intelligence to establish links with the Resistance.

Agnes's letters to the Irish legation also give a chilling insight into the shortages faced by the Irish community in Paris during the war years. She wrote to Irish diplomats in Vichy pleading for 'food, any sort... It was an activity in itself staying alive.'

There were certainly advantages to having an Irish passport: citizens of neutral countries were less likely to be detained or told to report to local police stations. But there were also disadvantages. The Irish government had imposed limits on the financial help going to the Irish trapped in France. And because they were Irish, or holders of Irish passports, they were denied access to British aid or the bounty of American Red Cross parcels.

One Irishwoman almost caused a diplomatic incident when she wrote to the legation in Vichy claiming that Irish people in Paris were 'dying of starvation'. When challenged, she was unable to name a single Irish person who had actually died because of lack of food, but that doesn't mean the shortages were not severe.

The lack of food underlines the selflessness of those active in the Resistance. They had little themselves, yet they eked out food and clothes to give to people on the run.

Irish religious communities in Paris also tried to help. St Joseph's church was helping fugitives, but it also did what it could to alleviate the suffering among its own Irish parishioners. The sisters at the Irish convent on the rue Murillo, in the eighth arrondissement, ran a hostel that helped Irish and British girls throughout the war.

Not too far away, Fr Patrick Travers kept the Irish College on rue des Irlandais out of German hands during the entire occupation. He set up what he described as one of the 'finest shelters in Paris... Nothing save a direct hit could damage it.' He cultivated vegetables on the college's grounds – 'I grew my own plants of tomatoes, salad, cucumber, vegetable marrows and Brussels sprouts' – and gave much of the crop away to his neighbours.

Fr Kenneth himself escorted Sgt Magrath and Sgt James to the train station on the next step of their long journey to hoped-for freedom. He gave them a little money, the appropriate documents and introduced them to a French doctor who gave them the name of a fellow doctor who would help them when they reached Nevers, a town near the demarcation line.

They holed up in Nevers for three weeks before crossing the line on 19 December, travelling across the River Loire in a small boat somewhere between Nevers and Clermont-Ferrand. The next day, another person drove them to the station to catch the train to Marseille. Once they arrived in that city, Dr Louis Nouveau sheltered them. He secretly noted the names of hundreds of airmen he sheltered on the pages of a nineteenth edition of a Voltaire volume.

Just before Christmas, the two men were taken to Toulouse and from there to Port-Vendres. With two guides and four Belgians, they finally made a 'diabolical crossing' over the Pyrenees into Spain. They were very careful not to ask too much about the people who helped them along the way in case they were captured. They could not give away names that they did not know.

They were ultimately taken to Barcelona and the British Consulate who, though shocked at the price, agreed to pay the smugglers 120,000 FF for each man's passage (worth about €3,500 today). The men went on to Madrid, then Gibraltar and finally arrived in Britain on 7 March 1942.

As Douglas MacArthur II, an American diplomat in Paris and later Vichy, said: 'The one requirement… most resistance organisations that I worked with had was that, if you were taken by the Gestapo, hold out for 24 hours if you can, but hold out for 12 hours [at least], because probably by that time it would be known that you had been taken and the network had been blown and there would be time for people to go underground.'

As it turned out, it was the British who did the rigorous questioning during lengthy debriefing sessions. When they got home, Magrath said British intelligence 'grilled us for four or five days'. After that, he finally got home.

'We were very, very lucky,' said Magrath.

Both men were awarded the Military Medal in May 1942. The citation read: 'Sergeant Magrath in company with Sergeant James, and in the face of many difficulties and physical handicaps, succeeded in escaping from the prison camp and showing the utmost determination made his way after many adventures through France and Spain to Gibraltar, from where he was repatriated.'

After the war, Bill Magrath went on to have a career in air traffic control and become Mayor of Salisbury in England. His story came to light after he sold his war medals, including the prestigious Military Medal, to raise funds for a cardiac unit at his local Salisbury District Hospital.

Sgt Oliver James got married shortly after his return home, but insisted on resuming his wartime career. He was fitted with a prosthetic arm, retrained and took off on another mission on 4 October 1943. This time he didn't come home. He was shot down and killed. He was 23.

America recognised the work done by Fr Kenneth Monaghan during the occupation of Paris. He moved to Germany after the war, working as a British army chaplain in the Rhine region. Later, he was posted to Wales where, again, he worked as chaplain at the RAF base in Brawdy. He died in 1969 in St Non's Retreat Centre, Pembrokeshire, South Wales. He was buried with military honours, according to his nephew, the late John Clancy who attended the funeral with another nephew, also Kenneth Monaghan, from Drumcliff, Sligo.

The Hannigan sisters stayed in Paris. Lily was one of the first members of the Irish Club when it was established in Paris in the mid-1950s. The American Legion in Paris, the US war veterans' association, offered its premises free for the club's monthly get-together for 'dancing, tea, wine and gossip'. Reporting on the gesture, the *Irish Independent* seemed to suggest that it was proof of US gratitude for Lily Hannigan's clandestine wartime work.

Lily's sister Agnes founded an agency in Paris which arranged student exchanges.

As for Miss Fitzpatrick? She was Judith Winifred 'Pat' Fitzpatrick from Killeshin, Co. Laois, a teacher who lived near St Joseph's church on Ave Hoche. Her proximity to Fr Kenneth Monaghan might explain her involvement, although her niece June Nelson later said she became involved in the Resistance through friends and a Sister Bernarde.

After the war, the Allies acknowledged her work in helping servicemen escape and she was awarded an MBE. She died in a car accident in France in May 1983 when she was in her eighties. She was brought home to her native Killeshin to be buried in accordance with her wishes.

The local priest, P.J. Brophy, remembered her as a woman with an iron will whose zest for life was infectious. 'She was a vigorous, independent-minded, immensely compassionate woman,' he said.

4
'I Risked My Neck'

'IF ANYONE EVER GOT A SWEET... WE WOULD MAKE SIX
PARTS OF IT. THAT'S HOW WE DID EVERYTHING DURING
THE WAR. WE SHARED AND WE STUCK TOGETHER. IN
PARTICULAR, THE IRISH.'
                                        DELIA MURPHY KIERNAN

Belfast, 1941: When 180 Luftwaffe bombers dropped wave after wave of high-explosive bombs on Belfast on the night of 15 April, Delia Murphy kept singing.

She sang on during an aerial bombardment that lasted five agonising hours, inviting the audience packed into the Ulster Hall for an Easter *céilí* to join in the chorus. She remained 'perfectly cool', the newspapers said, and sang the songs she had made her own. She even told the audience to defy the Germans to do their worst. The band and a troupe of dancers also kept up the performance until they got the 'all clear'.

Delia's bravery was heralded on the front page of several newspapers the next day alongside reports of the worst air raid on any city outside London at that point in the war. It was a night of 'tragedy, horror and heroism', the *Irish Weekly and Ulster Examiner* reported. The article went on to praise the ordinary men and women who, 'despite the hail of bombs and falling shrapnel, worked feverishly through the night to extricate the living and the dead from under tons of debris'.

A total of 745 people died. Some 1,500 others were injured and thousands of families were left homeless in the second of four devastating Luftwaffe raids on Belfast in April and May of 1941.

Delia's courage – and defiance – resonated not only in Belfast but in neutral Dublin. In October of that year, the Dublin Women's Social and Progressive League opened its session by giving Mrs Kiernan (her married name) a presentation 'as a token of the members' appreciation of her bravery during the air raid on Belfast early this year'.

On the same day, 4 October, the press reported that her husband, Dr T.J. Kiernan, Director of Broadcasting in Dublin, would soon be taking up his position as New Irish Minister to the Vatican. Delia Murphy Kiernan didn't know it then, but she would soon be drawing on the courage she displayed in Belfast to defy the Germans once again but, this time, in secret and at great risk.

The couple and their four children – Blon, Nuala, Colm and Orla – left for Rome days later. They boarded a seaplane at Foynes in Co. Limerick and flew to Lisbon. From there, they flew to Spain and then on to Rome.

'We are here safe and sound after a lot of ups & downs in three different planes,' Delia wrote in a letter to her friend Kathleen O'Connell, Éamon de Valera's secretary, in November. 'Rome is lovely & everyone here is on intimate terms with the Almighty. They stroll around the churches on Sundays – armed with two chairs as a rule – and don't take the least notice of the priest who is trying to preach a sermon. I'd like to see them doing that down in the Co. Mayo!'

By then, Delia and family had already been received by Pope Pius XII and, as she told her friend, the family was greatly impressed by his modesty and sanctity. Despite her irreverent tone, she was deeply religious and wanted to tell Kathleen O'Connell that the Pope's blessing, which he conferred on family and friends, extended to her.

Later, she would meet a leader of a very different kind, the Italian dictator Benito Mussolini. He sided with the Germans after the Fall of France in June 1940, even though public opinion was against him.

The Vatican, on the other hand, was an independent, sovereign state – the world's smallest at 108 acres – and it was neutral. When Italy joined the war, diplomats from 'enemy' Allied countries such as Britain were obliged to move into the Vatican's precinct. Ireland as a neutral country, however, had special status. The Irish legation was situated in the city of Rome itself, on the via San Martino della Battaglia near the railway terminus, but the Irish government had warned all Irish diplomatic staff of the need to remain impartial. 'Imprudent and unneutral expressions of views' could have serious implications for Ireland's neutrality, it warned in a circular in 1941, pointedly, adding: 'This also applies to wives'.

As the Vatican's new Irish minister took up his post, T.J. Kiernan must have mulled over the difficulties inherent in treading a diplomatic path between Axis and Allied forces in a country at war.

Delia, however, was not so much thinking of what lay ahead as what she was leaving behind. When one newspaper asked how she liked the prospect of living in Rome, she said she 'would prefer to be singing songs in Ireland'. She was leaving just as her singing career was reaching its height. She had just recorded 12 new songs with HMV, the music and entertainment company, which were due for release. Her plans for editing and recording more new songs were now 'in the lap of the gods', she wistfully told one reporter.

In spite of that, she settled into her new life in Rome with characteristic enthusiasm. She had an ease with people that made the endless round of diplomatic engagements, even in wartime, effortless. She was gregarious, outgoing and likely to burst into song given the slightest opportunity, the polar opposite of her husband who was courteous, retiring and very discreet.

The Murphy and Kiernan families had both objected to their marriage but the couple went ahead anyway, marrying in 1924. If their families feared their contrasting personalities would be an issue, it proved to be a combination that worked – in the private sphere, but also in diplomatic life. She was the welcoming hostess, chatty and personable, while he was the serious diplomat, dedicated and committed.

By Christmas 1941, Delia Murphy Kiernan had already established herself as the ideal diplomat's wife. Or at least that was the impression given by Sean Piondar who extolled the many qualities of 'Eire's Legation Hostess in the Vatican' in the Christmas issue of the *Waterford Standard*.

He wrote: 'Mrs Kiernan is a fine type of Irish womanhood: humorous, hospitable; proud of her home and fond of children; interested in Eire's language and cultural revivals; the friend and adviser of writers and artists and singers – the perfect partner, in fact, for one-time Radio Eireann Director TJ Kiernan, scholar and organiser, diplomat and economist.'

Piondar gave a sense that Delia was also much more. Although born in Mayo, she was, he wrote, 'Dublin's most versatile woman', a university graduate (B Comm from University College of Galway in 1923), a film star, a writer, a singer and an actress.

'Few who met the vivid, spirited woman for the first time would believe that she is the mother of four children altogether – and that, as well as having run a huge Dublin house and looking after her family, she was also a success in musical and film spheres,' he wrote.

One of the first to get a sense of this vivid, spirited woman was the dictator Benito Mussolini himself. 'I'll never forget [meeting him],' she recalled, 'I attended a reception in his honour, and I had to walk the length of a room that seemed a mile long, to be received by the high and mighty Benito. I was determined to put him off his majestic stroke and gabbled away to him in English. He had to call on his interpreter.'

He thought her charming, apparently, but others found Delia's approach too informal. As friend, actor Liam Redmond, put it: 'Delia was an extrovert, she liked people who had the same openness as herself, and they liked her. Women with social pretensions and prissy men did not care for her. She just thought such people ridiculous and, typically, she would seek out someone who was less hidebound by convention with whom she could have a bit of "craic".'

Yet, everyone was made to feel welcome at the Irish legation in Rome. Delia herself was charmed by her new residence, a three-storey villa with a roof garden overlooking the city. The carpet in the reception room had been hand-loomed by the Dun Emer Guild, the Irish Arts and Crafts textile studio in Dublin. The dining room – equipped with a dumb waiter, which pleased her no end – could seat up to 60 people.

'It was there I was your drawing-room hostess to dignitaries of the Church, Italian generals and leaders, [Erwin] Rommel and [Albert] Kesselring of the German High Command, and later, General Mark Clarke of the U.S. forces, and [Harold] Alexander of the British,' Delia said.

She hosted the Irish from the colleges on Thursday afternoons and, when food became increasingly scarce, she made sure they went home with food parcels.

For some, it proved to be life-saving. At least that is what Dr Thomas Ryan, later Bishop of Clonfert, a regular guest at legation receptions, thought. 'I would venture to say that there are many priests alive today working for God and the Church who owe their lives to her generosity and kindness,' he said later.

The scarcity of food was one of the most obvious signs of war in a city that otherwise appeared normal, at least on the surface. Michael MacWhite, Irish Minister to the Italian government, wrote in February 1942:

'A stranger arriving suddenly in Rome in these days would find it difficult to realise, from external appearances at least, that Italy is at war. Only comparatively few military uniforms are seen in the streets. Recently, however, German uniforms are more frequent as it is no longer possible to buy civilian clothing because of the rationing.'

The shops were open but they couldn't sell clothes, shoes, furs or any items that contained gold, silver or precious stones. In short, almost everything wearable or edible was near impossible to buy.

'Potatoes have not been available for several weeks,' MacWhite continued. 'The only vegetables on the market are

Brussels Sprouts, Cardoon [wild artichoke], Haricots, Cauli-
flower, Spinach, Artichokes, and such like unappetising garden
products. Eggs are limited to one per week and as they come
from Bulgaria they are rarely eatable. Hotels, restaurants and
Boarding houses are prohibited from serving either meat, fish
or eggs on Sundays and the afternoon of Saturdays. Workmen
doing odd jobs now ask for something to eat in lieu of any
other payment.' In essence, he concluded, 'everything appears
fine on the surface like a person who wears a starched front
with no shirt underneath'.

Under that misleading surface, however, Italians who
flouted rationing regulations were dealt with harshly. They
got sentences of up to five years' penal servitude. It was also
becoming clear that the Jewish population was coming under
increasing persecution. The country had introduced a raft of
anti-Jewish legislation in the late 1930s but, unlike other countries, Italy had been a relatively safe place for Jewish people.
The Italians did not support deportation.

That was about to change.

In July 1943, the Allies landed in Sicily, 'planting their feet
firmly on Italian soil', as MacWhite put it. Shortly afterwards,
on 19 July, some 500 Allied bombers launched an air raid on
Rome, killing thousands of civilians.

Bombs fell within yards of the Irish legation, blowing out
one of its windows, according to Delia. The Kiernan family took
refuge on the first floor as they had no basement shelter. The
family moved temporarily to a safer house near St Peter's Basilica.

A week later, Mussolini was voted out of office by his own
Grand Council and arrested. People rushed on to the streets in
night-gowns and pyjamas to celebrate the fall of the dictator.

Delia's husband gave this evocative description of the scene: 'A few minutes before midnight we were raised from our beds by wild shouting of exultation. Broken-down cars loaded with young men were careering through Rome shouting their heads off. Mussolini is arrested... People who have been waiting like a condemned-to-death prisoner reacted now with all the wild abandon of reprieve. Not only reprieve, but complete liberty. Little did they, or any of us, anticipate that Rome's travail was only about to begin.'

The rejoicing in the streets was quickly replaced by speculation and fear.

'Rome', Dr Kiernan wrote a few weeks later, 'was a city of the wildest rumours.' There was talk – in fact, it was more like hope – that the Allies were coming, but they were not. 'And so the rumours went round and round while German Battalions advanced towards the city.'

After Mussolini's downfall, General Pietro Badoglio stepped into the breach and negotiated an armistice, surrendering to the Allies on 3 September 1943. When news of it broke some days later, Mother Mary St Luke, an American nun living in Rome, summed up the mood of the city and a nation when she wrote: 'A sigh of relief went up from the crowds around the loudspeakers. Then a pause. People looked at each other questioningly – "Armistice or Armageddon?" What about the Germans?'

She hit the nail on the head. A month later, when Italy declared war on Germany, Hitler retaliated with lightning speed and German troops quickly occupied northern and central Italy. They swept into Rome and, on 16 October, arrested hundreds of the city's 12,000-strong Jewish population. More than 1,000 Jews were deported to Auschwitz's killing camp, and a further 800 would follow.

Meanwhile, several thousand Allied POWs escaped from internment camps when their guards left their posts after Italy's surrender. Many stayed put, believing the Allies were not far away, but an estimated 18,000 soldiers made a bid for freedom. They were now on the run and in need of assistance. Not all of those men turned up in Rome, but when they did, they knew to seek out a certain monsignor.

——— —

Kerryman and Vatican diplomat Monsignor Hugh O'Flaherty had been helping POWs and those in need since the conflict began but, as hostilities continued, he became convinced of the need to come down on the side of the Allies. The deciding factor was a newspaper photograph he saw in 1942 showing the forced labour of Jewish people on the banks of the River Tiber.

As he later told his friend Major (Maj.) Sam Derry, an escaped Allied serviceman: 'When this War started I used to listen to broadcasts from both sides. All propaganda, of course, and both making the same terrible charges against the other. I frankly didn't know which side to believe – until they started rounding up the Jews in Rome. They treated them like beasts, making old men and respectable women get down on their knees and scrub the roads. You know the sort of thing that happened after that; it got worse and worse, and I knew then which side I had to believe.'

The numbers of Jewish people deported would have been

much higher without Monsignor O'Flaherty's escape line and the support for the Jewish community in the Roman population.

The Rome Escape Line was set up around a Council of Three. It included O'Flaherty (codename Golf because he loved the game), Count Sarsfield Salazar of the Swiss legation (known as Emma) and John May, butler to the British envoy to the Holy See, Sir D'Arcy Osborne, and a man who knew the black market inside out.

It's not clear exactly when Delia Kiernan decided to help the monsignor, but this is how she described that moment:

'For a time, I wrestled with my conscience and prayed for guidance about what I should do to help Fr. O'Flaherty. A voice inside me said charity was something God intended for all humanity, in war and peace. And I remembered the words of St. Paul: "Now abideth faith, hope, and charity, these three; but the greatest of these is charity." What else could it be but charity to help those in trouble with the Nazis?'

She was well aware that the punishment for helping a fugitive or sheltering an Allied serviceman was death. As she said herself, posters reminding the population of that stark fact were splashed all around the city during the nine-month occupation of Rome. 'I doubt if they would have shot the wife of the Irish Minister, but they might not have hesitated with others in our group,' she said.

Prompted by events, the organisation filled up quickly with volunteers willing to risk their lives to help people escape Nazi terror. They came from all walks of life: the religious community, diplomatic staff, ordinary civilians, even an Italian aristocrat, Princess Evelini 'Nini' Pallavicini, and now the wife of an Irish diplomat and her daughter.

'I was in the thick of it,' Delia Murphy Kiernan later said. 'And [I] was determined to save the hides of others and not get caught.'

She went about her business as normal, making sure that none of 'the high-ranking German warlords', as she called them, ever suspected what she was doing. 'All of it was a challenge, from the scarlet robes of the cardinal to the glittering decorations of the generals… but I risked my neck and Her Excellency's immunity because a voice inside of me said it was my duty to help.'

—— ——

One of Delia's earliest missions was 'removing' boots from the *Wehrmacht* shoe repair depot right under the noses of the Germans. Shoes were scarce and the increasing numbers of escaping POWs desperately needed them.

When she got word from 'Golf' that help was needed, Delia went to the depot and managed to persuade the Italian shoemaker to part with several pairs. 'While my driver transferred the "booty" into the back of the diplomatic car, I engaged the German office staff opposite in idle conversation, making sure they looked anywhere but out of their window,' she later recalled.

She estimated that she managed to secure about 200 pairs of boots, but Irish priest and fellow network helper Br Humilis mentioned the figure of 900.

In any case, the operation continued over a number of weeks. The boots were brought to the Irish legation and then, under cover of night, they were taken in smaller quantities and thrown into the Vatican where they were collected for distribution. It's not clear who took them to the Vatican, but it was a person who was taking enormous risks.

Br Humilis, a Franciscan monk and bursar at his community at St Isadore's College in Rome, was one of a number of Irish priests involved in the monsignor's network (See Roll of Honour). He was also a canny operator on the black market and succeeded in securing large amounts of food, which were then delivered with the help of a farmer who had a cart with a false bottom.

The black market was so central to survival that even the nuns of Rome were praying to St Joseph to uncover bargains. And they said that their prayers were answered, Dr Kiernan remarked in one letter back to Dublin.

Br Humilis later said he knew of Delia's work with the escape network. 'She did help him [Mon. O'Flaherty] a lot that time. Besides getting them German boots and supplying them to the Allied soldiers, she got them food too. I don't know where she got it, but she did. It was risky and highly dangerous as an ambassador's wife to have herself implicated in anything like that. She could have got into serious trouble.'

Another Irishman, Fr Tom Twomey, an Augustinian priest from Tralee, Co. Kerry, told a story that casts a light on how Delia secured extra food. He was also involved in the network. He sheltered POWs at his order's house, the College of St Patrick's, or escorted them, dressed in Augustinian garb, to different hiding places throughout the city.

He knew Delia well and recounted how he once shared an unlikely bounty of 5,000 eggs with her. Someone had brought them to the college and after taking a few samples – 'to see if they'd sink or float' – Fr Twomey bought the lot. He asked Delia if she'd like some and she bought 1,000, having been assured they would keep in salt water.

'The legation car came and took them away,' the monk recalled.

The same car was put to a much more dangerous use when Delia used it to pick up a Scottish soldier with appendicitis and drive him to a hospital full of wounded German soldiers.

Maj. Sam Derry, himself an escaped British serviceman and vital cog in the escape line, explained how Delia came to be involved in the unlikely rescue mission. A young private, Norman Anderson, of the Cameron Highlanders, became seriously ill but refused to be brought to hospital in Rome because it meant he would lose his freedom. Monsignor O'Flaherty contacted a friend, Professor Albano, a surgeon at a hospital treating German wounded, who agreed to operate on the man but said he would have to be taken away immediately afterwards.

The difficulty, Maj. Derry wrote, 'was getting Anderson to and from hospital. Ambulances were out of the question, taxis were non-existent... and the few private cars were mostly in the hands of the Fascists... That left only the small group of cars belonging to the few members of the Corps Diplomatique... and one of those was in the possession of the Irish ambassador. The monsignor was on good terms with the strictly neutral Irishman, but he knew that there was nothing to be gained by a request that he should allow his car to be used for clandestine purposes. On the other hand, there was nothing to be lost by an appeal to Mrs Kiernan.'

Mrs Kiernan took up the challenge with gusto. 'I called for Fr. Spike in what must have been one of the fanciest ambulances in Rome – my roomy limousine with diplomatic licence plates, and the tricolour of Ireland fluttering from the fender,' she recalled.

Fr John 'Spike' Buckley was an Augustinian priest from Co. Mayo, who had been singled out for the task because he was a big man, strong enough to do the work of two stretcher-bearers. He was also the man in the organisation who cared for sick POWs, so he carried with him a supply of bandages and whatever medicine he could secure.

When the 'ambulance' got to its destination, the priest carried the patient into the operating theatre covered in a priest's cassock. Delia drove around the city for a few hours while he had his operation and picked him up afterwards. She had been told to drop him off with Henrietta Chevalier, a Maltese woman who sheltered fugitives and provided a makeshift nursing home for sick POWs in her already packed apartment.

The diplomatic car was on its way there when it was stopped at traffic lights by the SS. They looked inside and asked who was lying on the back seat.

Delia recounts Fr Buckley's reply with a degree of calmness that she can't have felt at the time: 'Spike explained that he was an Irish priest, and that we were taking him to hospital. The Scottish soldier looked pretty awful, and it was enough to convince the Germans, and they let us drive on.'

The Scot was at Mrs Chevalier's flat, along with five other escapees, when, days later, she received a warning that the Germans were about to raid her home. Mrs Chevalier, like many involved in the escape line, had come to the attention of the authorities, although she was never arrested. With just hours' notice, the five other servicemen were able to vanish into the city, but Private Anderson was still far too ill to walk.

Delia came to the rescue again, using the diplomatic car to spirit him away to the American College where escaper Colin Lesslie, of the Irish Guards, helped him to get back on his feet.

Sam Derry later summed up the operation to help Anderson, and Delia's role in it, like this: 'Rarely has a man owed his life to such strangely assorted factors as a scholarly Monsignor, with the incisive brain of a business tycoon; a giant priest, with the strength of a lion and the gentleness of a lamb; an Irish lady, whose humanity overwhelmed political propriety; a little Maltese widow, with a gallant heart as big as her own expansive family; and an Italian surgeon who, with his enemies all around him, risked his life to save a life.'

Meanwhile, conditions in Rome were getting worse as the winter tightened its grip in the early months of 1944. The city was regularly without water or electricity. Food had become so scarce that the Germans threatened to impose the death penalty on anyone who hoarded supplies.

The escape network went about its work regardless, succeeding in not only hiding but feeding and clothing thousands of POWs and fugitives. Sam Derry couldn't believe how much had been achieved: 'Tramping around Rome with [Monsignor O'Flaherty], I marvelled at how his organisation had so far concealed more than a thousand ex-POWs in convents, crowded flats, on outlying farms.'

In the final analysis, the escape line was credited with saving some 6,500 people.

Although it was set up to help those being persecuted by the Germans, Delia was willing to help anyone in need. On one occasion, an Italian brought her a German soldier he had found in a state of total exhaustion on the streets of Rome. At first, she suspected him of being a spy or an imposter but, after the monsignor and others asked him a series of questions, everyone was satisfied that he was who he claimed to be – a German solider, but also a priest who wanted to say Mass.

'We took him to the sacristy of a nearby church,' Delia said. 'There he shed his battledress and donned the vestments of Pentecost. And as I watched him slowly mount the steps to God's altar, I wondered about the foolishness of war and its sacrifices of life. I'm sure if women were allowed to rule the world there would be no more wars.'

Delia's daughter, Blon Kiernan (19), was also involved in the escape organisation. She clearly had her mother's courage, and also her ready wit. When Sam Derry first met her she was visiting Monsignor O'Flaherty. He asked her what she was doing there.

'Coming from you, that's rich, she laughed. Don't you know there's a war on? As a matter of fact, I'm neutral – my father is the Irish ambassador,' he wrote of the encounter.

But Blon Kiernan wasn't really neutral. After that first meeting with Derry, she passed on useful information she was able to glean thanks to the large network the Kiernan family had established in Rome.

Derry was keen to find out what the Germans thought about the prospect of an Allied operation to capture Rome during the Battle of Anzio in 1944. The escape line would have found it almost impossible to operate if the Germans decided to defend the city. On the other hand, if the Germans retreated from Rome, Derry could continue to protect the escapers until the arrival of the Allies.

Blon Kiernan was on good terms with the von Bismarck family and she agreed to visit Prince von Bismarck, first secretary at the German Embassy to the Holy See and grandson of the famous German chancellor Otto von Bismarck.

Derry doesn't say how she managed to wheedle information out of her host without raising suspicion, but the German diplomat was known to pass on intelligence against the Nazis. In any case, Blon Kiernan confirmed that the Germans would retreat to the north of Italy if the Allies advanced on Rome.

Blon also acted as an important conduit between the escape network and her father. In early 1944 one of its helpers, district nurse Concetta Piazza, was arrested while making deliveries of supplies. Luckily, the nurse had made her last drop-off before she was stopped and taken to Regina Coeli prison in Rome. All the same, she was charged with helping the Allies.

She wrote (on prison toilet paper) to the German Commander in Rome, Field Marshal Kesselring, appealing for her release on the basis that she helped all patients regardless of their allegiance. The note was smuggled to Monsignor O'Flaherty who happened to receive it while Blon was visiting him. She immediately volunteered to enlist her father's help. The letter was typed up and her father sent it to Kesselring. The nurse was released a few days later.

The Irish ambassador also came to the rescue when an Irish priest from Co. Offaly was arrested. Fr Ambrose Roche, an Augustinian student, tossed a packet of cigarettes to a prisoner as they were being marched through one of Rome's streets in early February 1944. He was arrested and jailed in Regina Coeli. Fr Tom Twomey, master of students at his college, became concerned for him and called to the Irish legation looking for help.

Dr Kiernan later wrote of his visit to the prison with a degree of humour: 'I had found it difficult to get into Regina Coeli to interview the priest, although I was well provided with cigarettes to ease my entry. The policeman on duty, to my complaint that it was a hard place to get into, dryly remarked that it was harder to get out of.'

Delia later said she also called on her German contacts to help get the priest – one of the monsignor's helpers – out of prison. The priest was released soon afterwards.

In later life, Delia Murphy Kiernan spoke about what she and her daughter had done during the war. She said she didn't want to speak about it until after her husband had died (in 1967) because it would obviously have put him in a very awkward position. She gave the impression that her husband did not know what she was doing, but was that just to protect his reputation as a neutral Irish Minister to the Holy See?

It is likely that he knew, at least in part, what was going on. An unsent letter written by Ireland's other diplomat in Rome at the time, Michael MacWhite, mentions Dr Kiernan's request for a fake passport so that a British POW could get into the Vatican.

It is a tantalising reference but there is nothing, in print at least, to suggest that T.J. Kiernan ever strayed from his steadfast neutrality. Indeed, he was praised after the war for his work. In letters to Dublin, he stressed that he had met diplomats from Axis and Allied countries and wasn't showing any favouritism.

By stark contrast, his wife was feted for doing the opposite and 'risking her neck', as she liked to put it, to protect
people from Nazi persecution.

Br Humilis said of her reasons, and indeed his own: 'She
did it for humane reasons to save lives. That was my thinking
too, because it made no difference to me if they were German
or English. I did it to save lives.'

When the Allies finally reached Rome on 5 June 1944,
Irish writer and war correspondent for the BBC Denis Johnston
called to the Irish legation and asked Delia when she first
became aware that the city was liberated:

'She tossed her head of black curls, and smiled the smile
that must have baffled many an Axis official. "They call me
your Excellency here. It is the way they have in the Diplomatic,
d'ye know. Well, I was out taking a walk in the morning to
see what was going on. And there was a lot of lads in uniform
lying on the pavement in front of the railway station, taking a
rest, d'ye know. And I thought they were Germans, until suddenly one of them sat up and said: "Say, sister. Come and park
your arse beside me." So then I knew I was liberated.'

This was certainly a fitting occasion for her to sing the songs
that she had sung throughout the war at diplomatic events,
parties, gatherings and Christmas dos so far away from home.
At some of them, she was joined by Fr Spike who had a wonderful voice. Her songs, 'The Spinning Wheel', 'The Moonshiner'
and 'The Blackbird', were known throughout Rome. There was
even a story that her own translation of 'Three Lovely Ladies
from Bannion' – she became a fluent speaker during her years
in Italy – was adopted so fervently that Italians came to believe
it was actually an old Neapolitan folk song.

There was talk of awarding her for her work. Both Field Marshal Alexander and British Minister to Rome Sir D'Arcy Osborne were keen to acknowledge Delia's role. For obvious reasons, it wasn't appropriate to award the wife of a neutral ambassador. Delia's husband was aware of the suggestion too, so he clearly knew she had been involved in the Rome Escape Line, even if he wasn't aware of the extent.

When Osborne asked Delia how he might recognise her assistance in some other way, she told him that she loved diamonds. When he arrived with a box sometime later, she asked if it was full of diamonds. It was a valuable Ming vase which, according to her biographer Aidan O'Hara, she took with her on all her husband's subsequent postings (Australia, West Germany, Canada and Washington).

In 1946, the Holy See made her a Dame of the Holy Sepulchre.

When her husband moved to Washington in the 1960s, she stayed on the family farm they bought in Ottawa, Canada. After her husband died in 1967, she stayed for two years before moving back to Dublin in 1969. She was still a star and featured regularly in newspapers. She told a reporter: 'I got several proposals of marriage since my return. They did not know my address, but wrote to me care of the Department of External Affairs.'

On 30 January 1971, she made a surprise appearance on *The Late Late Show*, the well-known chat show on RTÉ television. She spoke openly about how she had helped to smuggle escaped British POWs out of Italy. She drove them in her car, she said, hidden under rugs, and got through check-points because of the diplomatic immunity afforded her as wife of a diplomat.

It was to be her final public appearance. She died, unexpectedly, aged 68 on 11 February 1971 while planning a holiday to join her daughter Nuala in the Canary Islands. The next day, broadcaster and Delia's biographer, Aidan O'Hara compiled a half-hour tribute to her on his RTÉ radio show, *Morning Airs*. One listener remarked that it was ironic that she died so soon after her television appearance. 'It was almost as if,' they said, 'she had planned it as a last farewell to the people of Ireland.'

If anyone could pull off a curtain call such as that, it was Delia Murphy Kiernan.

IN HIDING

5
Callers at Dawn

'SHE STARTED OUT WITH ALL THINGS AGAINST HER, AND
SHE SHOWED WHAT YOU CAN DO IN THIS WORLD WITH
A WILL.'

PATRICK LEIBOVICI

Paris, 1940: When the police knocked on her door in the early
hours of 1 December, dance-troupe leader Margaret Kelly was
sure they had come for her husband. Marcel Leibovici, orchestral
conductor at the famous *Folies Bergère* cabaret, was half-Jewish.
The year before, he had renounced his Romanian citizenship in
order to marry Margaret, but he was not yet a French citizen.
He was a stateless person in a city under occupation.

The unexpected callers, however, had not come for him.
They had come to arrest her.

The police, French, young and under German orders, were
almost apologetic when they told Margaret Kelly that she had
to go with them to the local police station. They gave her time
to dress and pack, a rare concession during the early morning
arrests so often carried out by the Gestapo. Yet, there was
little consideration for the infant son she left behind, much
less the fact that she was pregnant with her second child.

At the police station, she joined a group of several other
women rounded-up that morning. They were questioned, half-

heartedly, and then taken by armed German soldiers to the Gare de l'Est station and marched towards a train. When they boarded, the soldiers locked the doors and stood guard along the platform.

'We were locked in for 24 hours on that station,' Margaret said later. 'Some of the women were acutely distressed – there was one lady who must have been in her eighties. We had had nothing to eat or drink. I asked one of the German women guards if this lady could have a warm drink, but she snarled at me. "Where do you think you are? Nobody gets anything here!" She was a monster.'

The train left the station the next day, but the women had no idea where they were going. It made slow progress and, by nightfall, arrived at its destination. The passengers were loaded on to army trucks and taken to a barracks at Besançon, an internment camp in eastern France near the Swiss border.

Margaret was assigned an iron bunk in a dormitory that held 18 women. When she saw a woodstove at the centre of the dorm, she cheerfully suggested that everyone gather around to make 'a nice cup of tea', she later told her biographer George Perry. It was typical of her overarching optimism – and audacity. The following morning, she pushed the latter to the limit when she told the female guard that she would not be part of any duty roster set up to carry out a series of daily chores.

She didn't wash and cook at home, so she wasn't going to do it here, she said. She held firm, confident that the guard would back down to avoid a scene. It worked. She was not assigned any heavy chores, though that, in part, might have been because she was five months pregnant. Yet, she also managed to persuade her German guards to bend the rules and allow her to see a civilian gynaecologist rather than rely on the appalling medical facilities at the camp.

It helped that Margaret Kelly could speak German. She also had an appreciation of German culture, having danced in Berlin for five years in the 1920s with the popular Alfred Jackson girls at the city's Scala variety theatre.

Even if she won certain dispensations, she still had to endure the unspeakable hardships at Frontstalag 142, or Caserne Vauban, as the military barracks was known. Frostbite, disease, food poisoning and vermin infestations were facts of daily life for the several thousand internees, mostly women and children. Hundreds died.

Their crime? Holding a British passport in occupied Paris.

——— ———

Margaret Kelly held a British passport, but she was an Irish citizen. She came into the world on 24 June 1912 at the Rotunda Hospital in Dublin. Her birth cert named her parents as Margaret O'Brien and James Kelly. However, three weeks after she was born, a local priest asked the Murphy family on the nearby O'Connell Street to care for her.

It was an unusual request, as the household consisted of three sisters and a brother, none of them married. Still, they agreed to what was initially supposed to be a temporary arrangement. The infant's mother took her to the Murphy household and paid for three months' care, but she was never seen again.

The child was called Margaret, presumably after her mother, and she soon acquired the nickname that accompanied her through life. When her doctor looked at her piercing blue eyes and called her 'his little Bluebell', the name stuck. She was a frequent visitor because she had poor health and, for a time, it was thought that she would never walk.

Mary Murphy, the eldest of the three sisters, took on the role of Bluebell's full-time carer, although in reality she was more like a loving surrogate mother. She supported herself and Bluebell with what she earned as a dressmaker, working from home. But it was difficult to make a living in Dublin and when violence erupted in the city during the Easter Rising of 1916, Mary decided to emigrate. She went to join relatives in Liverpool, taking the five-year-old Bluebell with her.

Mary found a job as a ward maid in a local hospital and Bluebell began school. Despite earlier fears, the young girl was able to walk, but her legs were still very weak. On a doctor's suggestion, she joined a dancing class to strengthen her muscles. Aged eight, she enrolled in Madame Cummings's dance school and, despite her young age, worked as a part-time golf caddy to pay for lessons.

It was the beginning of a career that would take Margaret Kelly around the world and earn her widespread praise as the founder of the acclaimed Bluebell dancing troupe at the glamorous *Folies Bergère* in Paris.

Her own life on stage started young. At 14, she got a job with a touring Scottish dance troupe, the Hot Jocks, and was later talent-spotted by Alfred Jackson, who brought her to Berlin. In 1932, he introduced her to the *Folies Bergère* and, shortly afterwards, she was asked to organise and lead a dancing troupe.

The Bluebell Girls, under her stewardship, went on to become one of Europe's most famous dance companies.

Margaret kept in touch with Mary Murphy in Liverpool and, on visits home, showed her photos of herself in *Folies Bergère* costumes. Her foster-mother inked in extra fabric around Bluebell's bikini briefs and skimpy top before showing them to the family. Nonetheless, she was proud as punch.

Meanwhile, Margaret Kelly met Marcel Leibovici, the pianist and orchestral conductor, at the famous nightclub. At first he acted as her financial adviser, but a relationship developed and the couple married in March 1939. When war broke out, she disbanded her dance troupe and the couple left Paris briefly after it fell to the Germans in June 1940.

When they returned a few months later, they found a city rendered darker – and quieter – by war. A curfew was in place and blackouts extinguished the neon lights that had once brightened the nightscape. The daily bustle of street traders, pedestrians and traffic had all but disappeared. In its place, sirens or the sound of military vehicles grinding their way along the main thoroughfares.

Shops, restaurants and the entertainment venues now had a largely German clientele. The swastika flew on many of the city's buildings and monuments, from the Eiffel tower to the Arc de Triomphe. Signs were written in German and the country ran on German time which, up to then, was an hour ahead of Paris time.

Rationing meant everything was scarce – food, fuel, clothing – but perhaps the most unsettling thing was the undercurrent of uncertainty and fear on the city's streets.

Marcel Leibovici avoided going outside, particularly after the Germans conducted a census of Jewish residents in September 1940. He made a point of not registering, but there was a real risk that he would be stopped and asked for papers if he walked freely in the city.

Following his wife's arrest, however, he was forced to risk a trip to see Count Gerald O'Kelly de Gallagh, a savvy Irish wine merchant from Tipperary who, despite orders to the contrary, had succeeded in staying in Paris when all other diplomats were forced to leave for Vichy in the free zone. He had been discharged from his diplomatic duties after a change of government in Ireland in 1932, but continued to offer consular assistance in a new role as 'special plenipotentiary'.

He ran Vendôme Wines from the upmarket Place Vendôme where he conducted business with many high-profile German officers. At the same time, he used his contacts and his diplomatic acumen to help many Irish people who found themselves in a tight spot in wartime Paris.

On Marcel's request, Count O'Kelly took up Bluebell's case and managed to secure her release along with three other unnamed Irish sisters of Mercy.

Margaret Kelly arrived home just in time to ring in 1941, but there was not much to celebrate in the new year. It was clear the city was no longer safe for her husband, who decided it was time to travel south to the free zone. He waited until the couple's second son, Francis, was born in April and left the capital by himself in May.

For weeks, Bluebell had no news, but then the new mother got word, through a clandestine grapevine, that her husband had arrived safely in Marseille.

Meanwhile, she was left to support two small boys and their live-in nanny Paulette Robin at her small apartment at 83 rue Blanche in the centre of the Pigalle district. The Moulin

Rouge, the famous birthplace of the can-can, was a stone's throw away. It was now largely frequented by German officers just like the *Folies Bergère* on the rue Richer. But that was not the only reason Bluebell turned down an offer of a job at her former place of work. Some months before, the theatre had made it clear they didn't want her to work on the premises while organising a dance troupe as her Jewish husband might attract unwanted attention.

Margaret Kelly was not impressed and, instead, found work at the Chantilly, a theatre within walking distance of her flat. She put together a cabaret act using the few resources at her disposal. The stage could accommodate only ten dancers, yet the troupe assembled sets, costumes and music accompaniment, albeit on a much smaller scale than before.

The audience was mostly French, but the Chantilly was not immune from controversy or violence. On one occasion, a row broke out between members of the audience – black marketeers and right-wing patrons. Shots were fired and several arrests followed. The venue was closed down, but only for a few days.

When a German colonel summoned Bluebell, she thought the worst. In fact, it turned out that he had received positive reviews of the show and asked the woman behind it if she would put on a similar show for the troops in Berlin. She managed to turn him down without causing further trouble for herself and continued to work and look after her family.

The year had begun hopefully with her own release from an internment camp, but it ended with the devastating news that Marcel had been arrested in Marseille. The only details she had were those that came through various contacts who passed on information as discreetly as possible. Marcel had been taken in for questioning during a periodic police round-up. His forged papers and, worse, his Jewish ancestry, must have been detected, Bluebell thought, because he was sent to Gurs internment camp in south-west France. A number of months later, thousands of Jewish people were deported from that camp to their deaths in Nazi concentration camps.

By the end of 1941, though, Bluebell felt a glimmer of hope when America entered the war following the Japanese bombing of Pearl Harbour. She said later that she was certain of an Allied victory. She was confident the Americans would bring an end to hostilities sooner rather than later.

Bolstered by that sense of confidence, she didn't think twice when a Jewish cousin of Marcel's called to her door asking for help. It was now compulsory for all Jewish people over the age of six to wear a yellow star, a hideous measure calculated to track and control the Jewish population. Bluebell hid the woman in her apartment and set about securing false papers for her.

She clearly had contact with people directly involved in resistance work. Many in the entertainment sector worked to undermine the occupiers. One of her fellow dancers and an acquaintance, Josephine Baker, was actively engaged as a secret agent. The showgirl, who caused a sensation dancing in a banana skirt in the city's music halls, used her own fame as a cover. Nobody would suspect a star to be a spy. She went to parties in the Italian and Japanese embassies and made secret notes, pinning scraps of paper to her bra.

'My notes would have been highly compromising had they been discovered, but who would dare search Josephine Baker to the skin? When they asked me for papers, they generally meant autographs,' she wrote later.

Later, as Bluebell and Marcel's cousin walked along the tree-lined Boulevard Haussmann, German policemen stopped them to do a spot-check.

Bluebell's papers were inspected and accepted, but one of the policemen thought he heard a trace of an accent when the other woman spoke French. Her false papers did not cause suspicion, but the way she had pronounced a few words did. In war, the fate of people – for good or ill – sometimes turned on such seemingly innocuous details.

Marcel's cousin was arrested and taken to Drancy, the transit camp for Auschwitz concentration camp. She did not come home.

Bluebell knew that it was only a matter of time before the Gestapo visited her apartment to ask further questions. Again, they came in the early morning. This time a member of the Gestapo joined two French policemen. They ransacked her apartment, but the search yielded nothing. Bluebell lied with such efficiency that she surprised even herself, in the process quelling any suspicion that she had sheltered a fugitive.

At Gurs camp Marcel Leibovici's command of language worked in his favour. He spoke German well and his captors used him as a translator. If the job brought with it certain privileges, it also left Marcel in no doubt about the fate awaiting the thousands of Jewish people incarcerated in appalling conditions at the camp. That is, if they survived long enough. One in four prisoners died at Gurs, some 1,100 people, while more than double that number, 2,600, were deported to Auschwitz.

Meanwhile, Marcel spotted an opportunity to escape; his interpreter job meant that he regularly left the camp to translate for the Germans trying to negotiate with a local population only too eager to use linguistic misunderstandings to trick them.

Marcel clearly had an established network as he was able to send occasional messages to his wife in Paris. He also had a friend in the city, fellow musician Guy de la Morenière, who was planning to get him out of the camp. When requested, Bluebell passed on one of Marcel's suits, without asking any questions.

The next time Marcel was out on a shopping trip, he slipped away while the German guards were having a cigarette. They had come to trust him, so they had become lax in terms of security. Marcel had agreed a meeting place with Guy. He changed into his civilian clothes and the two men waited until it was dark before making their way to nearby Pau and catching the train back to Paris.

Marcel could not, under any circumstances, return to his home on the rue Blanche. It was far too dangerous. Instead, Guy gave him the use of his sixth-floor attic flat on the rue de la Bûcherie, the street where the well-known Shakespeare and Company bookshop is today. In the Paris of 1942, the location was all the more notable as it was directly across the road from the German police headquarters.

Bluebell was not put off by the location, or the risk of cycling to and from the same address so frequently. She made the relatively short journey south, crossing the River Seine to her husband's hideout about twice a week, bringing food, fresh laundry and manuscript paper so Marcel could continue to write music.

Nothing was straightforward in an occupied city. Without a ration card, Marcel had no access to food, but Margaret cycled to the western edge of the city where she had a good contact who could give her extra provisions.

She would have to draw on her list of contacts again when she received yet another unexpected early morning call. This time, it was Guy calling to warn her that his office had been raided and the Germans now had Marcel's address. She would have to get him out of there as quickly as possible.

It is extraordinary that Margaret Kelly was able to react so quickly. She knew a woman who had a vacant flat further south, on the rue Berthollet, and came to an agreement to rent it. Marcel was spirited from his attic flat to the new venue without incident. Bluebell put her trust in the building's concierge and paid her 60 francs a week to look after Marcel's needs. She visited herself, too, whenever she could, making sure to vary her route to avoid suspicion.

In early 1943, Bluebell found out she was pregnant again and cut back on her work at the Chantilly theatre. She was pleased and looked forward to the birth of her baby, despite the many challenges she faced on a daily basis.

If there was a sense that she and her family could relax, it was shattered in July 1943 when she was summoned to Gestapo headquarters at 84 Avenue Foch. The building, on a wide boulevard in one of the wealthiest areas of Paris, was notorious. It housed the *Sicherheitsdienst*, the intelligence agency of the SS, as well as a number of torture chambers on its upper floor. Given that her husband had escaped from Gurs several months before, it was surprising Bluebell had not been interrogated sooner.

'I went because I had to,' she later told George Perry. 'Had I tried to get away from Paris I would have been quickly spotted with my English accent. There was nothing else I could do.'

She was brought into a room where a senior German official, flanked on both sides by armed soldiers, said that he would like to know where her husband was.

'So would I!' she replied, without missing a beat.

She said later that her ability to look a person directly in the eye had worked in her favour on many occasions and it worked again now, against the odds. Her interrogators must have noticed that she was six months pregnant, but they did not remark on it during an interview that lasted more than an hour. She left Ave Foch and prepared for another Gestapo raid on her apartment, but it never came.

A short time later, and against her better judgement, she brought her sons to see their father. She resolved never to do so again when one of them blurted out to an acquaintance that they had seen papa. When her daughter Florence was born on 22 October 1943, she didn't dare bring her to see Marcel. The infant was nearly a year old before her father saw her.

Meantime, Bluebell followed news of the Allies' progress on the banned BBC and managed to suffer through the shortages of food and electricity that became even more acute ahead of the liberation of Paris.

Difficult as that was, it was minor in comparison to the fate of those who had been rounded up and deported. By then, more than a quarter of the Jewish population of France had been murdered in Nazi extermination camps. Some 76,000 French Jews, among them 11,000 children, were deported, most of them to Auschwitz. Just 2,500 came home. The last convoy of people left Drancy holding centre on 17 August 1944 while the Battle of Paris was underway.

Bluebell had one final brush with danger when cycling home through Place de la Concorde, at the eastern end of the Champs-Élysées, when she found herself in the middle of a gun battle between the Resistance and German soldiers. She fell off her bicycle and lay as still as she could on the road for about half an hour.

When the shooting stopped, a young German holding a machine gun – he was no more than 18 and look frightened, she said later – approached her. He might have intended to help her to her feet, but she shouted at him to go away and he did just that.

When the city was liberated a week later, on 25 August, Marcel Leibovici rang his wife to tell her that he was coming home. The following day, General Charles de Gaulle, leader of the Free French, led a triumphant march down the Champs-Élysées.

The euphoria of victory was tempered with ongoing shortages and an unbridled rush to take revenge on the collaborators. There was bloodshed, beatings and summary executions. Women accused of sleeping with the enemy had their heads shaved as others jeered. Members of resistance groups tried to stop the grotesque spectacle, but not always with success.

Bluebell was stunned when she heard the elderly concierge who had looked after her husband was among them. She tried to make representations on her behalf, but discovered that the women had betrayed several other occupants of the apartment building to get a 50 franc reward. Bluebell had paid her 60 francs a week – a ten-franc pittance that proved to be the difference between life and death for her husband.

——— —

After the war, Bluebell went back to her role at the *Folies Bergère*, but the war had taken its toll. The theatre was run-down and shabby so when she got an opportunity to move her troupe to the lavishly remodelled Lido on the Champs-Élysées, she took it. The venue pioneered the idea of combining dinner with a show and it was a big hit in a city in need of some post-war spectacle.

From 1950, Bluebell collaborated with American choreographer Donn Arden to produce a series of dazzling shows featuring statuesque dancers – her 'girls' had to be at least 5ft 11' – wearing sequins, glitter, elaborate headdresses and little else.

In the meantime, Bluebell had a fourth child: Jean Paul arrived in 1947, but she continued to put in 12-hour days and think of new ways to attract audiences. She set up a troupe of male dancers, the Kelly Boys, and soon both troupes were performing all around the world. They were so well-received in Las Vegas that Bluebell set up a permanent company there.

Then tragedy struck. Marcel was killed in a car accident in 1961. She also had a close brush with death a few decades later when, in November 1980, a fire at the MGM Grand Hotel in Las Vegas claimed the lives of 84 people. Bluebell and her business partner Donn Arden were trapped on the tenth floor with about 30 others while they waited for the fire services to erect a ladder long enough to reach them. Inspired by the film *The Towering Inferno* (1974) – the press noted some of the survivors had recently seen a rerun – they soaked towels and stuffed them under the door to stop smoke entering the room. They all got out safely.

Earlier that year, Margaret Kelly had made a trip back to her native Dublin with a troupe of Bluebells who performed at the city's Gaiety Theatre.

'I always felt Irish and always called myself an Irishwoman and always wanted to come back here,' she told journalist Elgy Gillespie at the time. 'When I had the time I never had the money and by the time I had the money, I no longer had the time. And now it really feels like what an Irish-American would say: "Gee, it's great to be here!"'

She made tentative steps to find out more about her parents, but without much success. In any case, as she put it, she often thought she should try to find them, 'but then I'd remember that they never did anything to try and find me, so I'd forget it again.'

She felt no bitterness, though. 'Never for a moment do I consider that I had a deprived childhood. Mary Murphy always saw to it that I was well-dressed. And I always had enough jam butties to eat.' In turn, Bluebell supported Mary Murphy until she died shortly after the war.

Bluebell's fame grew in her later years. Rather than slow down, she continued to work long days so that her career spanned six decades. During that time, she trained thousands of dancers. In her seventies, she appeared on the British chat show *Parkinson* and did a high-kick worthy of a woman less than half her age. There were articles, a book, a BBC series on her life, numerous awards and an OBE, but it was perhaps François Truffaut's film, *Le Dernier Métro* (*The Last Metro*), that best encapsulated what she had done in hiding her husband and briefly, his cousin, during the war.

Her experience was one of the inspirations for one of the French film director's biggest screen successes. The title refers to the last metro that theatre patrons were obliged to catch before curfew. The film, released in 1980, was one of the first to deal with the occupation in Paris and it did so through the lens of a theatre in Montmartre, Paris. Drawing inspiration from Bluebell's story, its lead actor (played by Catherine Deneuve) hid her husband, Jewish theatre director (Heinz Bennent) in the tucked-away back-rooms of the theatre.

It's a story about the ambiguities of war but also one that shows how theatre – which experienced a wartime boom – provided a safe and warm space, as well as temporary relief, from the grim reality of daily life. *Le Dernier Métro* also captures something of the essence of Margaret Kelly, a woman who lived the phrase, 'the show must go on', even when faced with impossible odds.

She did that not just in wartime, but for all of her 94 years on this earth. As her eldest son Patrick Leibovici said of her: 'She started out with all things against her, and she showed what you can do in this world with a will.'

PROPAGANDA

6

'This is Vicky with Three Kisses for You'

'"THAT'S ADOLF HITLER," THEY CHANTED, "AND HE IS COMING TO KILL ALL THE JEWS." I KNEW MY FATHER WAS A JEW, AND STOOD AND SHIVERED IN THE SNOW.'

AGNES BERNELLE

London, 1943: Agnes Bernelle wasn't aware of it, but she was being followed. A man had climbed aboard the train carriage adjoining hers as she travelled to Bletchley station to make clandestine broadcasts designed to confuse and demoralise German troops and citizens.

For months now, she had been drawing in listeners with her seductive jingle. 'This is Vicky with three kisses for you, *mwah*, *mwah*, *mwah*,' she said, in her distinctive husky voice at the start of a radio show that was thought to be coming from somewhere inside Germany.

In truth, the radio station, *Atlantiksender West*, was an American propaganda operation targeting the *Kreigsmarine* (the German Navy) and it was broadcasting from a secret studio built into the chapel at Woburn Abbey estate in Buckinghamshire in England. A second station, *Soldatensender Calais*, targeted the *Wehrmacht*, or German Army. Twenty-year-old Agnes Bernelle had been recruited to work on both because she was a native German speaker with a background in singing and acting. She had the voice for it. And, as a German refugee with a Jewish father, she also had the motivation.

Her radio show was dominated by jazz, the 'alien' and 'decadent' genre much-hated by Hitler. The illicit choice of music drew a large audience, keen to listen to the music prohibited under the Nazi regime. Vicky kept the jazz and swing numbers coming, dropping in concocted news items and believable lies between tunes.

The idea was to casually include plausible disinformation, which, if believed – and it very often was – would sow confusion and lower morale.

Vicky had a turn for it. When she casually warned of a shortage of certain goods, it incited panic-buying. When she revealed that some high-ranking Nazi officials were getting extra food and clothing, it caused resentment and unease.

On one memorable occasion, she told German citizens to put samples of their morning urine into small bottles and to post them to the Minister of Health in Berlin. It was a wartime Aryan health check, she explained. It was convincing enough to be believed and listeners did what she asked, clogging up the German postal service for weeks.

She was the queen of fake news, to use a modern term. But like the codebreaking activities taking place at nearby Bletchley Park, her broadcast was top secret. She had been warned not to tell anyone, but now she was about to be discovered: on that fateful morning a man was waiting for her at the top of the steps as she made her way out of Bletchley station.

'Gotcha!' he said, as she approached.

There must have been a moment of immense relief when she realised the man standing in front of her was none other than her curious boyfriend, Irish Spitfire pilot Desmond Leslie. She would later marry him and spend her post-war years in Ireland. But in 1943, Leslie was standing in front of her, ready to challenge her. He was concerned she might be an enemy agent. And her English was just too good. Having noticed her frequent and unexplained absences from London, he decided to get to the bottom of it. Following her was much easier than he expected; he looked in her purse, found a return ticket to Bletchley and tailed her to the station.

When she saw him, her response was lightning-quick, as she recalled later: '"For God's sake, pretend you don't know me," I hissed, keeping my eyes resolutely averted but it was too late. The army driver who was picking me up had already spotted us. I didn't know what the penalties were for breaking security, but I was terrified that my superiors would suspect me of treason.'

She decided the best thing to do was to come clean. After all, Desmond Leslie was not only an Allied Spitfire pilot, but a cousin of British Prime Minister Winston Churchill. It was the right call. Her producer, Charles Kebbe, and his commanding officer, Ira Ashley, spoke to their superiors on her behalf. The incident was soon forgotten.

In fact, Leslie was even allowed to join Vicky in Buckinghamshire when he was on leave. Woburn was a restricted, high-security area so Desmond was encouraged to spend romantic weekends there to give Agnes a cover story for all her comings and goings.

Agnes Bernelle, however, was shaken by the episode. It was a chilling reminder that she was entirely on her own if her role with wartime American intelligence was discovered. She had been warned of that. She doubled down on security but never, for a moment, thought of abandoning her post.

——— ——

Agnes Bernelle was born Agnes Bernauer on 7 March 1923 into a wealthy family in Berlin. Her name, chosen by her German mother Emmy Erb and theatre impresario father Rudolph Bernauer, carried with it a hope that their daughter would pursue a career in the arts. They imagined that, one day, a German theatre programme for Friedrich Hebbel's classical play would carry the words: *Agnes Bernauer* played by Agnes Bernauer. It was a reasonable wish given that her father played such a key role in the cultural life of the city.

It all started out to plan. Agnes's early life was privileged and cosseted. She recalled being driven, by limousine, to her Jewish Montessori school and spending happy afternoons playing with her little gramophone and dressing up in her mother's exquisite beaded gowns. Her Hungarian father was Jewish and his wife was Protestant, although those differences did not matter then.

In the early 1920s, Rudolph Bernauer was directing the first 'talkies'. By the age of five, his daughter was already an avid movie-goer. At age nine, she had graduated to self-appointed casting director. Agnes regularly suggested who should star in her father's films; advice, she said, he often acted on. She moved in an artistic milieu, one full of the people Rudolph Bernauer had worked with in several decades as a theatre owner, writer and director.

Her best friend, Maria, was the daughter of an aspiring young actress at her father's theatre. Her name? Marlene Dietrich.

At the time, of course, Agnes had no idea of the international stardom awaiting Marlene, just as she had no idea that Albert Einstein, who passed on the pavement below her window regularly, would become a household name. Yet, young as she was, Agnes Bernauer was very aware of the changes that were happening all around her.

By 1930, she could already feel a sense of impending doom. Children, she recalled later, were hurling stones and snowballs at an enormous portrait of Hitler posted on a hoarding near her home. '"That's Adolf Hitler,"' they chanted, "and he is coming to kill all the Jews." I knew my father was a Jew, and stood and shivered in the snow.'

Although not yet a teenager, Agnes Bernauer was aware of the rise of Hitler's National Socialist Party. Between 1928 and 1930, it increased its vote eight-fold to win 107 seats in the Reichstag, the German seat of parliament. She, and her family, also quickly became aware of the Nazi's attitude towards the country's Jewish population.

It started as early as 1930 when Joseph Goebbels succeeded in derailing her father's plan to turn the Mozartsaal theatre at Nollendorfplatz into a cinema. On opening night, just before *All Quiet on the Western Front* was due to screen, Goebbels led a mob into the auditorium where they let off stink bombs and released dozens of mice. The next night, they did exactly the same thing. The project was abandoned and the entire investment lost.

When Hitler ran for president in 1932, he was already making use of the kind of propaganda that would play a key role in World War II. He travelled by air during his campaign to show that he was modern and effective.

He didn't win that election, but he was soon made chancellor in a coalition government. When the Reichstag was burned down in February 1933, allegedly by a Communist (though possibly by the Nazis themselves), Hitler used the fire to whip up anti-Communist sentiment. In that unsettled atmosphere, it was easier to introduce the Reichstag Fire Decree, which essentially outlawed all political opponents.

When Hitler won a majority in March 1933, ten-year-old Agnes Bernauer knew exactly what that meant for her and her family.

'Even before the count was finished Hitler's victory was plain,' she wrote years later. 'Huge torchlight processions passed through the city. I could hear the noise of marching feet, and listened to the shouting as I lay in bed.'

The next day, her father tried to leave the country with his long-time business associate Carl Meinhard. At one time, the pair had owned and run several theatres in Berlin while Rudolph raised extra money by writing and producing a number of successful operettas. He used to write his nationality as 'Hung-aryan', but the time for clever puns was over. Both men were arrested at the German border and put in jail. They were released after a few days but, as Jews, their passports were confiscated.

'It was not long before our German nationality was officially withdrawn,' Agnes wrote. 'With one stroke of the pen we were stateless and could not leave the country.'

Her elder brother, Emmerich, lost his job as an editor. Her father's name was erased from the posters advertising his productions. While his plays and songs were still being performed, he was not credited. His film colleagues, afraid of the consequences, stopped giving him work.

'Bad things were happening to Jews, yet I never noticed anyone objecting,' Agnes said later.

In 1930s Berlin, Agnes was just trying to fit in. She gave the Hitler salute whenever a teacher passed her on the school corridor, as was expected. She was even a bit upset when she was barred from joining Hitler Youth because she was no longer seen as German. It wasn't long, though, before she took a stand and urged her father to leave the country.

Young as she was, she had an understanding of how Hitler appealed to the masses. She had seen his image countless times, in black-and-white photographs, but the experience of watching him engage the crowd during a rally in 1936 was entirely different.

She wrote: 'His light blue eyes, his pink complexion, and above all, his auburn hair made him look much less repulsive than we expected... I hate to admit it, but Hitler was almost attractive when you saw him in real life.'

In mid-1936, her father managed to secure new papers for the family at the Hungarian consulate in Berlin. He left for London where he got work ghost-writing scripts. Agnes followed shortly afterwards and enrolled as a boarder at a school in Finchley. Her mother travelled back and forth, but made a final dramatic escape from Berlin in 1939 after the SS tried to recruit her as a German spy. She had been invited to dinner by a friend but when it became clear that he and two other SS officers sitting at the table were trying to coerce her into spying from London, she fled the restaurant. She went directly home, picked up a winter coat and her passport and spent the night in the waiting-room at the station, willing the morning train to come.

When she arrived in London the next day, she collapsed into her husband's arms – and safety. The SS did not try to re-establish contact, not even when war was declared a short time later. The family was grateful for that, but life became much more difficult when Hungary joined the German side in November 1940; the Bernauers were now considered 'enemy aliens'. Much as Agnes wanted to join the wartime effort in London, she found it impossible with such a label.

Her luck changed when she was talent-spotted by a journalist and introduced to a German anti-Nazi refugee organisation, *Freier Deutscher Kulturbund* (the Free German League of Culture). The league was set up by refugee writers, painters, musicians and actors who wanted to preserve German culture and stand in solidarity with other democratic movements.

Agnes Bernelle's career in the arts had begun. She performed on the league's tiny stage at a house on Upper Park Road. 'Some nights, at the height of the Blitz, the place would shake and rumble, but the audience never stirred except to applaud. Most of them were elderly people who had lost everything they possessed except their lives, and they were quite willing to risk even that for a few hours of entertainment,' she wrote later.

It was already clear that Agnes Bernauer was courageous and determined in wartime. Despite the many challenges, she continued to follow her passion – the theatre. She changed her name to Bernelle and got a series of jobs that would, in time, make her a very convincing black propaganda radio broadcaster.

In 1940, she got a short-term job as a secretary/production manager/understudy – 'the next best thing to acting,' she said – with Francis Goodheart Productions. The company continued to stage plays at St Martin's Theatre, one of the few West End theatres still open. If it was risky, it did not unduly bother Agnes.

During a run of Herbert Marshall's *Thunder Rock*, she took the Tube home with Irish actor Cyril Cusack after the show: 'We both got out at Golders Green station and walked together down the deserted Golders Green Road during the air raids while bits of shrapnel from ack-ack guns whizzed past our heads. I used to keep, in a sewing box, a jagged piece of metal that missed us by inches.'

Later in 1940, when the British government introduced internment for aliens, Agnes found herself having difficulty securing papers to find another job. She and her parents were now obliged to report to the local tribunal centre. When Agnes reported to the centre, she realised that she knew the people running it. She had entertained them earlier in the war.

It was a stroke of unexpected good luck. They willingly stamped her identity card, and those of her parents, with the letter 'B'. The coveted 'B' stamp meant the bearer would not be interned, although there were other restrictions. 'Aliens' were not allowed to own a wireless and they were not allowed to travel more than five miles from their home.

Agnes, though, had little time for rules. When filling in an application form for a travel permit to tour with a theatre company, she was asked if she kept offensive weapons at her house. 'Yes,' she wrote, 'I normally keep a submarine in the bath.'

Despite her tongue-in-cheek remark, she was granted a permit and went on tour with a production, *Potasch and Pearlmutter*, in which she played the juvenile lead, Irma Potasch. She recalled long eerie walks through devastated areas of Coventry and Hull and sheltering from dive-bombers in her landlady's garden in Cardiff, convinced that neither the house nor theatre would survive the onslaught. To her amazement, both did.

Soon afterwards, she was summoned by the British government to work in a munitions factory but, as she said herself, she felt she had something more important to contribute to the war effort. 'I could speak in English and German and still remembered most of my French and Italian. None of this was going to be very useful in a factory.'

A sympathetic doctor ruled her unfit, but her attempts to join the British Army and later St John's Ambulance Service, were both turned down because of her 'enemy alien' status. Determined to do her bit, she tried the Civil Defence, which enlisted her as an air-raid warden. She spent many days learning the difference between various missiles and incendiary devices and many nights patrolling her local area, Sneath Avenue, clutching a stirrup water pump.

When America entered the war in December 1941, everything changed for Agnes and her family. Rudolph Bernauer was one of the first German refugee artists to get a phone call from US intelligence agency, the Office of Strategic Services (OSS), asking if he would be interested in a job as a script-writer and translator for a possible new radio station. Rudolph mentioned his daughter's talents and, on a weekend in early 1942, without any idea of what lay in store, Agnes took a train to Bletchley.

A heavily camouflaged American army vehicle picked her up at the station and took her to a house at a secret location. When she arrived, a jeep full of excited American officers arrived at the door.

'Little did I realise what my presence in Buckinghamshire meant to them,' she wrote later. 'They were highly trained personnel with the recently established American Intelligence Unit, working on the "Enigma" project and on black propaganda behind a high security screen. They had not seen a woman since their arrival in England some months ago. No wonder they crowded around me...'

Agnes Bernelle was not yet aware of the top-secret work to decipher the Enigma, an enciphering machine used by the Germans to send secure messages, but she knew from that first night to say nothing. That was made explicit the next day when she was taken to Woburn Abbey, the Duke of Bedford's country estate. She was led to a studio built into the chapel in one of the wings where she recorded her first radio show.

She was warned not to tell anyone what she was doing or who she was working for, with the exception of her parents who had also been recruited to work with American intelligence. Her father was writing scripts and translating German songs into English, while her mother was appointed chaperone at a house in Newton Longville, which acted as the headquarters for all of the radio contributors.

Agnes was coached in her new role as Vicky, the seductive host who played real requests, interspersed with items of 'news' designed to mislead listeners who believed the broadcast was coming from within Germany or Occupied Europe.

Propaganda had already played a key role in the rise of Nazism in Germany. Hitler had used it very effectively, building a propaganda ministry that disseminated carefully curated information calculated to bolster his aims.

As soon as the war broke out, the Allies did the same. In 1940, British Prime Minister Winston Churchill set up the British Political Warfare Executive (PWE) at Woburn Abbey, a clandestine operation that produced propaganda designed to lower enemy morale and bolster that of the Allies. If both sides looked to science and technology to provide the most effective weapons and equipment, they also embraced a much older innovation – radio. It was accessible, cheap and easy to exploit.

By the time Agnes Bernelle began broadcasting, the so-called 'radio wars' were well underway. In Germany, the infamous Lord Haw Haw, aka William Brooke Joyce, was broadcasting propaganda to a British listenership, trying to undermine morale. His broadcasts were even monitored in Ireland.

It was 'white propaganda' because it made no secret of its origin or nature. In contrast, *Soldatensender West* was engaged in 'black propaganda', which meant it hid its origins to undermine the enemy. The station's boss, Sefton Delmer, called it 'psychological judo', although those who worked for him did not even know his name. Agnes knew him simply as the 'beard'.

Her objective, however, was very clear. She knew what she had to do, and that her broadcast went out on radio waves that could be neither traced nor 'jammed'.

'We had the entire "dirty tricks department" of British and American intelligence behind us,' Agnes explained later. 'This clever hoax gave us endless possibilities to bamboozle and confuse the Nazis, and to help Allied agents behind German lines.'

Vicky settled into a regular routine, broadcasting her show and auditioning for the few available acting roles in her spare time. Her employers encouraged it as it provided a convincing cover. In a sense, working at the radio station was Agnes Bernelle's ideal job: she was finally able to help the war effort while doing something she loved – performing.

At times, the radio troupe of writers, singers, pianist and sound expert put on whole sketches, pretending that they were being performed by soldiers and nurses near the front.

The station appeared all the more authentic as news bulletins were read by real German POWs who volunteered for the service. 'They were always brought to the studio blindfolded and remained so until they actually stood in front of the microphone to record their text,' Agnes later said. Her own request programme was convincing too as it used real information intercepted from field post by agents. Vicky was sometimes able to give anxious relatives news of their loved ones from the front.

That cut both ways, though, as there were times when she would lower the morale of a particular German battalion by letting slip they were possibly trapped, but that all was not lost. She would then play them a cheerful tune. 'I like to think that because of my programme some of the Germans surrendered when they were still alive to do so,' she said later.

She also sent coded messages to the Resistance, using record numbers and labels which were deciphered in the field.

As she said herself, it was difficult to know if any of her broadcasts had a measurable effect on the war. Her own prank, calling on German citizens to send urine samples to the health ministry, certainly caused chaos in the postal service. After the war, she heard of another tangible success.

One German submarine commander, who had been undetected off the coast of Scotland, surfaced without any good reason and later surrendered. When asked why, he said Vicky's programme had prompted him to do so. Drawing on real intelligence, Vicky had congratulated the commander on the birth of a son, playing a record in German for him entitled, 'Yes Sir, That's My Baby'. The commander had not been home in more than two years and the 'revelation' of a new baby that could not have been his was reportedly the last straw.

Goebbels, who had directly targeted Agnes's father's cinema, had by this time become Hitler's propaganda minister; now Agnes was using his tactics against the Nazi regime.

Other evidence of the success of black propaganda radio was much more unsettling. Years later, Agnes was shaken to the core when she visited the Plötzensee Memorial in Berlin. The centre commemorates the 2,800 people unjustly sentenced to death by the National Socialist judiciary from 1933 to 1945. She randomly began looking at the panels on the wall and was horrified to read of an ordinary German civilian who was executed for listening to foreign broadcasts.

'Had it been our station or the "white" propaganda put out by the BBC? What difference did it make? For years I had entertained my listeners with funny war stories – the submarine, the specimens – and now I was sharply reminded of the reality behind the laughs,' she wrote in her autobiography, *The Fun Palace*.

There was another broadcast that haunted her for the rest of her life, her son Mark Leslie says. Towards the end of the war, she was told to target the city of Magdeburg in a broadcast designed to cause mass panic. She looked at the script and said she couldn't do it. She was to tell her listeners in the central German city that they were about to be bombed and plead with them to get off the street and stay indoors. Only Nazi party members or people vital to the war effort had permission to evacuate.

She knew the broadcast would cause mass panic and a stampede from the city. She was deeply concerned about the effect on the ordinary citizens, and said so. 'She was conflicted,' says her son. 'Can you imagine how divided you'd feel? You're working for this great war effort to destroy a country that you love. Aggie [as she was known to family] never lost her love for Germany, the German people or Berlin.'

Despite her concerns, she was coerced into making that broadcast on 13 April 1945 and never quite got over it. What she didn't know at the time was that her broadcast played a role in saving her cousin, Ilma Gonda, her only Jewish relative to survive the Holocaust.

As she detailed in her autobiography, the war annihilated her family, on both sides. Her Jewish relatives on her father's side were either killed or tortured in the camps. Her mother's so-called 'Aryan' family fared little better, she said. Few survived. Her Uncle Franz was taken to work in a factory in Russia and never came home. Her favourite cousin, Rudie, died during the last week of the war, while 'brown-shirted Ernst Weise' was killed long before. 'My mother's family, more fortunate than my father's during Hitler's time paid dearly for their privileges afterwards,' she wrote.

The only exception was Ilma, who escaped death at the last minute. Agnes knew some of the details, which she set out in this account: 'My cousin Ilma miraculously survived five years of suffering, and just before the end of the war, when she and other living corpses were about to be driven into a Polish lake, she heard gunfire and saw the camp guards jumping from the train. American soldiers came out of the bushes and liberated the prisoners just in time.'

What Agnes hadn't realised was that Ilma was on board a train with some 2,500 other Bergen-Belsen survivors when her broadcast caused panic and stopped the train outside Magdeburg. Just as the driver got the green light to start the train again, two US Army tank commanders approached the train and the German guards fled.

Some 2,500 people, including Ilma, were liberated. The full story of the train and its passengers came to light in 2001 during an oral history project run by a history teacher, Matthew Rozell, in upstate New York. He posted photographs of the liberation on the internet and there, among the desperate and dishevelled survivors, was Ilma.

Aggie went to her grave not knowing that she had helped save her cousin's life, but the discovery made by her son so many decades later gives the family some comfort. Aggie's granddaughter, Leah Leslie, describes it as *kismet*, or fate.

———   ———

Agnes's own post-war fate began with wedding bells when she married her handsome Spitfire pilot Desmond Leslie just days after the war ended. They moved to her new husband's ancestral home, Castle Leslie Estate in Co. Monaghan, and began a new life. 'Their marriage sounds the stuff of fairytales,' Leah says, 'but it eventually imploded. A devastated but ever-resilient Agnes [and her three children] moved to Dublin, where she met the historian and author Maurice Craig.'

The couple stayed together for the rest of Agnes's life, although there were moments when she sought her own space. She had a curtain installed down the centre of their bed, which she pulled when she was cross with Maurice. Her granddaughter offers the detail as an insight into the character of a woman who made a deep impression on her as a little girl.

She made a lasting impression on the cultural life of Dublin city, too. She was known for her Weimer cabaret and interpretations of German composer Kurt Weill and theatre pioneer Bertolt Brecht. She was creative director at the Project Arts Theatre and sang with a host of stars, from Elvis Costello and Tom Waits to Irish punk rock band, The Radiators.

Agnes Bernelle might not have lived to discover the truth about her cousin Ilma, but *kismet* intervened once again in 1996 to unite her with a long-lost family artefact. Her father and his business partner Carl Meinhard had lost everything in the war – except their lives. Rudolph Bernauer escaped to London, but Meinhard endured five years at a concentration camp before going to live in Argentina after the war.

They had survived. That was what was important, so the last thing on Agnes's mind was the magical 'Jewel Book' she remembered from her youth. Her father was the first to give a limited-edition of *The Rabbi of Bacharach* by Heinrich Heine, with 17 etchings by artist Max Liebermann, to Carl for his birthday. When Rudolph's birthday came around, Carl regifted the book back to the man who gave it to him, unwittingly. Rudolph said nothing, but the following year he gave the same book back to Carl, adding a small diamond set into the soft, leather binding.

The following year, Carl added an emerald and presented it to Rudolph on his birthday. And on it went, back and forth on the friends' respective birthdays, until the cover was encrusted with a variety of precious and semi-precious stones. They also added a silver plate to record the dates of exchange.

Agnes never expected to see the book again. But, in the 1970s, she coincidentally met a visiting American stage director, Dan Mason, who told her that a book with 'jewels on the cover' had turned up at a New York synagogue. The next time she was in the city, she visited the synagogue. She couldn't believe her eyes when she saw the long-lost book among the artefacts at a Judaic Art exhibition at the Central Synagogue on 55th Street.

An American general, a Jewish man, had donated it to the synagogue. It's not clear how he got it, but it is believed he bought it from the original looters. Agnes was told she could have the book back – but 'at a price'. She didn't have the price at the time, and forgot about it. Years passed and on a visit to New York in 1996, three years before she died, she again enquired about the book. It was now in storage. When the synagogue's board of directors heard the story, they were so moved by it that they presented the book to her – without charge – in a ceremony that was covered by American media.

In an item on CBS News in 1996, Agnes Bernelle held up what she described as the only item of value that survived World War II and said: 'I never believed it would really happen, but here I am. Here we both are. Both survivors of the Holocaust.'

CODEBREAKERS

7

The Intelligence Factory

'SHE WAS AN EXTRAORDINARY WOMAN WITH AN EXTRA-
ORDINARY INTELLIGENCE.'
SHANE ROSS ON HIS MOTHER RUTH ISABEL ROSS
(*NÉE* CHERRINGTON)

Spring 1942: Ruth Isabel Cherrington was told to report to Station X, the cover name for Bletchley Park, where, unknown to her, thousands of codebreakers were working in a secret intelligence operation that would later be credited with shortening the war by at least two years. It was just an hour from Euston Station in London, but it was an entirely different world.

When Ruth, or 'Rubel' as she was known, arrived at the nearby train station, she was taken in what she described as 'a sort of a carriage' to a secluded country estate in Buckinghamshire. It would have taken her through an ornate gate, down a gravel path and past a large – and many said ugly – stately mansion that had been operating as the clandestine nerve-centre of codebreaking activity since 1938.

In the four years since then, staff numbers had grown to over 9,000 people, working around the clock in a series of wooden huts constructed around a lake on the estate's extensive grounds.

'It wasn't glamorous,' Rubel said of her own first impressions many years later when she was living in Ireland, where she made a career as a successful writer. 'They were all locked up, doing these codes.'

It wasn't particularly welcoming either. The atmosphere was focused and intense. Women with clipboards dealt with new arrivals and – to quote one of those new arrivals – 'there was no warmth to their manner, only a cursory good morning and the reading of lists'.

Rubel was assigned to Hut 15 where she began her duties, recording and analysing broadcasts on enemy radio networks. Like everyone else, she worked one of three shifts – 8 a.m. to 4 p.m.; 4 p.m. to midnight and midnight to 9 a.m. – six days a week. She was billeted in digs at nearby Fenny Stratford, less than two miles away.

It was slow, repetitive work carried out in difficult working conditions. The huts themselves were badly lit and airless. Respiratory complaints were common. The windows were covered with blackout curtains so, even within the enclosure itself, people working in one hut did not know what those in the hut next to them were doing.

That was key. If there was a single defining principle at Bletchley Park, it was the need for total discretion. Every member of staff had signed the Official Secrets Act, and there were constant reminders not to talk – at meals, on transport or even at 'your own fireside'. Another document to be signed on arrival warned: 'There is nothing to be gained by chatter but the satisfaction of idle vanity, or idle curiosity: there is everything to be lost'.

British Prime Minister Winston Churchill famously told workers during a visit to Bletchley Park, or BP as it was known, that they were 'his geese that laid his golden eggs and never cackled'.

If asked what they were doing, Bletchley workers had a series of stock answers: they were doing 'a frightfully boring job as a typist', or as a 'confidential clerk', or they were involved in 'communications'. If necessary, they had been told to say it was 'extremely bad mannered' to probe any further.

As the war progressed, however, people were much less likely to ask questions because a series of propaganda campaigns warned of the dangers of loose talk. Posters warning of the potential risks were printed across Europe and in America, showing a sinking ship along with familiar catchphrases, such as 'Careless Talk Costs Lives', or 'Loose Lips Might Sink Ships'.

'They were very, very strict about secrecy,' Rubel said later. 'You didn't really need to be a brain to go to Bletchley Park. You needed to be reliable and somebody they knew would never give away any secrets.'

Though Rubel Cherrington certainly did have a brain and, like many other women at Bletchley, she was an exceptionally bright university graduate. That, in part, was thanks to her parents who encouraged further education not only for their two sons but also for their two daughters. Rubel was born in Berkhamsted, north-west of London, on 13 December 1919 to Ruth Spinney and banker Selwyn Prescott Cherrington. As a child, she went to Saint Felix School, a private school in Suffolk, before taking the entrance exam for Cambridge.

'My father was very keen on universities and he wanted me to go. I said, "Well, I'll take the exam, but I won't get in." But I did get in.'

In the late 1930s Rubel went to study history at Newnham College in Cambridge where she, and the small number of other female students, sat in the front row. By then, she was already aware of the rise of the Third Reich, having witnessed it first-hand when her parents sent her to Munich from 1936 to 1937 to learn German. She heard Adolf Hitler deliver a speech and was horrified by his 'mob oratory', her son, journalist and former Irish Transport Minister Shane Ross, recalls.

Her German was obviously good enough to understand what he was saying. She was alarmed not only by his blatant authoritarianism but by the enthusiastic welcome for his hateful words. They were anathema to everything she held dear as a British subject, albeit one who would spend most of her adult life in Ireland. When she returned from Germany, this politically aware young woman, still in her teens, wrote a long treatise on Hitler's politics, setting out why his rise to power posed a threat to democracy.

'The experience had a lasting effect on her,' her son says.

Given her experience, it wasn't surprising that Rubel volunteered to join the Auxiliary Territorial Army, the women's branch of the British Army, as soon as she graduated with a degree in history from Cambridge University.

Her first posting was to Station X. The 'X' represented the Roman numeral X, or ten; Bletchley Park was the tenth property acquired by British intelligence in preparation for a war which, in 1938, seemed unavoidable. In September of that year, a group of over 150 people from the Secret Intelligence Service, or MI6, and the Government Code and Cipher School (GC&CS) spent three weeks at the country estate.

The location was ideal. The estate was near London, yet it was secluded and unlikely to be targeted in a bombing campaign. It was also near a major telecommunications network and it was situated on a well-connected railway line with links to the future recruiting grounds for codebreakers, the universities of Oxford and Cambridge.

The outside world was led to believe that the frantic preparations and sudden influx of people were due to a certain Capt. Ridley who was planning a lavish shooting party. The explanation was never challenged, even if some local eyebrows were raised when older men and young women were put up in the area's pubs and hotels.

'Captain Ridley's Shooting Party' spent three weeks at Bletchley Park, testing telecommunications and preparing the site for the arrival of many more people.

When the war broke out, those people arrived in increasing numbers. Early recruits came from Oxbridge but, as the war progressed and codebreaking became more mechanised, women were enlisted from the Women's Auxiliary Air Force (WAAF), the Women's Royal Navy Service (WRNS, or the Wrens) and the Auxiliary Territorial Service (ATS).

Given that Ruth Isabel Cherrington was a Cambridge graduate and an ATS volunteer, she was the ideal recruit. If she was struck by the fact that women made up three-quarters of the workforce at Bletchley Park, she never said so; although she was not one to challenge gender roles.

She got on with her work at Hut 15, listening to enemy wireless signals and noting the codenames used by the Germans. She wrote down what she heard, but she never knew who the people behind the aliases were: 'We weren't allowed to know...

it might have been somebody in charge of provisions or it might have been very important generals, for all we knew,' she explained in 2010, talking for the first time in public about her secret life at Bletchley during an RTÉ radio interview.

'There was an awful lot of donkey work to be done,' she added, dismissing any notion that the work was exciting. For the most part, she had to make 'copies of this, copies of that, and copies of the other', without knowing how any of her work contributed to the bigger picture.

Staff members could not tell anybody what they were doing quite simply because they didn't know themselves. 'It was important [work], but we didn't know we were breaking codes, we were never told… we didn't ask,' she said.

General staff, and women in particular, worked in a number of roles, from log readers and teleprinter operators to high-speed wireless operators and Morse slip readers. A lot of the day-to-day work involved listening to Morse code on wireless signals, then typing the message out in plain text. Several of the huts were equipped with banks of up to 30 teleprinters, which were constantly printing large volumes of paper. The noise was deafening.

While there was a sense that these isolated scraps of information were making sense to someone, Rubel, like her co-workers, knew better than to ask questions.

In Hut 6, for instance, Mair Russell-Jones, a German and music graduate from Cardiff University, was bewildered by the Enigma cipher machines sitting on each desk. It was the strangest-looking machine she had ever seen; 'like a cross between a gramophone, typewriter and a shop till', she said. She was told how to turn it on and off and how to input any codes received. Nobody explained that the Germans were using it to encrypt messages, or that cryptanalysts at Bletchley Park were trying to break that code.

It is not true to say that women did not occupy senior positions, however. For instance, Emily Anderson, the first woman professor of German at Galway University, played a key role at the war station. She is mentioned alongside the famous mathematician Alan Turing as one of the 'key people' of the last 100 years by Government Communications Headquarters (GCHQ), the UK's intelligence, security and cyber agency.

It offers this summary of the Galway woman's achievements: 'Emily Anderson joined MI1b, the Interception and Cryptanalysis section of the War Office, in 1918. She was the only woman Junior Assistant (JA) at the formation of the GC&CS in 1919, by far the most capable of the JAs, and was Head of the Italian Diplomatic section by 1927. She was considered the leading book-builder [a phase in the codebreaking process] in GC&CS and expected her own high standards in her colleagues and subordinates.'

She worked for British Intelligence during World War I and when a group of cryptanalysts were mobilised in 1939, Emily Anderson received a telephone message saying 'Auntie Flo is not so well'; the signal to report for duty. She was one of the first to arrive at Bletchley Park and led the Italian Diplomatic Section, using her knowledge of French, German and Italian to try to detect patterns in enemy wireless messages transmitted in Morse code.

Her exceptional mental agility and ability to work in a highly pressurised environment later earned her the title of 'Britain's greatest female codebreaker'. While she was known for her later groundbreaking translation of Beethoven's letters, the full extent of her wartime codebreaking work in Bletchley Park, and later in Cairo, became known as recently as 2023 in a revelatory biography by Jackie Uí Chionna.

In it, Dr Uí Chionna explains that Anderson's skill lay in being able to identify patterns in the seemingly unintelligible pages of transcribed Morse code that landed on her desk. She was particularly gifted at deciphering diplomatic intelligence, which was far more complex. She had the necessary knowledge of poetry, music and language to be able to interpret what was being said.

After the war, Emily Anderson was awarded an OBE for her work in Cairo at the Combined Bureau Middle East. She broke Italian codebooks which helped to change the course of the war in North Africa. While she is remembered – and honoured – at her alma mater in Galway, her achievements still pass under the radar.

That is partly because she didn't want to leave any trace of her work as a codebreaker, according to her biographer. 'She just wanted to disappear,' Dr Uí Chionna says.

Emily Anderson's experience, however, was the exception rather than the rule. For most other workers, life at Bletchley Park was far more humdrum. If it was dubbed 'the intelligence factory', the emphasis was more on the word 'factory' than 'intelligence'. It was a busy, noisy place where the majority of the thousands-strong staff worked on small and often seemingly menial tasks.

Many of them, in particular the women, didn't leave any trace of their work, partly because they had been told so often not to talk about it and partly because they didn't see the value of what they were doing. That is why it is instructive – and important – to shine a light on the foot soldiers on the intelligence frontline, such as Rubel Cherrington.

As she said later, it was difficult to work, day after day, not knowing what you were doing and not being able to say anything about it.

Despite the restrictions, though, staff did what they could to relieve the stifling secrecy and the boredom. Hut 2 was a designated recreation area where staff could get tea, sandwiches and, later, beer. It also housed a lending library and provided a venue for evening classes in German and Italian.

The Bletchley Park Recreation Club organised a range of out-of-hours activities, including dancing, sport, fencing, chess and music. There was also a drama group, which staged a number of original productions, while the resident poets and would-be writers put their quick wit to use to compose songs or poetry. A favourite, sung to the air of 'My Bonnie Lies over the Ocean', poked a bit of gentle fun at the singular circumstances.

It went:

> My bonnie is stationed at uh-uh
> And nobody knows it you see,
> Expect all the people of uh-uh
> And all his relations and me

A long poem, called 'A Bletchley Alphabet', dedicated verses to several members of staff. This verse for the letter 'V' provides a humorous peephole into behind-the-scenes activity.

V is the Visitor, distinguished Brass-Hat
Comes snooping around to see what we're at
We sweep the place clean with dustpan and broom
And move all the empties to some other room.

Another place where staff could relax a little was in the canteen. 'The atmosphere was jolly; there was lots of laughter and banter going around, especially with the military people,' Mair Russell-Jones said. She liked the food too. It was always hot, fresh and filling and 'there was always a main course and a pudding,' she said.

Rubel Cherrington was one of thousands who wore a uniform, but many others were dressed in civvies. Just as songs and poems caught on, so too did certain fashions. Russell-Jones gives this fascinating insight into a curious trend for brightly coloured legwear: 'The women were, on the whole, smartly dressed in frocks and jackets, but many of them wore colourful stockings. This turned out to be a real feature of Bletchley Park life… every day witnessed an array of colourful and sometimes gaudy leg adornments, and they served to raise spirits in an intense and generally serious atmosphere.'

Any bit of levity was welcome. Rubel's brother Paul had been evacuated from Dunkirk in 1940, one of the more than 330,000 Allied troops who made a miraculous escape from the Normandy coast back to Britain. She knew exactly what was at stake.

The reality of war was difficult. There was austerity, nightly blackouts, restrictions on travel and rationed food. 'The food was very, very dreary. But it was sustaining. I mean, it didn't kill you, but it wasn't nice,' Rubel recalled years later. But that, she said, was not what was difficult. 'It was watching all these young boys of 20 going off to war, knowing that they could be killed or, if caught by the Germans, tortured before being killed.'

Her soon-to-be husband, John Ross from Cork, was in the Irish Guards, but he didn't see action during the war. It was a relief to his new wife, but after they married in 1945, the couple's best man was sent off to France to fight. 'About four months later peace was signed and it was... marvellous. And he stood up in his trench and a German left over from somewhere, just shot him. He went down like that. John had to go and take his place, but it was... vindictive. I mean, there were people killing each other for no reason at all.'

When John Ross left the army, the couple moved back to Ireland and lived first in Sandyford in Co. Dublin and, from 1964, in Enniskerry, Co. Wicklow. Rubel had four children, Barbara Ann, Shane, Pippa and Connolly, and settled into family life. Her degree in history and her wartime experience faded into the background. Her husband knew she had worked at Bletchley Park but nothing more.

If the war was ever mentioned, it was John Ross's experience that was evoked. 'He always said he was doing Winston Churchill's signals,' his son Shane Ross recalls. Rubel, on the other hand, was self-effacing and reticent.

While she spent all of her married life in Ireland, she remained interested in British life and politics. She was an 'unashamed monarchist', her son says, and was delighted when he met Princess Anne at the Dublin Horse Show at the Royal Dublin Society in 2016.

That sense of Britishness made her uncomfortable at times, particularly at the height of the Troubles in Northern Ireland.

Yet, she created a happy home and held firm to her principles and beliefs.

'She didn't believe in illness, or doctors, or death,' her son says. She didn't believe in feminism either, he adds. 'She said she didn't need to be feminist because she never had any problems. She believed it was a wife's duty to make a marriage work and she would defer to her husband and would never put herself in a position where she was competing with him. But she was much, much cleverer than him – the whole family, in fact. She was extraordinarily bright.'

That fierce intelligence blossomed again when Rubel was in her late fifties. When her husband teased her that she hadn't used her 'history degree for five minutes', it was the prompt she needed to begin historical research again. That led her to submit a number of articles on Irish houses to *Country Life* magazine, which, in turn, led to a long and successful career as a writer. She became a well-known gardening and cookery columnist and wrote several books, including *Irish Wild Flowers* and the *Little Irish Baking Book*. She wrote the introduction to the very well-received *An Irish Florilegium: Wild and Garden Plants of Ireland*.

Her experience of the war, however, was ever-present. Although she spoke little about it, it shaped her attitude to life. When her youngest son, Connolly, died suddenly at the age of 47, she bore it with characteristic stoicism.

'During the war we were cannon fodder, really... And so many [young boys] just disappeared, never seen again... That's why, though it was terrible upon his death and I just miss him awfully... some people might have it worse. A long lingering illness, I think is worse. I'm sure it is. And the sort of things that went on at the end of the war were worse as well,' she told broadcaster Miriam O'Callaghan on the RTÉ show, *Miriam Meets*, in 2010.

In the same interview, her son Shane Ross said his mother, and anyone who had lived through the war, seemed to be much more accepting of death. They were more accepting of the challenges in life too, he said; they looked at economic downturns and recessions as challenges to be endured and overcome.

Ruth Isabel Ross certainly seems to have seen any hardship she experienced after the war as a paler version of what had gone before: 'I wouldn't say war is futile because it does decide something sometimes. But the tragedy of wars is something that nobody who hasn't been through one knows what it is. So, so dreadful.'

When wartime information was declassified in the 1970s, many of those who worked at Bletchley Park began to speak of their time there. There were biographies, documentaries and later an Oscar-nominated film, *The Imitation Game*, starring Benedict Cumberbatch and Keira Knightley, which brought Alan Turing's work at Bletchley into the limelight.

Rubel still said very little, but her work was no longer a secret. Her great-granddaughter Issy Ross wrote a school project on Bletchley Park, using her own name to explain the workings of the Enigma cipher machine.

Her explanation is as crystal-clear as you'll find: 'The enigma machine looks like a keyboard inside a wooden box. It has 26 letter keys and 26 letter bulbs and lots of plugs, and

3 rotors on the inside. When a letter is typed on the keyboard it lights up as a different letter of the alphabet on one of the bulbs. But the operator of the machine used the plugs on the inside of the machine to change the letters and bulb connections every 6 to 24 hours. For example, for my name "Issy" on a particular date: at 12pm the code for my name could be "JXXF". At 6pm, the code for my name could be "PRRL".'

She described how Alan Turing's bombes – electrical and mechanical machines made of 10 miles of wire, 100 rotating drums/rotors – were used to crack the code. And, in turn, how those discoveries were considered the most important victory by the Allied powers during World War II.

Several decades after spending long hours in dimly lit huts, Bletchley Park workers were finally able to see how their work had been part of a much bigger picture.

Rubel Ross said she hadn't particularly liked her work – although she wasn't unhappy either – but she just got on with it because one just got on with things. It was an outlook that informed her post-war life too. A few years before she died, aged 96 in 2016, she was asked if she had enjoyed her life:

'Oh, yes,' she said, 'I've had a wonderful time. Absolutely. I mean there have been stresses and difficulties and all sorts of things. Disappointments [too]. You have not to mind that, just to sort of shrug [your] shoulders and get on with the next thing.'

SPECIAL AGENTS

8

'A Cool and Lonely Courage'

'O'SULLIVAN HAS NEVER YET BEEN KNOWN TO LET CIRCUMSTANCES BEAT HER.'

WAAF WING COMMANDER

22 March 1944: When Maureen 'Paddy' O'Sullivan parachuted in thick fog into occupied France, she hit the ground with such force she was sure she had broken her neck. It was the last thing that went through her mind before she passed out. When she came to, a short time later, her first terrifying thought was that she had been discovered; she sensed a figure bent over her and felt breathing on her face. When she opened her eyes, relief flooded her body: a curious cow in a field near Le Bourg, in the northern Creuse area of France, was standing over her.

Her money belt, packed with two million francs, broke her fall, but she was not where she was supposed to be. She was about a half a kilometre from the agreed meeting place. She set out to find her contact. Luckily, she started to walk in the right direction and, soon afterwards, met two Frenchmen who were gobsmacked to find that 'Paddy' was a woman.

Initial reservations were soon forgotten when they saw the drop of supplies that had landed with her. Their network, the Fireman circuit, which operated around Limoges, had a pitiful armoury of just two revolvers.

They worked quickly to recover two wireless sets and 22 containers of weapons. Then, they took Paddy to a safe farm for a meal before going to a village south of Limoges to introduce her to the leader of the circuit, Maj. Edmund (Teddy) Mayer, aka Barthélémy.

Mayer was furious that London had sent him a 'girl'. The work, he said, was much too tough for a woman. And leaving aside that not-inconsiderable issue, he was unconvinced by his new field agent. She just didn't look the part. It was crucial that agents looked and sounded French.

There was no faulting Maureen Patricia O'Sullivan's command of French. After her mother Adelaide Johanna (née Repen) died a year after her birth in Dublin on 3 January 1918, she spent her early years with her father, journalist John O'Sullivan, on Charleville Rd, Rathmines, Dublin. However, she later spent her formative years with an aunt in Belgium. She received most of her education there, apart from a short spell at Rathmines Commercial College in Dublin when she was 15.

She started to train as a nurse in London in 1939, but signed up for the WAAF two years later. Perhaps she was keen to do her bit to fight Hitler, given that she already had personal experience of war: one of her three elder brothers, Paddy, joined the International Brigades during the Spanish Civil War and was killed at the Battle of the Ebro in 1938.

Her early schooling gave her a distinct advantage for clandestine work. She had fluent French and English and some Dutch and Flemish. The latter would prove life-saving later on.

It was her looks, though, that were bothering Mayer. His

new agent had blonde hair and blue eyes. Paddy herself wasn't convinced that the civilian clothes she had been issued looked sufficiently French. Before each mission, great attention was paid to dressing field agents in local attire.

Fashion was highly individualistic, varying widely from country to country. The idea of a uniform high street was decades away, so something as seemingly innocuous as a seam or how a button was attached could give you away. The French generally attached buttons with the thread going in two parallel lines, for example, while the English favoured crisscross stitching.

The SOE went to great lengths to tailor garments that looked local. They hired clothing companies, often ones run by refugees, to make sure that details on garments such as labels, zips and collars looked authentic. Female agents also had their hair cut in particular styles, and they were told not to dye their hair or manicure their nails, as that would make them stand out in wartime France.

Before she set off on her mission, Paddy's pockets were searched to make sure nothing incriminating – a bus ticket, coin or receipt – was forgotten.

But nobody had told Paddy not to smoke. Although she suffered from chronic asthma, she was a very heavy smoker. She did not know, however, that most French girls did not smoke and if they did, they were not able to afford cigarettes, which were prohibitively expensive. Had it not been for Mayer, she would have slipped up several times. He warned her that it would look very suspicious if she smoked too much in public.

Mayer had several other reservations, but Maureen Patricia O'Sullivan was determined to stay. 'Here I am,' she told him, 'and we'll just have to make the best of it.'

The early days of her mission didn't go at all well. Mayer was shocked by her lack of training. She couldn't set up an aerial, change a fuse and, worst of all, she couldn't ride a bicycle. The latter was a huge shortcoming as agents regularly cycled tens of kilometres daily as couriers and wireless operators.

It wasn't an obstacle as far as Paddy was concerned. She set about learning in Limoges – and incredibly was taught to ride a bicycle by a German soldier, she told her sons after the war. He saw her struggling and came to her aid. If he hoped for something in return, he went away disappointed, but his student was at least now mobile.

By the time Paddy, aka Josette, landed in France several women were operating in the field. In fact, the SOE had already faced down considerable opposition to recruiting female agents, largely centred around concerns that women, if armed clandestinely, would not be protected under the terms of the Geneva Convention if captured.

There was less doubt about women's ability to do the job. The first female agents, Krystyna Skarbek and Virginia Hall, had proven capable and very effective. Polish-born Skarbek carried out several dangerous missions for Section D of MI6. In 1939, she skied across the Tatra mountains in Hungary into occupied Poland and delivered money and information to resistance networks.

Virginia Hall, meanwhile, sent vital reports from Vichy France, where she posed as a reporter for the *New York Post*. She had lost a leg in a hunting accident and walked with a limp on her wooden prosthetic. She made an unlikely agent, but her false leg was no barrier to helping resistance fighters and gathering intelligence. In fact, it was an advantage, as it diverted attention. At first unsuspecting, the Nazis soon became aware of an agent 'who could be four different women in an afternoon', to quote her biographer Sonia Purnell.

She was so skilled that the Gestapo ordered 'Wanted' posters with her image and the words: 'The Enemy's Most Dangerous Spy – We Must Find And Destroy Her!'

So when SOE recruiting officer Selwyn Jepson suggested including female agents, British Prime Minister Winston Churchill agreed it was 'a very sensible thing to do'. Indeed, Jepson believed women had a far greater capacity for 'cool and lonely courage' than men.

Women were first admitted to the SOE in April 1942. Maureen O'Sullivan was serving at the RAF station at Compton Bassett in Wiltshire, England, when she was called up for SOE training, F (French) Section, in May 1943.

Women received exactly the same training as men. Both men and women were woken in the early hours of wintry mornings in Inverness-shire, Scotland, where they experienced 'the same mud, muck soakings in peat bogs on fieldcraft and the same sore muscles and aching joints', as Maj. Aonghais Fyffe, security liaison officer for training schools in Scotland, put it. 'They were all just bods in battledress.'

Not everyone saw them as equal, though. To judge from some of the comments on Maureen's training reports, those in authority were often sexist and paternalistic.

At the end of 1943, for instance, a Capt. Clitheroe wrote of her: 'A tough type of woman, at the moment growing quite a successful moustache. Seems to be popular with all students. Is more of a boy than a girl. Not particularly intelligent, and does not seem [to] take her work very seriously. Irresponsible, and not sufficiently level headed to warrant any undue confidence.'

Two months earlier, though, her appearance was described as 'childish' and though bad-tempered at times and undisciplined, 'serious and earnest at bottom'. Two months before that again, at the end of August 1943, her superior described her as 'a pleasant intelligent Irish girl with a mind and will of her own. Purposeful and determined once she is convinced that what she is doing is right.'

She was said to be accident-prone, though, and it was considered inadvisable that she should ever jump from a plane.

Her report card from paramilitary special training school in Scotland was also rather mixed. She was handicapped in rope work because of her 'very weak arms', it said. On the plus side, she did well in map-reading, boating, schemes and tactics, and had shown an improvement in fieldcraft. She had also overcome her nervousness at weapon training and her theoretical knowledge of explosives and demolition was good, but she was still afraid of the noise and the recoil when using a rifle.

As part of her training she was sent on a spurious mission to Manchester, she later told her son John Alvey. 'What she did not know was that her trainers had told the Manchester police that she was a German spy. She was arrested and kept naked in a dank cell and abused for being an "Irish bitch". The trainers told the police the truth after a couple of days.'

Despite her ordeal, the final analysis from her commandant (on 8 October 1943) was pretty damning: 'An exceedingly temperamental student, who appears to be suffering from an inferiority complex... owing to her temperament, the advisability of her employment <u>abroad</u> is very doubtful.'

There was one exception. Maureen Patricia O'Sullivan showed outstanding keenness and was considered well above average at signalling. 'She would make a first-rate W/T [wireless telegraphy] Operator.'

Maureen Patricia O'Sullivan did indeed make a first-rate wireless operator. Her ability to work as an agent quickly became clear in France because when London offered to send Mayer two men six weeks later, he turned down the offer: 'Having trained her, I will keep her.'

He did not regret it. The woman who could not change a fuse or ride a bicycle went on to become one of the best agents in France, staying in the field for seven months at a time when wireless transmitters had a life expectancy of just six weeks.

Once she had learned to cycle, she began to operate in the Limoges area, moving from safe house to safe house, sometimes cycling up to 50km a day. She never stayed anywhere for more than a fortnight and sometimes much less if word came through Mayer to move on.

She was equipped with false identity papers, a London-issued handbag with a false bottom to hide documents, and a cover story – she was a doctor's *dame de companie*, or assistant, who had been given a month's holiday to look for a Belgian parent apparently lost in the area. She never used that story. Instead, she fabricated a new one that seemed more plausible given her circumstances.

She said she was a former pupil of the local school-teacher's wife. They had supposedly met in Alsace. 'In this way,' her military file noted, 'she was able to stay in the area and no-one suspected her.'

Soon, she was operating seven different radio sets, which she kept hidden in seven different houses. At one, she hid the set under a pile of sticks in the yard; at another, she buried it after use. While she was transmitting, someone always kept watch. At another location, she put the garden gate on the latch so that it creaked to warn her if someone was approaching. In other houses, the occupants hid her behind a thick curtain or kept the wireless on to obscure any sound she might make.

She transmitted from a grain barn too while the daughter of the house kept watch. The girl would sing if anybody was coming. The attendant at a grocer's shop did the same while she worked secretly on the upper floor. If he started to sing a popular hit of the time, *'J'attendrai* (I will be waiting)', she knew there was danger.

On one occasion, the Germans searched the house where she was staying. An old lady sat on the radio set on a chair, covered by her voluminous skirts, and abused the intruders in patois. The messages for transmission were hidden in a large soup bowl. The Germans smashed up the house, but found nothing.

Paddy memorised transmission codes in the form of poetry so that she didn't have to 'carry the silk', as other agents did. Single-use codes were often printed on a small piece of fine silk, known as 'the silk', which could be easily concealed. Agents developed ingenious hiding places. Phyllis Latour, another member of SOE F Section, said she wrapped her encoded silk around a knitting needle, fed it into a shoelace and used that to tie up her hair.

Maureen's colleague, Marie Louise Thomas, who cycled up to 140km daily as a courier, hid her messages in the tube or tyres of her bicycle.

It was exhausting and dangerous work.

Once, the two women were stopped by the *Maquis* who ordered them to give up their bicycles. Maureen was exhausted and with 20km still to go, she flatly refused and cycled on with her friend. The men were so taken aback that they let them go.

She would not have escaped so lightly at the next check-point if the Milice – a paramilitary group set up to fight the Resistance – had found the coding sheet hidden in her camouflage bag. Luckily, it was a single sheet and the man who searched her bag did not find it.

Maureen must have thought her luck had finally run out when she was stopped at a German control a few days after D-Day on 6 June 1944. She rarely carried her own wireless set, but on that particular day it was strapped to her carrier in a suitcase.

She approached the check-point and showed her papers. They were given back to her and then the *Wehrmacht* guard asked her what she had in the suitcase. She said it was full of clothes and just as the guard was about to open it, a German lieutenant stepped forward.

'*Ah, Mademoiselle,*' he said, '*vous resemblez à une Fräulein.*' ('Ah, miss, you look like a young German lady.')

Without missing a beat, Paddy said that her mother was German and that she had died when she was a baby, both of which were true. And then, in a mixture of Flemish and German, she flirted for her life. She spoke to the lieutenant for close to half an hour. He was so taken with her that he made a date for the next day. The suitcase was completely forgotten, and Paddy cycled away.

Her close call illustrated the advantage of being a female agent at a time when stereotypes of women kept her above suspicion. She was not the only one to capitalise on the perceived gender roles of the 1940s. Other agents turned the chivalry, or sexism, of the enemy to their advantage. They feigned helplessness or played the 'dumb girl' to allay suspicion.

When French resister Hélène Renal was stopped in 1944, she did just that: 'I played the complete imbecile who knew nothing, who did not understand what it was about, who had never heard of the Resistance. That worked more or less.'

By contrast, Maureen's courier, a boy of about 16, was captured and tortured to death by the Germans, but he gave nothing away.

During her time in France, Paddy, or to use her wireless plan name, Stocking, transmitted some 332 messages to London and trained three other operators. She was also involved in a mission to blow up a train, pressing the plunger at the appropriate time.

The man who, at first, thought her entirely unsuitable was full of praise for her in the end. 'Due to her patience, her natural intelligence, her hard work and willingness to learn, she improved rapidly and after a couple of months became a first class W/T operator who could be entirely trusted to carry out her job thoroughly, and all the credit for that is entirely due to herself,' Mayer wrote.

When she arrived back in London, she didn't hesitate to highlight the many shortfalls in her training at her debriefing session with Capt. Howard on 29 December 1944. She said the reason she got such high marks in her exams was because she had 'a parrot memory', but she did not really understand how certain things worked.

She said security training and further technical training were vital; she didn't want other agents to face similar dangers because of a lack of preparation. Two of the four female agents who had been infiltrated into France at the same time as her did not come home. Violette Szabó and Lilian Rolfe were arrested during their respective missions and later executed at Ravensbrück concentration camp in 1945. Of the 470 agents sent into France, 118 failed to return. Fourteen of those were women.

In spite of that, Paddy was keen to volunteer for a new mission: this time a parachute drop into Germany using the codename Saunders.

She got further training and her finishing report of 6 March 1945 was much more positive than it had been a few years previously. Though there were still a few barbs. It read: 'This student has a good brain which she can use if she wants to: a bearing which she can successfully adapt to clandestine conditions; a manner which is largely bluff and conceals all her normal female reactions; and a temperament which can be difficult unless controlled by a personality she is prepared to acknowledge.'

The report also gave this interesting insight: 'Her prime motive appears to be sheer love of adventure which covers most of her activities. Nevertheless, she would do a "first-class" job in Germany.'

Maureen Paddy O'Sullivan was to be denied another wartime 'adventure', however, because the press, hungry for stories of wartime exploits – particularly female ones – blew her cover. It is instructive to see how newspapers treated stories about the women of the SOE. If the 39 female agents infiltrated into France had upended stereotypes about the role of women in war, the press seemed intent on putting them back in their place. They highlighted women's physical attributes or depoliticised their action by framing it as the pursuit of adventure.

In March 1945, the *Daily Mail* ran a photograph of 'Paddy the rebel' under the headline: 'Sky-girl spied for 7 months'. The article began: 'A vivacious personality, good looks, calculated daring, and a knowledge of foreign languages made 25-years-old Maureen O'Sullivan, WAAF officer, one of the most valuable pre-D-Day parachutists for the Allied Commanders in London.'

It continued in gushing prose, detailing how she had 'crawled through hedges and ditches watching the movements of German troops, and sending and receiving coded messages to and from London through her portable wireless'.

Most damning was this line: 'Back in her Irish home, she told me yesterday some of the stories of her amazing exploits in France before the invasion.'

In fact, Paddy hadn't told the press anything. She had signed the Official Secrets Act and was adamant that she had never spoken to any journalist. Her details, and those of other SOE female agents, were leaked, it was thought, by others. Whatever the truth of it, her superiors were unhappy. They worried that she had been 'over-publicised' and was 'becoming too much of a glamour girl'.

The wisdom of allowing her to go to Germany was discussed, back and forth, in a few documents before deciding against it.

Nonetheless, Paddy was recommended for an MBE for her courage and bravery. Her wing commander at the WAAF wrote: 'S/O [Section Officer] O'Sullivan has never yet been known to let circumstances beat her... Her early efforts were most discouraging, and at one point it was feared that she would have to return for further training. It was at this point that Paddy O'Sullivan stuck out her determined chin with that Irish flexibility which is characteristic of her... She had to live in atrociously insanitary conditions, but she never grumbled or complained. She was inspired by her work, and if the circuit did a magnificent job it was due in no small measure to her persistent efforts and untiring devotion.'

In September 1945, Maureen Patricia O'Sullivan received her MBE from Princess Elizabeth. When she said she was Irish, her family said that the future queen replied: 'Paddy the rebel!', echoing the *Daily Mail*'s headline.

Just after the war, Paddy's name was put forward to tour America with other former female SOE agents on a publicity/propaganda mission. She would be an excellent choice, her wing commander said. The SOE, however, disagreed, claiming she was indiscreet, adding that 'she was a citizen of Eire [Ireland]'.

Paddy moved to Calcutta in India where she worked as a liaison officer to the French. This time, she did grant an interview to the Air Force PRO, believing the article was for an internal readership. When it circulated more widely, there was a brief kerfuffle and a rush to edit out certain details, including the fact that agents were trained in picking pockets.

There was much more upset when a report in the *Evening News* in Britain suggested that the French francs Paddy brought with her had been forged. One official, referred to as 'F', wrote: 'I need hardly draw attention to the repercussions, particularly among the French, of the word "forged". As you know, the French are only too prone to believe all they see in the Press is gospel truth, because they cannot understand why we don't control the Press more effectively.'

While in India, Paddy met Walter Eric Alvey and married him in 1946. The couple later moved to Leeds in England and had two sons, John and Robin. She took her sons with her on a trip to France, returning to the house where the old lady had hidden a radio set under her skirt. The trip and her stories inspired her sons to play 'Parachute into France', a game that involved jumping off the sofa and later, when they upped the stakes, the precarious heights of the shed.

Media interest in Maureen Alvey continued, but her husband turned down an offer from Eamonn Andrews to appear on the popular TV programme, *This Is Your Life*. When she found out, years later, she was furious.

After her husband died in the 1970s, she moved to Bray in Co. Wicklow, hoping to settle back into the country of her birth. She taught French and worked as a translator. If she was seen as an Irish rebel in the British SOE, some in Ireland considered her, if not quite British at least aligned to that country because she had served in its army. At least, that was a theory put forward by her half-brother Tom O'Sullivan in the *Irish Independent* in 2002 to explain why her house had been burgled. He said her house had been ransacked and some of her wartime memorabilia stolen.

She later told her son, John Alvey, that she moved back to England because the priests really annoyed her, 'always coming round to collect money and preach'.

Her nationality had not been an issue when she was being parachuted behind enemy lines a few years previously, but it appeared to matter now. But then, Maureen Patricia O'Sullivan had spent a lot of her life crossing boundaries of one kind or another; she was an Irish child schooled in Belgium; a woman in the male arena of war; an Irish citizen in the British army, and later, when she moved to Ireland, 'a stranger in her own country', as her son John Alvey put it in 2002.

If there was one constant in her life, however, it was her connection to the camaraderie she appeared to have found in the army. While many said nothing about their wartime experiences, Paddy spoke to groups on a regular basis in Leeds, giving the money she raised to the RAF benevolent fund.

She may not have missed the horrors of war, but she certainly had deep admiration for the people she met during her days as an SOE agent. She summed it up best herself in one of those articles that caused a furore: 'I was terribly frightened at times, but there was a wonderful spirit of sharing danger with men of the highest order of courage, which made it a privilege to work for them.'

9

The Moonlight Hours

'RATHER INCLINED TO ACT THE WILD IRISHMAN, HE WAS
NEVERTHELESS QUICK AND CUNNING AND HE COULD
TALK HIMSELF OUT OF ANYTHING.'
                    ONE OF BRIAN RAFFERTY'S SUPERIORS

France 1942: The parachute drop went according to plan, but little else did. SOE agents Brian Rafferty, Christian Sydney Hudson and George Jones landed safely when they parachuted into central France, on 24 September, but a suitcase containing Rafferty and Hudson's effects could not be found. All three left the landing site regardless and made their way to a safe house at Le Crest, south of Clermont-Ferrand.

A short time later, Rafferty and Jones moved on from the safe house, while Hudson stayed behind. It was a decision that cost him dearly as the French police had since come upon the missing suitcase and were able to track Hudson down to the safe house and arrest him. He would spend the next 15 months in solitary confinement.

The Headmaster 1 resistance circuit was left without a leader. Hudson's mission had been to organise sabotage operations, destroying anything that might be of use to the enemy, and to accumulate a large stock of weapons for use by the Resistance in the Massif Central in south-central France. Now, there was a gap. Capt. Brian Dominic Rafferty, Hudson's number two, stepped in to take on the role of leader.

A few months earlier, his superiors had given him a mixed report. They thought the 22 year old 'rather inclined to act the wild Irishman', but they saw real potential too. As Sgt Searle put it, on 19 March 1942: 'This student likes to give an outward impression of laziness, yet he is actually most reliable and in possession of a happy, excellent character. He gives the impression of a leader who would inspire confidence and carry out a job with extreme courage.'

Now, having just turned 23, he had a chance to prove his mettle, dealing with circumstances that were beyond challenging. He had landed in a region, though still inside the unoccupied zone, where Gestapo activity was intense. There was local support for the Allies, but Rafferty had been warned that some of them were not above denouncing their neighbours in anonymous letters. Aware of these challenges, he took charge of a circuit that would go on to become one of the biggest in central France.

Despite his reputation – 'an excellent man of the type who likes to hide his qualities under a cloud of buffoonery', as another superior said of him – he proved to be cautious in the field. The conditions, he wrote, 'have made "go slow" the wise rule for this region for the moment'. All the same, he and his wireless operator, George Jones, still managed to travel large distances to organise sabotage groups around Clermont-Ferrand and, further east, in the Jura.

He also directed parachute drops of weapons and equipment, a high-risk clandestine operation that had been perfected by specially trained SOE air teams.

Drops took place at night in full moonlight to guide pilots, but in remote areas so they were unseen. Rafferty was always on the look-out for suitable locations. In a surviving report, he gave details of one landing spot that might be suitable: it was flat, hidden from a nearby road and couldn't be seen from any inhabited dwelling. It also had suitable cover nearby, which was vital for those gathering dropped supplies.

A plane did not need to land to deliver equipment, but it flew low while discharging specially designed containers that were packed with shock-absorbing material to protect the contents.

If the reception committee had a ground-to-air radio, it made contact with the pilot. If not, it relied on flashlight signals or fires to direct the clandestine operation. Speed was of the essence as signalling might quickly attract attention.

It was also necessary to have a team to pick up the containers, which, with their load of machine guns complete with magazines and ammunition, could weigh over 20 stone, or more than 120kg. Some containers could be unclamped and divided into separate, more-portable segments, but others had to be transported whole.

Back in London, SOE engineers were constantly developing equipment that was robust, light and easy to conceal. Portable wireless sets were hidden inside briefcases, which were well-worn and battered to distract attention. Metal drums were also used to hide ammunition or explosives. They were mislabelled – oil, paint or creosote, for instance – and a sample of those liquids were inserted in a bung-hole to fool anyone who inserted a dip-stick into the container.

For all the innovation and support, the reality on the ground was extremely difficult. In early November, not even

General Charles de Gaulle's BBC rallying call on 18 June 1940 was credited with providing the spark that ignited a resistance movement. *(Alamy Stock Photo/Adoc Photos)*

Samuel Beckett's resistance work
went 'to the extreme limit of daring'.
(Hulton Archive/Stringer)

When Sgt Bill Magrath, a 19-year-
old from Co. Fermanagh, set out
on an RAF raid in 1940, he knew
he wasn't coming back.
(Courtesy of Ole Rønnest MBE)

Fr Kenneth Monaghan, a Passionist
priest from Co. Sligo, took enormous
risks to help Allied soldiers on the run.
(Diocese of Menevia Archives)

Delia Murphy Kiernan, wife of the
Irish ambassador to the Vatican,
'was determined to save the hides
of others and not get caught'.
(Courtesy of Leo and Carole Cullen)

Delia Murphy Kiernan with her husband Dr T.J. Kiernan at
Dublin Airport in the 1940s.
(Courtesy of Leo and Carole Cullen)

Margaret Kelly, aka Bluebell, founder of the world-famous Bluebell
dance troupe, hid her Jewish husband in occupied Paris.
(Getty Images/Hulton Deutsch)

Agnes Bernelle married her sweetheart Spitfire pilot
Desmond Leslie just days after the war ended.
(Courtesy of the Leslie family)

Agnes Bernelle, of Berlin and Dublin, used her native language to broadcast black propaganda to misinform German troops and send secret messages to the Resistance. *(Courtesy of the Leslie family)*

Concerned she might be an enemy agent, pilot Desmond Leslie followed his future wife Agnes Bernelle in 1943, only to discover she was involved in resistance work. *(Courtesy of the Leslie family)*

Rubel Cherrington was assigned
to Hut 15 at Bletchley Park
where she recorded and analysed
broadcasts on enemy radio networks.
(Courtesy of Shane Ross)

Thousands of codebreakers worked at Bletchley Park, a secret
intelligence operation near London that would later be credited
with shortening the war by at least two years.
(Getty Images/Bletchley Park Trust)

Special agent Maureen Patricia
O'Sullivan married Walter Eric Alvey in
1946. (*Courtesy of John Alvey*)

Maureen Patricia O'Sullivan in the field after D-Day in 1944. Her
boss, Major Edmund (Teddy) Mayer, to her right, was furious
London had sent him a girl, but later said she made a first-rate
radio operator. (*Courtesy of John Alvey*)

Captain Brian Dominic Rafferty was 'inclined to act the wild Irishman', but he was also a leader who inspired confidence. (*The National Archives, ref. HS9/1225/2*)

Resistance leader Claude de Baissac was the father of Irish special agent Mary Herbert's daughter. The baby girl was born in occupied France. (*The National Archives, ref. HS9/75*)

Sgt Pickering revisits the stone outhouse in northern Italy
where he and Captain John Keany hid in 1945.
(From The Bandits of Cisterna *by William Pickering
and Alan Hart)*

Monica de Wichfeld, of London and Fermanagh, was condemned to death for helping the Resistance in Denmark. *(Courtesy of Christopher Massy-Beresford)*

Robert Armstrong, gardener and resistance member, was sentenced to death for helping Allied men get to safety. *(Courtesy of Doug Armstrong and Ronan McGreevy)*

Andrée Dumon, alias Nadine, worked with Irish *résistante* Catherine Crean in Brussels. Both were arrested and imprisoned. *(From* I Have Never Forgotten You *by Andrée Dumon)*

Dubliner Mary Cummins, who spent years in camps and prisons for her resistance activities in Belgium, married Count Guy O'Kelly de Galway after the war. *(Courtesy of Dorothy Seagrave)*

Mary O'Shaughnessy, left, survived the horrors of
Ravensbrück concentration camp and later went to
live with fellow former camp inmate Anne Spoerry,
right, in Kenya. (*Courtesy of John Heminway*)

Waterford woman Anna Duchêne (née Hodges),
right, was 71 when she sheltered two airmen in
her home in Brussels. She is photographed here
with her sister Edith. (*Courtesy of George Vecsey*)

Aufziehen der Wache auf den Champs Elysées

On 14 June 1940, the Germans entered Paris unopposed.
(*Alamy Stock Photo* / *Lordprice Collection*)

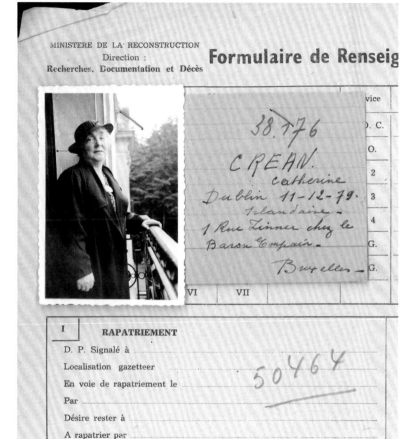

Catherine Crean, of Moore Street in Dublin, was arrested
for helping Allied airmen in Brussels.
(Courtesy of Archives de l'Etat en Belgique
[State Archives, Belgium])

Co-author John Morgan brought a photo of Catherine Crean across the Pyrenees into Spain in September 2023. She helped many fugitives to make that journey; now it was time for her to see 'freedom'.

The Mayor of Killarney Marie Moloney and Mary G O'Sullivan admiring the plaque unveiled in 2022 on Mission Road, Killarney, Co Kerry, commemorating local woman and *résistante* Janie McCarthy. *(Courtesy of Michelle Crean / Killarney Advertiser)*

two months after Rafferty landed in France, the Allies invaded North Africa. The Germans and Italians responded by occupying the free zone in France. The *zone libre* (the free zone) became the *zone sud* (the southern zone) while the *zone occupée* (the occupied zone) became the *zone nord* (the northern zone).

But the biggest blow to Rafferty's mission came a month later when his radio operator George Jones had a serious bicycle accident on his way to transmit a message to London.

'I am afraid he is permanently disabled,' Rafferty, aka Michel, wrote in a report a short time later. 'It is impossible for me to exaggerate the pluck and tenacity shown by Isidore (Jones's field name) through all the trials to which he has been subjected. He was still very ill when he got back to work and I had the greatest difficulty in getting him to wait that long.'

Isidore was by his side again, but Rafferty was now concerned about the stream of new faces presenting as couriers. He felt they were not security-conscious and he scoffed that some of them spoke French with a German accent.

His own French was excellent, having studied in France as a child and later as a student at the Sciences Politiques university in Paris. He studied at Christ Church in Oxford, too, and had been thinking of a career in diplomacy.

That all changed when war broke out. In early October 1939, he volunteered for the Officer Cadet Training Unit and was later appointed captain in the Royal Berkshire Regiment at Ballykinlar, Northern Ireland. He joined the SOE in March 1942.

A sub-division called F Section sent some 400 agents into France to help local resistance groups through their own circuits. Before they were sent into the field, recruits completed specialist training – in four stages. It included sabotage, weapons, explosives, parachuting, map reading, tactics, Morse code, demolition training, wireless telegraphy, even silent killing (it was not how hard you hit an opponent, but where you hit them that was important, trainees were told).

Recruits were also encouraged to drink freely so that their superiors could assess whether or not they could keep a secret under the influence.

Special Training Schools were set up in a number of big houses around England, requisitioned for the purpose. Those manors played such a central role in training that the wits of the organisation joked that the acronym 'SOE' stood for Stately 'Omes of England. Paramilitary training took place in Scotland and lasted up to five weeks. In all, though, agents were expected to be ready for action after six months' training, if that.

As well as physical training, agents had to speak the language of the country in which they were posted. Capt. Rafferty passed that test with flying colours. 'He could pass for a Frenchman and should be a valuable asset to the organisation,' his training report noted, although it was his Irish heritage that appeared most often in his performance reviews, usually with a disparaging adjective before it.

'Tends to the anglophobia which might be expected of his ancestry, but this should not produce any difficulty as long as it is known,' said one.

Military historian MRD Foot was more positive, even if he drew on a cultural stereotype: 'of Irish descent, Rafferty had all the charm, vivacity and most importantly, all the fighting spirit of his race.'

Although he was born in Hull, England, on 1 September 1919, the eldest of Thomas A. Rafferty and his wife Keyna

Mary Rogan's three children, it is clear that his ancestry was important to him. At the same time, he was equally at ease in France and England. He was also well-travelled, having spent time in Spain and Switzerland.

Perhaps more important than all of those observations was this one: 'He is a lot tougher than he looks, and will not let himself be defeated,' as his final report from Special Training School at Whitehall, London, said.

Resilience and self-belief were essential in the field. As MRD Foot pointed out, the word resistance comes from the Latin word *resistere* – to stand fast, doubly so. A good agent had to have a strong sense of inner certainty to succeed. Sound judgement, a sharp instinct and quick wits were also vital. Courage was a given, as was discretion.

Sometime in early 1943, though, Rafferty was concerned about a lack of the latter within his circuit. One safe house had been ruined, he wrote, and he was very concerned that some new couriers were writing down the addresses of other houses. Worst of all, one of them had an envelope addressed to 'Isidore', George Jones's field name, which was not supposed to be divulged to others.

Rafferty's field name was Dominique; his operational name was Aubretia and the name on his false documents was Bertrand Dominic Rémy. He had other names too and it was as 'Michel' that he expressed concerns to his superiors about the planned sabotage of the Michelin tyre factory at Clermont-Ferrand. He was waiting for the support of a replacement team that had not yet come. 'We have not failed to let you know of our anxiety about the Relève [relief],' he told his superior.

He later carried out that operation with more-than-hoped-for success, burning some 300 tonnes of the factory's tyres at a time when rubber was particularly scarce. Another resistance circuit, Plane, dropped leaflets to encourage French workers inside the factory to do what they could to compromise the quality of the tyres on the production line.

If Rafferty led many effective sabotage operations, he had less success trying to spring his comrade Sydney Hudson, aka Marc, from jail.

'The unfortunate Marc lingers in what my "peeping Tom" described as a mighty fortress which even a regiment could not invest. This is a really unsatisfactory business and you can be sure I am doing my utmost to get him out,' he wrote. Rafferty mightn't have been able to rescue his colleague, but Hudson succeeded in breaking out of jail himself. He later escaped across the Pyrenees to Spain, then on to Gibraltar and finally back to London.

Rafferty, however, proved adept at staying out of jail. He gave a witty insight into the remorseless pressure of being constantly just one step from arrest. 'We boys are being hunted high and low these days… all Max Factor's, Elizabeth Arden's or Madame Rubenstein's wares or manipulations would hardly change my features and complexion to that of respectable middle age.'

It all took a heavy toll on his body, though: 'After anxious months of helplessly watching my retreating waist-band, I am just about keeping to the figure of an often sylphchewing [dieting] fellow. My greatest enemy is my bike on which I average 300 kilos [it seems he meant kilometres] a week. Morale good though at times waves of homesickness creep past brought on by my anxiety for parents and so on,' he wrote in a report from the field.

That anxiety would soon shift in the other direction when Capt. Brian Dominic Rafferty was reported missing in June 1943. Earlier that month, or in late May, according to some reports, Rafferty and Jones were arrested.

Jones later escaped from prison, but Rafferty had no such luck. In Dijon prison, he was beaten brutally. It was reported that his arm was broken and he was 'unrecognisably bruised and in a lamentable condition', but he gave nothing away. Weeks passed before he revealed his own identity, which allowed his fellow resistance members ample time to regroup.

His resistance groups, in the Massif Central and in the Jura, survived his arrest. They were taken over by another organiser and developed into two of the most successful circuits in France.

When his captors realised that Capt. Rafferty was a British agent, he was moved to Fresnes prison outside Paris. Later, in April 1944, he was moved with 13 other Allied officers to Flossenbürg in north-eastern Bavaria, a concentration camp that, at its peak, held more than 50,000 prisoners.

A Danish officer later told the war office that the officers remained there 'in conditions of great hardship, but they were neither required to work nor did they undergo any form of ill treatment. All were extremely hopeful of being liberated by the advancing armies when suddenly on 28 March 1945 orders were received to execute some of the prisoners and to evacuate others to a camp further inland.'

The following day, Capt. Brian Dominic Rafferty and 13 other Allied prisoners of war were hanged.

Even before news of his death filtered through to London, Major General McVean Gubbins wrote a citation recommending that Capt. Rafferty be awarded the Military Cross. 'This loyal and courageous officer made an important contribution to the organisation of French Resistance, and deserves high credit for his bravery and devotion to duty,' he wrote.

Sometime later he added: 'Since this citation was written we have been informed that Capt. Rafferty died in enemy hands on 29th March 1945.'

Colonel Buckmaster wrote to tell Rafferty's parents of his execution: 'They are known to have met their death with the same courage with which they had faced up to these long months of imprisonment during which time they had always kept up their morale. This is a most tragic end which has filled me and all who knew him with the greatest sadness and bitterness.

'As you know during his time in the field Brian proved himself to be a most able and gallant officer and the work which he and his friends had begun was carried on by others and finally led to the successful invasion of the Continent with the minimum loss of lives, both to the Allied armies and the civilian population. I hope you will take pride and comfort in this.'

The response from Brian's father, Thomas, gives a heart-rending insight into the grief suffered by parents during war:

'The tragic circumstances of Brian's death, coming shortly before the cessation of hostilities, seems to make the burden more difficult to bear, especially as we had not given up hope of his safe return. However, such was not to be and like many others he had to make the supreme sacrifice.

'We much appreciate your noble references to his personality and his work and it is a satisfaction to think that he and his comrades helped to pave the way, in some small measure, for the final overthrow of the enemy. I also take this opportunity of expressing my appreciation of the very kind and sympathetic manner in which your colleague in Paris, Capt. Hazeldine, broke the news to me and the nice manner in which he dealt with my frequent enquiries for information.

'My daughter has given us an account of her recent conversation with F/O [Flight Officer Vera] Atkin and we hope that you can get supplementary information from the repatriated Danish Officer or any other person who had been in contact with Brian in Flossenbürg, Fresnes or the district in France in which he was operating, or capture.'

That repatriated Danish officer did not have any further information and when a photograph of Brian was circulated, Flight Officer Vera Atkins wrote to Capt. Hazeldine, on 31 May 1945, to explain why they were often of little use when tracing people who had suffered the hardship of prison.

'I find it extraordinary that photographs which one would imagine would be of great help in identifying people are really of so little use,' she wrote.

'It is no doubt due to the fact that the appearance of women is pretty considerably changed and the men also grow beards and lose weight to such an extent that they cannot be recognised by their former photographs. At this end, I find it easier to get some detail of the chap, ie a nickname, his home town, or any other fact that can be checked with existing records.'

There is nothing in Capt. Rafferty's military file to suggest that his parents ever learned any more about the last days of their 25-year-old son.

He is remembered, though, with memorials at Valençay in France, Brookwood Memorial in Surrey and at the museum of Flossenbürg camp. He was also posthumously awarded the Military Cross and the Croix de Guerre with a citation to the Free French Forces.

10

Passing the Baby

'AT GIBRALTAR [MARY] BOARDED A FELUCCA WITH A STRONG SMELL OF SARDINES AND AN UNUSUAL HEAD OF STEAM.'

SQUADRON LEADER BERYL E. ESCOTT

October 1944: Colonel Maurice Buckmaster, the head of F Section, received a letter to say that one of his agents, Mary Herbert, had 'gone to ground good and proper'. Nobody knew where she was, but she was said to be 'extremely well, in no need of money, and comfortable'. The letter-writer, from the section's administration office, went on to say that attempts were being made to get her address, before dropping the bombshell: 'I was also told that she produced a baby last November!'

Mary Katherine Herbert, courier for the resistance network Scientist, had indeed 'produced' a baby. A little girl Claudine (which was also her mother's fieldname) was in fact born in early December 1943 in a nursing home outside Bordeaux at a time when the Germans had infiltrated several circuits, arresting agents and many of their French contacts.

Becoming a new mother in an occupied country in wartime was difficult enough, but Mary Herbert also had to fabricate a new cover story – and find documents to prove it – that explained the presence of her baby daughter. And she had to find a place to stay. She made contact with friends in Poitiers and, believing it to be relatively safe, travelled north to stay in the flat of Lise de Baissac, a fellow SOE agent who had recently been called back to London.

Once installed in Lise's flat, she went to the black market, bought ration books and false identity papers for herself and her infant. She was now Madame Marie-Louise Vernier, a French widow (and new mother) from Alexandria in Egypt.

Then, the unthinkable happened. On 18 February 1944, the Gestapo swept through her apartment block at 19 bis rue Boncenne in the early hours of the morning, arresting several residents, including her. They came to the door while she was feeding her infant. Without giving it a second thought, they separated her from her baby and took her to Gestapo head-quarters in Poitiers. They assumed she was Lise de Baissac.

Lise was sister to Claude de Baissac, SOE agent and leader of Scientist circuit, who also happened to be the father of Mary's baby. Brother and sister had been recalled to London in 1943 after a number of breaches in their respective networks.

It turned out that a member of the network had given away the location of several arms dumps and other informa-tion that led to the early morning swoop. While Mary was taken away, her baby was put into the care of French Social Services – although she wasn't aware of that at the time.

In any case, the most pressing issue now was making the Gestapo believe her cover story. Like many SOE recruits, she was a gifted linguist. She spoke French, Italian, Spanish, German and Arabic, which she had learned while studying for a diploma at the University of Cairo before the war. That stood to her as she explained to her interrogators that her 'queer accent' in French was because she spoke English, French, Spanish, Italian and Arabic when she was in Egypt.

That 'was enough to upset anyone's pronunciation', she said.

They continued to question her before putting her into solitary confinement. There was no chair to sit on, only a stone slab that served as a blanket-less bed.

She stuck rigidly to her story and was so convincing that the Gestapo released her two months later in April 1944. As she had argued herself, how likely was it that a woman who had just given birth could be an active agent? After her release, she spent a frantic few days trying to track down her baby. She eventually found her, well-cared-for, at a convent orphanage.

After their reunion, she relied on the friends she had made through Lise de Baissac in Poitiers to help her find a safe place to live with her child. She also knew two elderly sisters who arranged for her to hide out on a farm in the countryside outside Poitiers.

When Mary Herbert had set out for France some 18 months before, she might have considered the risk of incarceration, but she could hardly have foreseen that she would be jailed just after giving birth. The SOE had contingency plans for myriad eventualities, but motherhood was not one of them. That seems clear from the organisation's reaction to news of Mary's baby, the only one born to the 39 female SOE agents in France. Security in F Section didn't want anything to do with it and, as one document said, it was 'passing the baby' on to leader Colonel Buckmaster to 'clear up'.

It was impossible to predict what might happen on the ground, or how those sent there would deal with it. Mary

Katherine Herbert had been among the first agents to be trained and sent to France. When she joined the SOE in March 1942, her CV already held a lifetime's worth of experiences.

Born in Ireland on 1 October 1903 to Ethel (née Rodger) and Brigadier General Edmund Herbert, Mary was very well educated and travelled widely. She studied at the University of Cairo and was a graduate of the Slade School of Fine Art (University College London). In her twenties and thirties, she acted as an escort to orphaned children who were emigrating to Australia. After that, she moved to Poland to work in passport control at the British Embassy in Warsaw. Then, she returned to London to take up a job as a civilian translator at the Air Ministry.

Her ease with languages – she later added Russian to an already-impressive list – meant she was a perfect fit for SOE work. She joined the WAAF in September 1941. Her request to join the SOE was accepted the following March. Squadron leader Beryl E. Escott offered this description: 'At thirty-nine, she was quite tall (5ft 7in, 1.7m), slim, with short fair hair, pale face and, as far as SOE was concerned, [she had] the gift of being inconspicuous. She was also highly intelligent, patriotic and very religious.'

While her trainers thought she showed promise, they were concerned that she was 'too fragile for resistance work'. She proved to be the opposite.

In October 1942, Mary Herbert and four others – Marie-Thérèse le Chêne, Odette Sansom, George Starr and Marcus

Bloom – were transported by submarine to Gibraltar. From there, they transferred to a traditional sailing boat, which followed a course along the western coast of Spain en route to southern France.

Escott described the journey rather poetically: 'At Gibraltar they boarded a felucca [a small Mediterranean boat] with a strong smell of sardines and an unusual head of steam. After several days they arrived at a cove near Cassis, on a moonless night with only the phosphorescent spray breaking on the rocks and high cliffs. The felucca hove to with silent engines, leaving them to be propelled to the shore by cockleshell boats with muffled oars, landing on Halloween, 31 October 1942.'

When they arrived they were taken to Cannes. 'The town,' Liane Jones observed in A Quiet Courage, 'had kept its holiday character despite the war; in fact, war had filled its streets, cafes and clubs with moneyed refugees from the occupied north. Beauty salons and fashion shops and expensive pâtisseries continued to ply their trade, albeit with some rather strange raw materials in their products.'

Those monied refugees weren't aware of it yet, but the freedoms in the so-called zone libre were about to come to a sudden end. While the Vichy government was still in place, all of France was now under German military administration. It meant life would be much harder for agents operating in the field, although there was an upside for the Resistance too.

Under the new administration, a law had passed a month earlier that would help to significantly boost the numbers of those willing to fight a guerrilla war against the occupiers. On 4 September, the Germans introduced a measure requiring all French men, aged 18 to 65, and single French women, aged 21 to 35, to make themselves known so that they could bolster the workforce in Germany if deemed necessary.

That was deemed necessary a few months later, in February 1943, when hundreds of thousands of French workers were deported to Germany under a work programme known as the STO (*Service du travail obligatoire*). Many tens of thousands dodged the compulsory measure by escaping from occupied France or going into hiding, where they joined the *Maquis*.

Meanwhile, back in Cannes, the five SOE operatives were guided into the back of a beauty salon where they were intro-duced to the leader of the Cannes network, Peter Churchill. He had been parachuted into France that August to set up a resistance network. His first impression of Mary Herbert was that she was frail and very obviously English, he said later.

He was impressed by Marie-Thérèse le Chêne, though. She was a grey-haired woman (she was in her fifties), full of common sense and good humour, he said. He was particularly taken by Odette Sansom, who would become his courier – and, much later, his wife. Mary Herbert was not the only woman from this group to start a relationship that was against SOE regulations.

The members of F Section rested in the back-room of the beauty salon before setting off on their respective missions. Mary was bound for Bordeaux. She made it just across the demarcation line before Germans mobilised their tanks and, in their thousands, moved in the opposite direction to occupy the free zone.

Mary Herbert met Claude de Baissac in December 1942. She was using the codename Claudine, but SOE agents had a number of aliases: one for their false identity papers, another – often the name of an occupation – for use within the network, and a third, or even fourth, that was generally just a first name. Mary Herbert was known as 'jeweller' while the name Marie Louise Marielle appeared on her documents. She changed that surname to Vernier after her child was born.

We can't say what she thought of Claude de Baissac, or Jacques, or David, when she first met him, but he had a reputation as being a difficult taskmaster.

Liane Jones, who interviewed his sister Lise after the war, described him as a man who was not easy to work with: 'He was proud and determined; his own capacity for hard work and leadership made him demanding on others. Maurice Buckmaster called him "the most difficult of all my officers without any exception". But he was an irresistible force.' He had successfully recruited large numbers to Scientist, and he kept London supplied with vital information about German naval movements.

Scientist also had a plan to sabotage the docks in Bordeaux, but that was scuppered by Operation Frankton, a British operation which, unknown to de Baissac, planned a commando raid on German ships in the port. Only two of the ten men involved in the operation, including its Dublin-born leader Herbert 'Blondie' Hasler, survived.

Whatever about the frustration of not being kept in the intelligence loop, the raid in early December meant the Germans were now on high alert. Working in that atmosphere, Mary Herbert began her job as a courier, cycling hundreds of kilometres in a week to deliver messages, money and sometimes even wireless sets.

Part of her work included scouting for safe houses and finding hidden locations suitable for night-time drops of supplies and arms. She often attended those moonlit parachute drops, too. She travelled widely around the region and sometimes accompanied de Baissac to Paris. Having a woman with him was good cover, though the pair were also a couple by then.

Mary became close to Claude's sister, Lise, too, who worked as a courier near Poitiers. She was seen as a capable and well-organised operator, not least by her brother, which was praise indeed. Mary often visited her. They became friends and comrades, even if there were certain subjects they did not raise for the sake of security.

In the field, Mary was considered courageous and diplomatic. And she had the capacity to remain cool and unperturbed when necessary. On one occasion, while carrying a wireless set in a suitcase, a German naval officer picked it up and carried it to the train, entirely oblivious of what was within.

Her personnel file notes that she was a 'P2' agent, the highest of three rankings in the Resistance. New agents were designated PO. As they gained experience and responsibilities, they were elevated to category P1 followed by P2, although many did not make it that far.

In the spring of 1943, Mary Herbert realised she was pregnant and told de Baissac. They discussed marriage, but agreed that it would pose too many bureaucratic challenges in wartime France. In any case, a short time later, de Baissac and his sister were recalled to London as several networks were understood to be in danger.

Mary was left on her own but she continued to work, relying on trains when she was too heavily pregnant to cycle. The physical challenges, though, must have been the least of it. The father of her baby was in London. And both of them were only too aware that they had breached SOE rules, although later Lise told an interviewer that Mary, then aged 39, had wanted a baby.

Claude de Baissac did not return to the field. Instead, Roger Landes was appointed leader at a time when the network was becoming increasingly insecure. Mary confided in him about her pregnancy. Though shocked, he was supportive and did not tell London. This arrangement continued until the network was blown, leading to Mary's arrest, as well as the murder of some 300 resistance members.

After her release in April 1944, Mary Herbert went to ground, living quietly in the countryside until France was liberated.

In September 1944, Claude and Lise de Baissac returned to France and went in search of Mary. They borrowed a car and, on information from a friend, traced her to her rural hideaway where Claude saw his daughter for the first time. The couple married, in London, on 11 November 1944, though they both returned to France shortly afterwards.

The SOE released Mary Herbert from duty. She was 'outposted' with effect from 31 December 1944. Her boss Colonel Buckmaster wrote: 'It is proposed not to raise the matter officially with the French, at any rate at the moment but to leave her where she is in view of the impossibility of moving the child. She appears to be perfectly happy in France and ardently to desire to stay there. As far as we are concerned, we have no objection.'

After the war, France awarded Mary Herbert the Croix de Guerre, but there was no recommendation for a British honour. F Section's evaluation of their officer consisted of a single line: 'Charming, but solely of interest to Claude De Baissac.'

Mary and Claude de Baissac did not remain a couple. There was a 'friendly separation', according to Lise, and later a formal divorce. Mary moved back to the UK and supported herself by giving French lessons. In 1950, her mother died, leaving her estate to Mary and her sister, Elinora. The details made the *Gloucester Citizen* because her mother also left her maid £2,000, her car, her spaniel Tim, and her half-hoop diamond ring.

The news item stands out because it is the only obvious mention of Mary de Baissac after the war. That wasn't at all unusual. Many of the women of SOE F Section quietly retreated to civilian life after they had done their duty.

11

Two Pairs of Silk Pyjamas

'HE HAD NO INTENTION OF LETTING IRELAND'S NEUTRALITY
STAND BETWEEN HIM AND THE THRILLS OF BATTLE.'
SGT WILLIAM PICKERING ON JOHN KEANY

Italy, 4 February 1945: Capt. John Keany was second in line as six special agents prepared to parachute 100 miles behind enemy lines in occupied northern Italy. They watched as the aircraft light went from red to green. Then they jumped, at one-second intervals, from the door near the tail of the DC3 Dakota: Hope, Keany, Giovanni, Millard and Salvadori. Pickering was last, giving him time to reflect on his stupidity for finding himself in such a situation, as he would later put it.

All six were wearing Irvine Statachutes that, they had been assured, would open automatically. Pickering wondered about that as he stepped out into space and felt the icy blast of the cold night air on his exposed face. 'Before I had time to think further my parachute had opened and I felt the welcoming tug of the harness on my shoulders. That slight pain produced a surge of relief as I realised I was not about to become a "Roman Candle",' he wrote later.

A Roman candle was the slang phrase used to describe a parachute that did not open, leaving its wearer to fall to earth like a spent firework.

But luck was with the crew – at least for now. All six sailed through the air on a crisp moonlit morning and they landed without incident. They were Maj. Adrian Hope and his wireless operator, Corporal 'Busty' Millard; wireless operator Sgt William Pickering and a man referred to only as Giovanni; and the famous anti-fascist historian Lieutenant-Colonel Max Salvadori and his aide, Capt. John Keany of the Royal Irish Fusiliers.

All of them had turned down the suicide tablets offered in the event of capture, but they were 'armed to the teeth', as Pickering wrote. The agents had a Marlin sub-machine gun, a .45 Colt automatic pistol, a Commando fighting knife and a comb with a hidden saw inside it.

The six men had been parachuted into north-west Italy on a British special forces mission to help the Italian Resistance. Codenamed 'Operation Chariton', they were ordered to make contact with the National Committee of Liberation and help them in their fight against the Germans, who had occupied northern Italy since 1943.

Capt. Keany spoke Italian, a language he mastered in his posting as personal assistant to the governor in Eritrea in East Africa. He joined the Royal Irish Fusiliers at the start of the war and spent three years in Africa, from August 1941 to May 1944. In the years just before the war, he spent time in Berlin and Paris so he spoke French and German too. He had graduated with an honours degree in both languages from Exeter University in 1939.

As his colleagues observed, John Keany was also a powerfully built man, ready for action. 'He had no intention of letting Ireland's neutrality stand between him and the thrills of battle,' Pickering said of him later.

The Irishman's attitude to war might not, in reality, have been quite so cavalier. His father was shot dead in Cork, in February 1921, during the Irish War of Independence. Michael Keany, or Keeney as it was sometimes spelled, was a Royal Irish Constabulary District Inspector in Clonakilty in West Cork. A few months before his death, he had been promoted and was transferred to Tuckey Street in Cork city.

On 12 February, Michael Keany returned to his former home in the West Cork town to make arrangements to move his family to the city. As he was leaving a hotel with his eldest son Edward (19) late on a Saturday evening, he was shot dead. Edward was also shot and seriously wounded, but he later recovered.

John, born on 14 April 1915, had not yet turned six. Sometime after her husband was murdered, Margaret Mulcahy and her family moved away from Cork and, later, Ireland. Keany went to public school in London from 1925 to 1929.

The party landed in thick snow near Piedmont in February 1945 where anti-fascist resistance fighters immediately led them to the cover of a nearby wood. German troops were already cresting the top of a hill half a mile away, yet the Italians still had time to collect the cylindrical tubes dropped with the men. They contained much-needed supplies, guns and ammunition.

Sgt Pickering was impressed by the Italians' speed, but a little taken aback by their clothes. 'They looked like a chorus of brigands from some *Gilbert and Sullivan* opera,' he recalled. But their appearance was deceptive. The Bandits of

Cisterna, as they called themselves, were disciplined, effective and feared by ordinary German soldiers.

Pickering and Keany paired off and were spirited away into hiding at a farm outside the village of Monesiglio, just 400 metres away from occupying German troops. On the first night, Sgt Pickering used his quartz crystal transmitter to send an encrypted message to London saying that the party had landed safely. At the SOE HQ in Baker Street it was received, interpreted and a return message sent to the Chariton team. Operators in the field made sure transmission lasted less than an hour so that the Germans' radio-direction finding equipment could not locate their hideout.

As soon as the men started to transmit, however, it was picked up by the Germans who knew, by the wavelength, that coded messages were being sent to and from England. 'Keany and I knew we were immediately at the top of the wanted list for the Germans in Monesiglio,' Pickering wrote.

Over the next three weeks, the two men settled into a routine of sorts: transmitting at night and hiding during the day. Their hosts, Tal and Luigia Biestro, were taking an immense risk in sheltering and feeding them. Other neighbours had been shot dead or had their houses burned down for doing the same. Despite the ever-present danger, the Biestros welcomed them into their house at night and hid them under four feet of dry leaves in a stone outhouse during the day.

Partisans came and went from the hideout, delivering messages and receiving them. On one occasion, they brought the men's parachutes, which had been retrieved from the landing site. Normal practice was to bury them on landing, but there hadn't been time.

It was perhaps a sign of just how secure Capt. Keany and Sgt Pickering felt in their new surroundings that they took the unusual step of visiting a seamstress, under cover of night, to ask her to fashion items of clothing out of their silk parachutes. The woman was a known sympathiser – and trustworthy. She said she would be able to make a dressing gown and two pairs of pyjamas. '"We'll see you in a few weeks when the war is over," said the ever-confident Keany,' his colleague Sgt Pickering recalls.

There were other trips to the nearby town of Monesiglio, south-east of Turin, to drop off radio batteries at an electrical shop to be charged. The fact that they passed off without incident was a mixed blessing, Pickering noted, because it 'emboldened Keany to the point that he ordered me to accompany him one night for a drinking session... even by Keany's laid-back standards, this seemed a little reckless.'

There was something to celebrate too. Intelligence from the Resistance's network of spies confirmed that the Germans thought the 'new British broadcasting team' was operating miles away, rather than within a mere 400 metres. The search party was far away, which prompted the two men to let down their guard and chance an evening out. They made their way discreetly through farmyards and back streets to a bar situated right in the centre of a German garrison.

Sgt Pickering stayed sober enough to refrain from singing 'Rule Brittania' and managed to talk Keany out of singing 'Danny Boy'. After a night of mirth, they set out for their hut, zig-zagging and giggling as they went, looking like 'a pair of music hall drunks', to use Pickering's description. It was reckless and high-risk, but they got away with it. The next day, however, they had one of several close brushes with German troops.

The Germans were closing in on resistance groups, which made it ever harder to find a safe location for night-time transmission. They could use the farmhouse attic only so many times before their luck ran out, so the two men chose a small hill nearby as a potential site. On their way there, Keany ducked behind some bushes to answer a call of nature. Pickering joined him and as they were mid-flow, a group of about a dozen Germans passed within three metres of them.

'Keany and I stood statue-still with our fully-loaded "weapons" held tightly in our hands to stem the flow… our ploy worked and the Germans never spotted us. Perhaps I could add a chapter to the SOE manual entitled, "What to do if the enemy approaches while you are urinating".'

There were other close shaves too. On occasion, they jumped into a ditch as a patrol of the Mussolini-supporting *Brigate Nere* (Black Brigades) passed by. Pickering said his face was just inches away from the men's muddy boots. Keeping absolutely still was the best camouflage, they were told in training, and it was a tactic that paid off now.

There was another terrifying close call as Keany and Pickering went in search of a safe transmission place. It was increasingly difficult to use the area around Monesiglio as the Germans had further increased their efforts to round up resistance groups. Nevertheless, the partisans guided the ever-courageous pair to a farmyard to make a transmission. Pickering, as he always did, jammed a stone into a loop at the end of a long piece of copper wire and threw the other end high over a tree to maximise signal strength. About 15 minutes into the transmission, a partisan came running towards them, frantically warning that a German vehicle was approaching.

The two men quickly tried to pack up their wireless, but the aerial was caught on one of the branches. The more Pickering pulled, the more it jammed. Everyone, bar Keany, had already run for cover. He stayed behind to cover his colleague. And also to try to remove a tell-tale wire that would mean almost certain death for the farmer and his family.

Just as the German lorry came into earshot, Pickering settled his nerves to try one last time. The wire came loose and the two men ran to a nearby orchard for cover – and to safety.

Before the mad scramble to escape, they had time to receive a message from headquarters in Bari in southern Italy. Information and instructions about an up-coming mission were released on a need-to-know basis. As they stopped for a bite to eat, Keany deciphered the message.

They were on their way to Milan.

They had come to know their hosts very well and said a warm goodbye before setting off on a hazardous journey. A network of resistance partisans guided them across tough terrain and the raging River Tanora to the Castle of Cisterna, a stronghold on a 2,000-foot hill which housed the famous bandits of the same name. There, they met their comrades Maj. Adrian Hope and Busty Millard again, but parted ways after a few days. Disguised as peasants, they set off for Villanova d'Asti on a donkey and cart with their radio and weapons buried under a load of root vegetables.

'Keany,' Pickering wrote later, 'was laughing as usual as we set off at dusk. "To be sure and aren't I feeling at home now," he said with an exaggerated bog Irish accent. "These vehicles are all the rage in County Cork."'

They set off at dusk, on their way to a safe house in Brusasco, about 40km to the north. As they made their way through the town, a train passed under a bridge and was blown up about 200m down the track. A blinding flash lit up the night sky and they worried the explosion would bring reinforcements into the area. Just as they were starting to feel safe, a voice shouted at them in the dark, ordering them to stop and put up their hands.

To their utter relief, six members of the communist Garibaldi Brigade came out of the hedges. They too were fighting Hitler and the Italian fascists, but things got a bit heated when the group discovered a Marlin submachine gun under the turnips. They wanted to keep it and offered a World War I pistol in exchange. Capt. Keany's fluent Italian – and steely nerve – got them out of a potentially tricky situation. He acknowledged their need of weapons and took out a notebook to make an elaborate list of all the patrol needed. Then he promised them a plane would arrive in the coming days; it would signal as it dropped the supplies and they were to flash agreed Morse letters with a torch.

Peace was restored and when they were back on the road, a baffled but impressed Pickering asked Keany: 'How on earth are you going to persuade HQ to send all those weapons and supplies to the Reds?'

Capt. Keany, with a disarming smile, tore the pages of notes out of his pocket book, scrunched them into a tidy ball and tossed them over the hedge.

An hour later, they arrived at an isolated farmhouse and used a series of prearranged flash-lit signals to alert the occupants of their arrival. When a set of agreed signals were sent back, they went to the farmhouse; there they ate and slept in an outbuilding with two other comrades. At daybreak, they all set off again to join a division of the Justice and Liberty resistance forces.

They felt a little more at ease when they joined the 120-men division. There was greater safety in numbers, even if it also meant they could only move at night. And progress was slow. Too slow for Keany who was anxious to keep going. Resistance leader Renato was against it and advised caution. Keany retorted: 'I'd sooner be shot at going forward rather than standing still or retreating.'

They turned out to be prophetic words. The following day, 8 March 1945, Keany and Pickering and a number of partisans were ambushed as they hid on a large hill near Viale, just north of Villanova. Pickering had seen a large number of Germans enter a farmhouse nearby. That wasn't unusual as regular searches were taking place in the area. A little later, he saw even more Germans going into the house, but nobody was coming out. He mentioned the fact to Keany, who told him not to be silly as the Germans couldn't creep up a hill unseen or unheard.

'To the best of my recollection, those were Keany's last words,' Pickering wrote later.

Somehow sensing danger, he moved a few steps away from Keany and then the Germans opened fire.

This is his official report of what happened:

'At 0930 we saw 70 enemy troops approach farm house quarter mile away after which 16 of them headed towards us. We believed ourselves to be 90 strong and therefore waited for them to approach. It was not until they opened fire on us that we discovered most of partisans had left leaving Keany, Renato [resistance] leader..., his squad leaders and myself, in all 12 men. We had no cover so ran for next hill 200 yds away, during which time enemy were firing and killed 4 of our party including Keany.'

The surviving men beat a quick retreat. Sgt Bill Pickering was in shock: 'An uncontrollable shaking swept over my whole body. For 45 minutes I had been a man of action, risking life and limb for his country. Now I was a frightened young lad a long way from home.'

And he had lost his closest comrade: '*Poverino* (poor fellow) was repeated over and over by the stunned partisans, who had come to believe Keany's faith in his own immortality. Some men actually broke down and wept at the loss of the laughing Irishman we had all come to love.'

Three days later, they returned to retrieve the body. Dr Gino Predazzi, a doctor and surgeon, examined it and recorded five bullet wounds to Capt. Keany's face, neck, arm and chest. 'These wounds, in my opinion and according to my knowledge, caused immediate death,' his report of 11 March 1945 noted.

Keany's personal documents and money had been taken, but later an envelope containing cipher pads and five quartzes from the radio set belonging to his mission was found buried near his body. Somehow, he had found time to hide them before the ambush.

When news of his death filtered back to the farmhouse where Keany and Pickering had spent their first three weeks, Tal and Luigia Biestro were deeply affected. A few days later, on 25 March, Luigia wrote a poignant letter of sympathy to

Keany's mother, offering a different view of the devil-may-care man of action described by his comrades.

It began:

Dear Mrs. Keany,

I feel impelled by a feeling of motherly love to introduce myself to you in this letter.

At the moment I am unknown to you, but I was very well known to your dear son, and I offer you my deepest sympathy.

I would like this letter to bring a small measure of consolation to you in your grief. Your son lived in my house from the 5th to the 25th of February, and during this period I was fortunate enough to come close to him and to get to know his gentle goodness and his profoundly religious outlook. On the 10th he got up early and went to Mass and Communion; I know that this will be a comfort to you and that it will also help you to know that the rectitude of his actions was an example to all who came near him.

She also told Mrs Keany that her son had spoken so willingly about his family whom, she wrote, 'he loved so dearly'. Her own faith – Roman Catholic, like the Keanys – was evident in the rest of the letter as she said she believed that John Keany had received his just reward and that he was looking down on them.

The postscript added another layer of poignancy: 'As soon as things settle down we will go and visit his grave and give you precise information. With deepest sympathy.'

The Italian resistance division also provided a report of the incident to the British war office. Paolo Braccini of the Justice and Liberty Division added another unsettling operational detail. Four of their seven weapons had jammed in the encounter. As Braccini wrote: 'Unfortunately out of the 7 individual automatics which we had left to repulse the enemy attack, four jammed; this made our barrage insufficient and made it necessary for us to carry out an extremely difficult retreat.'

Following Keany's death, Pickering joined up with Maj. Hope's mission. He carried out duties as a radio operator and also fought alongside the Italian partisans who called him 'English Billy', or *il biondino* ('the Blond One') – until the Allies entered Milan on 29 April 1945.

Of the six men who parachuted into northern Italy some 12 weeks before, two were dead. Capt. Keany had been killed in action while Maj. Hope died in a freak accident. He was shot during an impromptu party to celebrate a successful weapons drop. An Italian partisan was approaching the major to shake his hand when his gun slipped and accidentally went off, killing him. At his funeral, near the Castle of Cisterna stronghold, Italian partisans gathered from miles around to pay their last respects and they later named one of their divisions after him.

Meanwhile, Capt. John Keany was buried at Cinaglio cemetery, in Piedmont. Maj. A.N. Maughan-Brown enclosed a photo of it when he wrote to his brother in Berkshire in England to tell him of his courage and his contribution. 'It is largely due to the efforts of your brother and many others like him who voluntarily went into enemy occupied territory to organise the partizan forces that these successes were achieved so quickly and the defeat of the enemy ensured,' he wrote.

Capt. John Keany was awarded a medal by the Italian partisans in July 1945 and there is a memorial to him in the War Cemetery in Milan.

The inventory of personal belongings left behind includes Capt. Keany's army-issue jackets, trousers, pyjamas, Bush Jacket and handkerchiefs. It did not include the promised pairs of silk pyjamas and dressing gown. After the war, though, Sgt Pickering made a return trip to the seamstress in Monesiglio to collect them. In his memoir, his former comrade pays tribute to Capt. Keany's courage, his sense of humour and their joint effort in helping Italy.

Capt. John Keany himself, however, had the final word. Several newspapers, including the *Belfast Telegraph*, noted in late June 1946 that Capt. John Keany, Royal Irish Fusiliers of Sundial Avenue, Norwood London, who died on war service left £20 in his will to the Secretary For War 'as a slight consideration for the benefits I have derived from joyriding in Government transport'.

LEADING THE WAY

12

From the Ritz to a Prison Cell

'FOR NEARLY THREE YEARS, HARDLY A DAY PASSED WITH-
OUT HER INVOLVEMENT IN ONE OR ANOTHER ILLEGAL
ACTIVITY IN THE REGION.'
CHRISTOPHER MASSY-BERESFORD

Denmark, 13 May 1944: When Monica de Wichfeld was condemned to death for helping the Danish Resistance, she simply
took out her enamelled Tiffany compact and powdered her
nose. All the newspapers made much of that detail. It was
interpreted as an act of defiance – which it was – but there
was another, perhaps more pressing, reason for her gesture.
Its mirror allowed her to see her younger son, Viggo, sitting
directly behind her at Dagmar House, the Gestapo headquarters in Copenhagen, and give him a reassuring smile.

Once she had done so, she looked towards the three judges
dressed in SS uniform and asked: 'Anything else, gentlemen?'

The counsel for the prosecution told her she had the right
to appeal for clemency. She asked if the three much younger
male resisters, who had also just been sentenced to death, had
the same right. When told they did not, she responded: 'Then
it is of no interest.'

She reached back to hold her son's hand, and waited
for his sentence. He too had been held in jail, but was to be

released on the grounds of his youth and the minor nature of the charges laid against him.

We can step inside the makeshift courtroom thanks to Christopher Massy-Beresford, Monica's surviving nephew and custodian of some family essays and memorabilia that animate the life of an extraordinary woman who worked with, and later led, one of the few resistance networks in her adopted country.

She became ever more deeply involved, from funding illegal propaganda newspapers to allowing her estate on the southern Danish island of Lolland to be used for parachute drops of supplies. She also got away with harbouring Allied airmen and sheltering refugees and Jews, without even her husband knowing, for nearly three years.

In early 1944, however, she was betrayed by a captured SOE agent who disclosed the names of over 40 members of the Resistance, including hers, allegedly under torture.

When two Gestapo officers stormed into her bedroom to arrest her on 13 January 1944, she ordered them out while she dressed. When she emerged, immaculately turned out, she gave one of the officers her suitcase, which he carried down the stairs. She maintained the same composure during the four months she was held in a small, damp cell in Vestre prison in the centre of Copenhagen. And she gave nothing away under questioning.

Under the heading 'Refused to tell tales', a *Times* correspondent wrote: 'An ardent smoker, [Monica] was deprived of her cigarettes when in prison, but a bargain was proposed – she would be permitted to smoke if she would give certain information. Neither then, nor in the hours of gruelling interrogation at her trial, did she allow the smallest scrap of information to escape her.'

'Show trial' is a better description of the proceedings because the hearing was little more than a deliberate display of Nazi force calculated to quell resistance activity.

The press had been invited, so news of the death sentences handed down to Monica and the three Danish members of the Resistance was widely reported – and condemned. The Danish population was outraged that a woman had been sentenced to death, the first woman to be given such a sentence in several decades.

A few days later, on 20 May, Monica's fellow resistance comrades – liaison officer with the British SOE Georg Brock-hoff Quistgaard, radio operator Arne Lützen-Hansen and ammunition supplier Carl Jørgen Larsen – were executed. Outside the prison's walls, there was increasing pressure to grant Monica de Wichfeld a reprieve, but the woman herself was resigned to her fate.

'I have learned that there is no such thing as black or white, only grey,' she wrote in a letter to her friend Claire Schlichting as she awaited news of her expected execution. 'No one is evil through and through... It is for this reason that I am not afraid to face my God; he knows my sins – and if he has a sense of humour, which I am sure he has, he will just smile at me and let me pass. Say therefore to my children that they must not be unhappy, for I am not.'

She went on to explain that it was not that she didn't want to see her family in prison, but she couldn't bear to see them suffer: 'Viggo brought me to the verge of tears when he asked to say goodbye to me the other day. Ivan and the girl [her daughter Varinka] are stronger, but my husband and Viggo are weaker. And I *must* remain strong for other people's sake.

I have had such luck. – All those I love are free, but there are so many others whose loved ones are either here or dead, or about to be executed, and it is of *them* that I must think and try to help.'

The *Belfast Telegraph*, which had noted how she 'took out her powder and lipstick and coolly attended to her appearance' after being sentenced, also referred to her courage and fortitude, attributing it to 'the unquenchable spirit of her Ulster blood'. That strength of character was evident from a very early age.

——— ———

Monica Emily Massy-Beresford came into the world on 12 July 1894 in the family home in Eaton Square, London. She was the first child born to George Massy-Beresford, a landowner with estates in Northern Ireland and Scotland, and Alice, daughter of John Mulholland (the 1st Baron Dunleath of Ballywalter), one of Ireland's wealthiest early industrialists.

Tristram Hugh followed in 1896, John Clarina in 1897 and, eight years later, Desmond George. All four children grew up at St Hubert's, the family estate on the shores of Lough Erne in Co. Fermanagh, and they spent family holidays in Bundoran, Co. Donegal. Monica had wonderful memories of shrimping and fishing for mackerel by moonlight during those carefree summer trips.

'She was a spirited and fearless child with a penchant for mischief and an unpretentious ease that ensured she was universally loved,' Christopher Massy-Beresford writes in a moving summary of his aunt's life, which brings together the surviving documents that tell her story.

Among them are some childhood memories of Christopher's father, Tristram, who had become Brigadier Tim Massy-Beresford in 1941. Tim wrote of the magic and remote paradise at St Hubert's where the large family home 'with its deep windowsills, faded chintz, and a profusion of flowers, food and servants' was surrounded by gardens with lawns that swept down to Lough Erne. The family had to cross the lake to get anywhere – from the grocer to the dentist.

In this isolated fiefdom, Monica, the oldest child and only girl, was the 'undisputed leader', he wrote. 'She had all the ideas and saw to it that we carried them out. More often than not, these were things strictly forbidden, often dangerous, like bathing on some remote rocky shore... or jumping from a particularly high trampoline in the barn... She knew no fear and egged her brothers on. From an early age she had a clear-cut personality and a will she could impose not only on her brothers but on other children who happened to be around or came to visit.'

The boys were sent to boarding school and Monica was home-tutored by a governess, Miss Jell, who encouraged her young charge to think independently. At 16, Monica and a travelling companion, Sheila Brooke, travelled to Tours in France, where she learned French, followed by a year (1909/1910) in Dresden to learn German.

As Christopher recounts: 'Her year in one of Europe's most sophisticated cities turned into a social whirl of visiting the opera, going to parties and dances, and learning how to deal with the opposite sex. No longer a gauche teenager, Monica soon developed a knack of wrong-footing young Germans she didn't want to dance with.'

When she was 21, she moved to London. It was 1915, and like everyone else, she was committed to doing her bit to help the war effort. She worked in a soldiers' canteen in the city's East End, although she still moved in elite social circles. Later that year, she was introduced to Jørgen Wichfeld, a Danish diplomat – at his own engagement party. He was so taken with Monica that he broke off his engagement and the couple were married the following year, on 15 June 1916. They spent the rest of the war in London but shortly before it ended, Monica received devastating news. Her brother Jack (John Clarina), to whom she was closest, had been killed in action on the Somme in August 1918.

Christopher continues: 'Jack's death had a profound influence on Monica, such that she became agnostic and – despite her happy memories of the year she had spent in Dresden – she developed a deep and abiding dislike of Germans. Monica later took Danish nationality, but she added the "de" into her married name because she wanted to discourage her English friends from thinking she had married a German.'

After the war the Wichfelds stayed in London, where their first son, Ivan, was born in 1919 before moving to the family's large estate of Engestofte on Lolland in 1920. Their daughter, Varinka (or Inkie as she was always known) was born there in 1922. Their second son, Viggo, followed in December 1923. Monica helped to manage the estate and tried to tackle its considerable financial problems.

These deteriorated throughout the 1920s and the Wall Street crash of 1929 ended any hope of resolving them. The family was obliged to rent out Engestofte and move to Italy to live with Monica's mother, Alice, in the spacious villa in

Rapallo on the Italian Riviera. She had retired there after her husband's death.

Monica soon went about restoring the family fortunes, in part because she wanted her sons to be educated in Britain, recalls Christopher Massy-Beresford. Ever resourceful, she soon made a name for herself – and much-needed money – selling cheap costume jewellery, with a big markup, and beauty products. They became the *dernier cri*, or all the rage, as one of her friends, the Paris decorator and hostess Elsie de Wolfe, declared.

'Throughout the 1930s, she worked in Paris, commuted every fortnight to Rapallo for long weekends with her family, all the while enjoying a sort of pan-European lifestyle that included socialising with numerous rich and famous or well-connected people (to whom she discreetly managed to sell her products to pay the school fees!),' Christopher says.

As she later put it herself in her final letter to her friend Claire: 'I have driven in a Rolls to dinner at the Ritz with all my jewels one night, and I have pawned them the next day to buy medicine for my ailing husband.'

Yet, despite her difficulties, she was still mentioned in London's social columns in the company of the King and Queen of Denmark. In December 1933, 'The Letters of Eve' diarist in *Tatler* magazine wrote: 'Among the visitors we were specially glad to welcome over here were the King and Queen of Denmark... Hats off to them for braving the terrors of the North Sea at this time of year, to perform the graceful gesture of doing their shopping in London.

'They must have just missed Madame de Wichfeld, who left us after a very flying visit and whom we so seldom see now that she lives mostly in Paris or Rapallo. She was very popular here as Monica Massey-Beresford [sic], and married Mr. de Wichfeld when he was attached to the Danish Legation in London. Really lovely hands and a most attractive speaking voice are, perhaps, the most striking points of her engaging personality, and these are charms not too easy to find, especially allied to typical Irish looks. (This is intended as a compliment, not as another insult to Ireland.)'

Monica's comments to her mother, however, were not well-intended when she found herself seated beside Mrs Wallis Simpson at dinner, the woman who caused a constitutional crisis in Britain when King Edward VIII abdicated to marry her.

'Dearest Mother,' she wrote on 2 March 1937, from the Carlton Hotel in Cannes:

'I sat beside her at dinner and she came and talked with me afterwards... she was called to the telephone to talk to the "King," as she calls him (while the proper King and Queen are referred to as "the Yorks")... I could fill several letters with the things that were said... Her mailbag has now dropped to 500 letters a day but they still have to have an extra postman... Some letters are threatening, others rude, and others again from admirers or from the clergy (shame on them!)... who wish to conduct the [marriage] ceremony.'

She went on to say that she found Mrs Simpson 'common and vulgar beyond words'. Monica de Wichfeld was not one to temper her views. That applied to politics too. After a visit to Berlin in the 1930s where her son was staying with an anti-Nazi family – she made sure of that – to learn German, she wrote to her brother Tim to say he was getting on well. 'We adored seeing him, but I hated the atmosphere in Berlin, charged with hysteria. It can't be very long now before the madman moves on to the next step.'

After the war was declared, the family stayed on in Italy, but Monica did not hide her dislike of fascism. And, it seems, she started to file reports to British intelligence as early as 1940.

Her brother Tim, by then a brigadier in the army, wrote: '...I cannot possibly tell you how it all came about, but I know that in 1940 our intelligence became aware that Monica was making useful observations on the attitude of certain types of Italians to the war, and they commissioned her to send (via America) regular reports. I seem to remember that some of them made their way to the BBC as background material for their broadcasts to Italy. You can tell from this that my sister had no intention of remaining idle through the war. This activity of hers, small as it was, may well, for all we know, have been a step which led to the job she did when she returned to Denmark...'

When the war finally forced the family to leave Italy in 1941, they returned to an occupied Denmark where life went on almost as before. The king was still on the throne, the government was in situ and the Danish police helped the Nazi occupying force deal quickly and harshly with any suspected resistance activity.

'Monica found the atmosphere deeply shocking,' according to her biographer, Christine Sutherland. 'She wanted to be in what she called "the real world" – fighting, not meekly consuming the fruits of collaboration.' Her resolve was strengthened when America entered the war in December

1941. She was worried about her brother Tim, too, who had been posted to Singapore and was soon taken prisoner there by the Japanese.

Monica secretly listened to the BBC, hoping for news. The daily reports of air raids, rationing and growing resistance to the occupier in other countries sharpened her resolve to get involved. At first, she found it difficult to make contact with the underground movement, but then found out that a tenant on her estate, the Danish writer and communist Hilmar Wulff, was producing the resistance newspaper Free Denmark (*Frit Danmark*), which was in dire need of money.

Using her contacts and business acumen, Monica began to raise funds for the magazine in the winter of 1942. Everyday politics were put to one side: the communist and the 'lady of the manor' began to work together. 'From the very first [Monica] placed the fight for Denmark's freedom above politics,' Wulff said later, adding, '... she combined a freedom of spirit so broad and so extensive that it transcended all social considerations.'

Meanwhile, Monica discreetly made contact with other resistance members. She agreed to help Erik Kiersgaard, an insurance salesman who was setting up a sabotage unit at the neighbouring island of Falster, by storing arms and explosives. She was introduced to other leading members of the Resistance through Count Carl 'Bobby' Moltke and agreed to allow her estate to be used for arms drops. Her own home was designated a safe house for parachutists and she sheltered fugitives from the Danish police and the Nazi occupiers.

'Bobby' introduced her to Flemming Muus, a Danish businessman who had joined the SOE in Britain. He was parachuted into Denmark in March 1943. By then, the spark of resistance had grown closer to the flame evoked by General Charles de Gaulle in 1940.

On the island of Lolland that was, in no small way, due to Monica de Wichfeld, who continued to set up new groups. She enlisted the help of the local minister, Pastor Marcusson, who allowed his secluded vicarage to be used for sabotage training. She recruited a sympathetic hospital director and one of the local vets whose van was used to transport weapons and explosives, as well as some 30 others whom she thought might be able to help in various ways.

By 1943, as the Resistance gained pace, parachute drops were taking place on Jørgen Wichfeld's Lolland estate without his knowledge. Monica kept her husband in the dark because she was fully aware of the risks involved if caught. She didn't tell her children either, although Viggo later found out. Independently, Varinka had joined the Resistance in Copenhagen, where she became Muus's personal assistant (and later his wife; they married secretly in 1944).

Flemming Muus was impressed by Monica's ability to carry out clandestine work. When she suggested that marked supplies be dropped by parachute into the nearby Maribo Lake and later retrieved, Muus thought her idea ingenious.

'I was amazed,' he wrote in his memoir, 'for I happened to know that something very similar was being planned in England at that very moment by some of our most brilliant RAF brains. This was one example of Mrs Wichfeld's talent of instinctively putting her finger on a vital point.'

Her nephew takes up the story: 'For nearly three years, hardly a day passed without her involvement in one or another illegal activity in the region. Monica organised the distribution of anti-German literature, assisted in the distribution of arms and explosives from air-drops and sheltered people on the run, including Jews.'

The mood in Denmark had changed. News of German defeats in the summer of 1943 galvanised support for the Resistance.

A wave of demonstrations, strikes and resistance-organised sabotage, called the 'August Uprising', swept the country. The Germans responded with an ultimatum to introduce the death penalty for resistance, which prompted the Danish government to resign. Worse was to come. Hitler ordered the deportation of the country's entire Jewish population, some 7,800 people. While the Reich's Danish representative, Dr Werner Best, was committed to Hitler, he leaked plans of the round-up to avert further unrest.

What happened next was extraordinary. Over a period of a few days in early October 1943, most of Denmark's Jews escaped. Many thousands of ordinary Danes, quietly and discreetly, helped their fellow citizens to abandon their homes and businesses at short notice before enduring nerve-racking trips in small boats and bad weather to Sweden. The implementation of Hitler's repugnant policy towards the Jews failed when it came up against the strength of Danish democracy and the willingness of Sweden to let in all the Danish Jews who made it across the water.

The rescue represented what Holocaust studies scholar Professor Therkel Straede described as one of 'the most miraculous and heroic acts of courage to emanate from what was the worst genocide ever perpetrated by human against human'.

At Engestofte, Monica hid a number of Jewish people at her home, although the network warned her that it was too dangerous. She passed them off as staff, sheltering them in the servants' quarters.

Increased resistance activity had consequences; it brought with it ever-more intense German crackdowns. That didn't put Monica off her work. She continued to travel to Copenhagen to liaise with Flemming Muus, too, although she commented to her son that she felt she had been too lucky; something bad was going to happen.

That kind of premonition of impending danger was common among resisters, who often developed a kind of sixth sense. Monica was not wrong. SOE agent Jacob Jensen, who had worked on Monica's estate for a short time, and two other resistance members were arrested in December 1943. Allegedly under torture, it was Jensen who revealed a number of names, including that of Monica de Wichfeld.

She had not fully trusted Jensen when she met him. During her two-day trial, it was his word that condemned all four resistance members to death. All charges, though denied by the accused, were deemed 'proved by Jacob Jensen's testimony'. (Jensen was imprisoned in Denmark and survived the war. He died in 1977.)

After the execution of her three comrades, Monica was resigned to her fate. In a prison cell in Copenhagen, she wrote: 'We do not die, we only sleep a little, to live again as spring follows winter, and when they see my hands or my eyes in their children or hear them say something with my voice, they will no longer grieve.'

The people of Denmark, including the royal family with whom she had been linked in *Tatler* so many years before, had other ideas and they mounted a campaign for her reprieve. Initially, she was not for turning until she was persuaded to apply for clemency on the grounds that her death would lead to more unrest and the arrest and imprisonment of Danish civilians.

Within weeks, Monica de Wichfeld's death sentence was commuted to life imprisonment. On 2 June 1944, she was deported to Germany with two other Danish women, Elsa (Pia) Baastrup-Thomsen and Greta Jensen, both of whom were sentenced to six years for hiding a parachutist. Monica's biographer noted that she walked from the prison with the bearing of the queen, with a warder following behind carrying her suitcase.

We can accompany those women on their journey – part of the way, at least – because Pia later wrote of it in a memoir. Spirits were good at first, she wrote, because relatives had filled the women's suitcases with warm clothes, food, cigarettes and medical supplies. They didn't know then that their precious supplies would be confiscated.

Both Greta and Pia were slightly in awe of their fellow prisoner. As Pia wrote: 'Mrs. Wichfeld, an older woman, [was] still beautiful, with particularly wonderful eyes. Her hair was blue-black with whitish streaks at the temples. While in prison I had always admired her proud carriage, and how she always greeted us when we met in such a charming and endearing way.'

When the three women reached Cottbus prison, north-east of Dresden, Monica made the most of their incarceration. She turned the cell she shared with the two younger women into what Pia described as a mini-university: 'We learned English, Italian and French history, studied the rise of Mussolini and of Hitler, and followed in the footsteps of Mrs. Wichfeld's travels from Ireland and Scotland to England and Italy.'

Yet the daily prison regime was brutal. The women were awoken before 5 a.m. and forced to work long days unravelling miles of string which was to be used to bale hay. 'We always managed to leave a couple of knots in each batch, hoping they would wreck the harvesting machine,' Pia wrote. Despite the appalling conditions – the red-bricked prison was later nicknamed the 'Red Misery' – Monica managed to hoard scraps of food and fashion decorations from scraps of paper to mark Christmas.

The celebration was short-lived as the New Year brought with it a 'descent into hell', Pia wrote. In January 1945, as the Russians approached, the Germans decided to move 180 of their women prisoners, including Monica, from Cottbus to Waldheim. They were loaded onto unheated cattle wagons, without food or water. After three days of stopping and starting along its 100-mile cross-county route, the train eventually arrived at Waldheim.

Pastor Emil Viereck met them at the station. He was appalled at the sight of these starving, freezing women being herded down the street by armed soldiers. The journey from station to prison, in freezing conditions, was too much for Monica de Wichfeld. She collapsed and was later taken to the prison's rudimentary sanatorium.

Her nephew remarks on the timing: 'Monica was still alive but close to death when, for the three nights starting on 13 February 1945, she would have heard the noise and sensed the intensity of the bombing of Dresden. The 1,300 bombers that flew in waves of nine, every 10 minutes for three consecutive nights, would have roared over Waldheim on their approach to the doomed city. The furore of the bombing was such that, even 50 miles away in Waldheim, everyone must have realised that the war was in its final death throes.

'[Monica] might have had poignant memories of her youthful years in Dresden, so glamorous and exciting in 1910 at its zenith, but now – 34 years later – collapsing in flames to its nadir. She would also have had the satisfaction of knowing that she had made a significant contribution to Denmark's Resistance and that her sacrifice had not been in vain.'

On 27 February 1945, Monica de Wichfeld died of tuberculosis of the lung. Had she lived just six more weeks, she might have been among the 15,000 or so neutral prisoners rescued by the Swedish Red Cross and the Danish government.

About two weeks later, Jørgen Wichfeld received a letter from the prison chaplain informing him of Monica's death, and stating that she had been buried in grave number 316 in the cemetery of the women's section of the prison. Monica had requested the pastor's presence shortly before she died and he had given her Communion to which she was, he wrote, *ganz aufgeschlossen* (entirely receptive).

Biographer Christine Sutherland added the detail that the pastor had opened the window of the sanatorium on the night she died so that she could see the full moon she remembered so well from her childhood in Ireland. It sounds like a novelist's flourish, but on the night she died there was indeed a full moon.

Her biography ends with another mysterious detail. It suggests that a Danish commission travelled to Waldheim to repatriate her remains, but that when it dug up the designated grave, it was empty. The last line reads: 'Her body has never been found.'

In October 2007, 62 years after her death, Christopher Massy-Beresford travelled to Waldheim to retrace his aunt's last steps. He walked the kilometre from the station to the prison (their location is the same now as it was then); a 20-minute walk at a normal pace. But, in February 1945, he estimated that it must have taken the 180 women prisoners who disembarked from those unheated cattle wagons very weak, thirsty and hungry, at least three times as long.

Christopher was now hoping to trace Pastor Viereck, or one of his relatives, to find out more. Before he arrived, he had contacted the local paper in Waldheim, which published an item about his visit. 'As the member of the family who now knows most about the Wichfeld family and as a German speaker, I considered I was probably the only person able to probe this matter further.'

When he finally arrived in late October, there was a strange quietness about the town. After the war, Waldheim fell just inside the East German frontier and remained part of East Germany until the fall of the Berlin Wall in 1989. The town was tidy and peaceful with an attractive bridge over the river and some Art Nouveau buildings painted in a variety of pleasant colour washes. Yet, to this day, it is still notorious throughout Germany as a prison town.

'It was a strange feeling, arriving at the town where such a close member of the family had spent the last few weeks of her life,' he wrote in an account of his journey.

Christopher's visit got off to a discouraging start. Nobody responded to his newspaper call for help. He also discovered that Pastor Viereck had died in 1950: 'My faint hope that

Viereck might have had descendants still living in the area and that he had kept some sort of diary faded away.'

After a number of conversations, including with the pastor of the town's main church and its then Mayor, Christopher realised that the only place he might find more information about Monica was in the prison's own records. After two days of difficult telephone calls, he eventually gained admission to the prison. Finally, his search yielded results thanks to a fruitful meeting with Georg Zetzsche, one of the prison's administrators who, among many other duties, was assembling a museum of the prison's history.

After a two-hour conversation and subsequent correspondence, along with his own observations, photos and deductions, Christopher Massy-Beresford was finally able to write a more complete version of his aunt's final days.

This is an edited version of his final report written at his home in Beckington in Somerset, England, in 2016:

On their arrival at Waldheim station, the group of 180 Scandinavian women… was herded on foot to the prison. Pastor Viereck had met them and was horrified by their condition. He alerted the prison staff and obtained permission for them to be revived with unlimited hot soup when they eventually arrived. They were taken immediately into the chapel of the woman's section of the prison, from which Monica was removed a day or two later to the prison's sanatorium.

After she died, Monica was initially buried in the graveyard of the women's prison. However, burials there ceased a few months later and the Communists then built over it some kennels for the prison's dogs. These kennels were demolished early in the 1980s and the site eventually formed part of a new road – a sort of minor town by-pass route – that was completed in 2007 (the year of my visit). It was in the course of excavations for this road that mortal remains were discovered which were carefully examined and found to be of females who had died in 1944/45.

'So I think we would be justified in making the assumption that parts of Monica were among those remains and accepting that the funeral which then took place in the St Nicholas churchyard on 21st April, 1995 [as officially planned and recorded by Waldheim's Town Council] was indeed, and at last, a thoroughly correct and proper finale to her sad demise – just over 50 years after her death.

Christopher Massy-Beresford was only five and living in Canada when his aunt died, but his research trip, recent lectures and essays have contributed to commemorating her colourful and eventful life, which, in his words, 'ended prematurely after three years during which she acted with cool, formidable courage and magnificent altruism'.

There was one other surprise. While looking through the records, Christopher saw that another Irish person had also been imprisoned in Waldheim. The man's name: resistance member Robert Armstrong.

13
Carve his Name with Pride

'[ROBERT ARMSTRONG] HELPED NUMEROUS AVIATORS
RETURN TO ENGLAND. WHEN THERE WERE ALLIED DEATHS,
HE LOOKED AFTER THEIR BURIAL IN THE CEMETERY –
AND AS AN ACT OF DEFIANCE TO THE OCCUPIER, HE
DECORATED THEIR GRAVES WITH FLOWERS…'

EUGÈNE DENNIS

28 November 1942: The first thing Irish gardener and resistance member Robert Armstrong did when he met Sgt Arthur B. Cox was take the coat off his own back and give it to him. The young American airman was tall like the six-foot Armstrong and, in wartime France, it was exceptionally difficult to find civilian clothes to fit broad-shouldered men.

A few months later, a photograph was taken showing a smiling Cox on his way out of occupied France. He was still wearing the coat, but it had been adjusted to fit his waistline.

Armstrong's gesture, and the effort to tailor the coat so it wouldn't look out of place, are minor details in the grand scheme of history, but they illustrate the extraordinary measures taken by resistance members to help stranded Allied servicemen get to safety.

It wasn't just those directly involved in the Resistance who helped, though. Several ordinary civilians took huge risks to help Sgt Cox when his aircraft was shot down during a mission to bomb Lille on 9 October 1942. Shortly before the aircraft made landfall over France, it was attacked. In the ensuing chaos, the 23-year-old American was thrown from the bomb bay doors; he hadn't meant to jump, he explained later. 'I think I fell out at 15,000 feet and opened my chute at 10,000 feet. The chute carried me over a village in full view of everyone.'

He came down in a tree, managed to cut the shroud lines of his parachute and then he started to run. He ran from about noon until five o'clock, covering some 15 miles. Then, exhausted, he crawled into a haystack and slept until the next morning.

Like so many other shot-down aviators, he was completely at the mercy of the people he met when he set out that October day. He was in luck. Sgt Cox came across a series of sympathetic French people who directed him to the home of Marie-Thérèse Debrabant, a teacher in Douai in northern France. He stayed there for weeks while Marie-Thérèse made a number of unsuccessful attempts to contact the Resistance.

Some eight weeks went by before she managed to get in touch with Robert Armstrong, an Irishman and head gardener at Saint-Roch war cemetery at Valenciennes about 40km away. Known as Bob, he called to see the fugitive on 28 November with another man called Mr Lindsay, the alias used by shopkeeper and fellow *résistant* Marcel Maillard. The two men regularly worked together to help parachutists return to England.

Robert Armstrong had the credentials so valued by the Resistance – an ability to speak English and French. And he had an Irish passport, which meant – initially, at least – that he was less likely to be interned and was not considered suspicious by the Germans.

When Bob arrived at Marie-Thérèse Debrabant's house in Douai, he was able to bridge the communication gap and, more importantly, put the American airman through his paces to ensure he was not an enemy imposter. He did that by bringing him a map of the United States and asking him to point out his home town, Fountain City in Tennessee, Sgt Cox explained later.

Once Bob and his companion were satisfied, they took photos of Sgt Cox to use for false identity papers, but they turned out badly. Another two months went by before the men returned to take new photos; a delay that demonstrates the long days of waiting and the careful planning needed for each dangerous escape.

Sgt Cox remained in hiding, leaving the house on a single occasion to go to another house for dinner. On that single trip, he was stopped by French police and asked for his identify card. His hostess, Madame Debrabant, had warned him not to say anything under any circumstances. She told the police he was mute – the tried-and-very-much-tested ploy favoured by the Resistance – and that he had no identity card. The police let him go.

Meanwhile, Bob Armstrong arranged the details of the airman's onward journey through France along the Pat O'Leary escape line. Despite the Irish-sounding name, the line was founded by a Belgian doctor, Albert Guérisse, who apparently christened it after a Canadian friend. By then, hundreds of Allies had already been shunted along a path that brought them into Spain where they left for England through British-controlled Gibraltar.

Guérisse personally helped Sgt Cox make it safely across the Pyrenees in February 1943 but, a month later, he was betrayed and arrested himself.

The infiltration of the Pat O'Leary line led to many arrests – and deaths – and the line was definitively shut down. It was a terrible blow to lose such a vital network, but Robert Armstrong had seen the rise and fall of a number of resistance organisations since he first got involved in June 1940.

Like his compatriot Janie McCarthy in Paris, he worked with the Saint Jacques network until it was blown in 1941. And then, just as she had done, he sought out new groups to continue the fight against German occupation.

It was clear from the start of the war that Robert Armstrong was going to do whatever he could for the Allies. Under different circumstances, he might have enlisted but he was 44 years old when the war broke out and a troublesome injury, sustained in the previous world war, still nagged at him. His hip had been shattered by a shell in the Somme, leaving lasting after-effects.

He had also lost his brother in the previous war. Robert joined the 1st battalion of Irish Guards shortly after his younger brother, Private James Henry Armstrong, joined the 2nd battalion. Both battalions fought in the Battle of Loos in 1915, suffering terrible losses. James Henry Armstrong was among the thousands of dead. He died on 2 October and was buried in France.

Robert was brought back to London and treated for his injury. He left the army a few years later and when, in 1920, the Imperial War Graves Commission advertised for gardeners, he applied for the job. It made sense. He had worked as a gardener before the war and the commission's undertaking to honour the war dead, of all ranks, must have resonated with him.

He wasn't keen to return to Ireland either, with a War of Independence raging. He was born into a Protestant family on

7 October 1894 in Newbliss, Co. Monaghan. In the 1920s, his parents were living at Currygrane near Edgeworthstown, Co. Longford, the family home of staunch unionist, Field Marshal Sir Henry Wilson. Though, as Robert illustrated himself, the Armstrongs did not always do what one might expect.

When neighbour and revolutionary leader Seán MacEoin was on the run, Robert's father hid him at Currygrane. Much later, MacEoin would try to repay that kindness when Bob Armstrong found himself in deep trouble.

Robert Armstrong was the kind of man who made an impression. That was clear from the references sent to the Imperial War Graves Commission when he applied for a job. He held a range of posts – in Wicklow, Limerick and the Royal Hospital Kilmainham, Dublin – and, without exception, his former employers described him as honest, willing, industrious and hard-working.

He would prove to be equally conscientious when he began work at the war cemetery at Valenciennes in France in the early 1920s. He wasn't long in France when he met and married Belgian woman Claire Maricq, but their marriage ended in divorce in 1932.

During that time he had considered moving to Belgium, but when the couple parted he stayed on in Valenciennes where he was well established with a wide circle of friends. That was why he decided to stay when he found himself in the middle of a second world war, he told his Irish family.

He returned to see them at Christmas in 1939, but was back in France for the New Year. He kept in contact when he could, in particular with his sister Augusta Lindsay.

It is interesting that one of his colleagues in the Resistance had the codename Mr Lindsay. Historian Caitlin Galante

DeAngelis speculates the alias was a nod to Robert's younger sister. He had designated her his next-of-kin and he sent her a monthly payment of £2 to help her make ends meet.

Augusta Lindsay worshipped Bob, her son Harry Lindsay told writer Ronan McGreevy in 2015. 'Anything Bob wanted, Bob got. Our house was very rigorously controlled financially. When Bob came home, that went out the door. Bob always brought my mother a bottle of perfume from France and this was absolutely treasured as if it was holy water.'

He remembered his uncle as a flamboyant and physically strong man; a 'natural rebel', the kind of person who would get involved in a resistance movement. It was even said he had helped Seán MacEoin with his IRA activities on trips home in the 1920s. It wasn't a surprise to anyone to learn of his resistance activities in France.

Harry Linsday also gave this fascinating insight into one of his uncle's wartime activities in Valenciennes. The mother superior at the town's convent apparently refused to co-operate with the Germans. They retaliated by trying to starve the nuns out of their defiance by blocking deliveries of food.

'Armstrong threw food over the wall to them until he was caught by the Germans and given a hiding,' his nephew said.

If Armstrong said he wanted to stay in France at Christmas 1939, the situation had changed drastically by May 1940 when German troops began their blistering assault of Europe. As bombs were falling on Valenciennes, he was stunned to receive orders from the War Graves Commission, telling its gardeners in France to stay at their posts.

He went to the commission's office in Arras to request permission to leave. If not for him, then for the two gardeners who served under him. He made his way there through the chaos of a panicked civilian population on the move. Despite clear evidence that the Germans were coming and it was time to evacuate, his request was turned down.

In the week that followed, about half of the 393 war grave gardeners returned to England, while the others were trapped on soon-to-be-occupied soil where they had to fend for themselves.

Robert Armstrong drew on his wide circle of friends, who responded with generosity. He lodged with one of them, Monsieur Penez at 69 rue Durin, where 'he was treated as the child of the house', according to another friend, Eugène Dennis. But he had no money and contact with Ireland was all but cut off.

Augusta Lindsay wrote several letters to the Imperial War Graves Commission to try to get news of him, without success.

Then, in early January 1941, the family received word from the Irish legation in Vichy to say that he was 'very well sends love'. It was a huge relief, but the tables had turned. This time, Augusta Lindsay's big brother was asking her to send money to him if at all possible.

She eventually managed to get a sum of £30 from the Irish government's hardship fund. By then, Bob had another occupation, albeit unpaid – French *résistant*.

——— ———

He was part of *Libération Nord*, a large resistance movement operating around the north of France. After the war, one of its leaders said Armstrong had given great service, going to parachute drops, carrying out acts of sabotage, distributing propaganda tracts and helping Allied aviators.

One of those aviators, Flight Lieutenant Brian Desmond Barker, a Halifax bomber shot down on 9 March 1943, found his way to a café in Valenciennes and asked for help. They sent for Bob Armstrong, who helped to arrange his passage to Paris. From there, others helped him escape into Spain and back to Britain some four months later.

Bob Armstrong also worked regularly with another Irishman, William O'Connor. The two men had much in common. They were both veterans of World War I. They both stayed on in France after the war, finding work with the Imperial War Graves Commission. And they both joined the Resistance early in the war.

William O'Connor was born in Dublin in 1893 and served in France during World War I. After the war, he stayed on and married a French woman. The couple had three children. He, too, was employed as a war graves gardener but at a cemetery in Douai, not far from Valenciennes.

It is interesting that O'Connor, like his compatriot, got involved in the Resistance from the very beginning. Having fought the Germans once, they found an indirect way to do so again. By June 1940, the same month as General de Gaulle's famous appeal, he was already working with a group known as *Voix du Nord* (Voice of the North).

He was involved in a wide range of activities: gathering intelligence, transporting weapons, cutting telephone lines and, from 1942, helping airmen.

In mid-1943, what was already dangerous work became even more so. The Germans swooped on 80 members of

Organisation civile et militaire after the resistance group executed a Nazi double agent discovered in its midst. There were more arrests, interrogations and torture.

Many resistance members stayed silent under the worst depravations the Germans meted out. They reacted with remarkable ingenuity when the Gestapo turned up to search their homes; distracting them from incriminating documents, throwing papers on the fire or, in one case, even eating a photograph rather than put the person in it at risk.

Some people did reveal names under torture, however, and there were informers at work, as well as double-agents. It's not clear how William O'Connor's activity was discovered but on 1 September 1943 he was arrested at the cemetery in Douai and taken to a court in Arras. He was sentenced to 18 months' hard labour for helping the British and sent to a number of different camps.

He endured beatings during interrogation and his fingers and teeth were broken. He also contracted typhus in Siegburg prison in Germany, but was liberated in April 1945 and repatriated to France a month later.

A fellow resistance member, Emilie Nisse, said of him: 'He demonstrated great Francophile sentiments and rendered service with real devotion. He always tried to help me and, on several occasions, transported arms and munitions.'

It was remarkable enough that two Irish gardeners working for the Imperial War Graves Commission in northern France were resistance members, but there was also a third Irish gardener, Thomas Crowley, who occasionally helped out. Caitlin Galante DeAngelis mentions him in her illuminating book, *The Caretakers*, which tells the story of war grave gardeners who helped Allied airmen.

Meanwhile, back at Saint-Roch cemetery in Valenciennes, Robert Armstrong continued to tend the graves of those who had died in World War I. Now, however, he was looking after the graves of a new generation of dead – the Allied airmen shot down over northern France. When the funerals were held for the first Allied soldiers, the Germans treated them with respect, even burying them with military honours.

That changed, however, after the graveyard became a focus for French patriotism. The Germans responded by banning the public from Allied funerals. In turn, the people of Valenciennes expressed their anger by flocking to the cemetery in their thousands on Armistice Day, 11 November 1943. They placed thousands of chrysanthemums, the traditional flower of memorial in France, on some 34 Allied graves.

Bob considered it an act of defiance to decorate the Allies' graves with flowers – and made a point of doing so, one of his friends said in a letter after the war. It wasn't surprising, then, that he reacted with fury when he saw a German kick memorial flowers away from a grave. He punched him, or so an account of the incident claims.

Whether Bob Armstrong assaulted a German officer or not is unclear, but he was certainly a wanted man by then. His cemetery colleague Emmanuel Dossche was summoned to Gestapo headquarters for questioning. When he was released, he went to warn Bob and tell him to flee. Instead, the ever-defiant Irishman presented himself to the Germans on 26 November 1943, believing the interrogation would be little more than a formality.

A few days later, French workers said they saw him being taken from the station in handcuffs. His face was bleeding and he was guarded by four Germans, they said. He was sent to Loos prison in Lille and later questioned – and most likely beaten – at Gestapo headquarters.

The Germans had closed in on all of the people who had helped American Sgt Arthur Cox escape in 1942. The teacher who had sheltered him in Douai, Marie-Thérèse Debrabant, was arrested and deported to Germany. Separately, the day after Bob's arrest, another man with Irish connections, SOE agent Michael Trotobas, was shot nearby, in Lille. (See Roll of Honour.)

Monsieur Penez and Eugène Dennis hired a lawyer, Maître Delcourt, to defend Bob in a German court. After six months in jail, he went on trial and, on 16 May 1944, the Irish legation in Vichy received a telegram to say that Robert Armstrong had been sentenced to death.

When the news filtered through to Ireland, his sister and the rest of his family were distraught. Seán MacEoin, then a Fine Gael deputy in the Irish government, made representations on his behalf.

Con Cremin, the Irish Minister in Vichy – and later Berlin – also tried to intervene. At one point, it looked as if Robert Armstrong would be released along with two other Irish nationals, Mary Cummins and Robert Vernon, in exchange for 10 German agents in Ireland. The exchange never went ahead.

According to Eugène Dennis, Armstrong's lawyer won the right to an appeal. His death sentence was later reduced to imprisonment with hard labour. The repeated calls from Con Cremin, now based in Berlin, most likely secured the reprieve. Unfortunately, a short time later, his friends, family, lawyers and the politicians all lost sight of him. He was sent to

Saint-Gilles prison in Brussels. 'After that, we heard nothing more,' said Eugène Dennis.

The Germans moved Bob Armstrong from prison to prison – Saint-Gilles to Aachen then Cologne, then on to Rheinbach and Kassel-Wehlheiden, his health deteriorating with each transfer. A prison guard gave him a terrible beating at one of the prisons so when he arrived at Waldheim, he was in very poor health.

When the war was over, the first thing his friends in Valenciennes did was try to find out what had happened to him. News of his fate came in the form of a poignant letter to Marie-Thérèse Debrabant, who survived her time at Waldheim. It was written by a fellow inmate, a Dutchman whose signature was recorded as 'illegible'.

'You asked for information about Bob Armstrong,' he wrote. 'I knew him in Cassel-Wehlheiden from November to December 1944. He had come from Rheinbach on 15 September.'

He went on to say that Bob was made to work outside, rebuilding a barracks that had been bombed by the Americans. At first, the weather was fine and prisoners managed to find potatoes and rutabagas (the root vegetable, swede) to supplement their meagre diets. But then winter came, with snow, wind and rain, and the work was much more challenging.

'Armstrong was not strong enough for it,' the Dutchman wrote. 'He had a big boil on his leg that had not been looked after and he grew thinner with each day. Because he couldn't work as hard as demanded, he was occasionally pushed by the guards, among whom there were some very cruel ones. On the 14th of December when he left with us to go to Waldheim, the situation got much worse. The day before we left, the guard floored him because he was taking too long to eat his meal. He could hardly move.'

When the prisoners arrived at Waldheim, the Dutchman and others carried him to the hospital.

'We hoped he would get better there because the medical treatment at Waldheim is better than at Cassel. But alas, he was already too weak and his leg was nothing more than an open sore. He died about two days after his arrival. I'm not sure of the exact date, but I think it was 16 December. All the camp comrades were very moved and we prayed for him. You can tell his family that he always kept his courage and his good humour.'

There were numerous tributes to the courageous, daring, rebellious, affable Irishman. Warm admiration leaps from the pages of several post-war depositions made by fellow resistance members and friends.

In a letter to Maj. John White, for example, Eugène Dennis summed up a widely expressed sentiment when he said: 'Among his friends... we could list the whole of Valenciennes.'

The two men had been friends since 1924 and Dennis said Robert Armstrong had given steadfast service to the Resistance: 'He helped numerous aviators return to England. When there were Allied deaths, he looked after their burial in the cemetery – and as an act of defiance to the occupier, he decorated their graves with flowers...'

Capt. Gaston Lepine, who led the Bureau des Opérations Aériennes (BOA) resistance network at Valenciennes, said Bob was a man who would do the impossible to make himself useful, and find an opportunity to harm the enemy. He kept nothing from Bob during their weekly meetings, the captain said after the war.

In Ireland, his sister Augusta Lindsay wrote letter after letter to the Imperial War Graves Commission trying to find out what had happened to him. The official confirmation of his death came a year later in 1946 but she found out before that because Bob's friends wrote to her.

In the difficult months that followed, there was talk of treating Robert Armstrong's death as a war crime, but it came to nothing. The War Graves Commission had a case to answer, too, because Bob had requested but been refused leave to evacuate.

There was also the question of his estate and an ensuing row among siblings about how it should be divided between them. When they finally reached agreement, the Irish government asked for reimbursement of the £30 in hardship funds it had sent him. It was paid from his estate.

In contrast, in Valenciennes, the community raised some 10,000 French francs, a considerable sum in post-war France, to help fund a memorial to Robert Armstrong at the Saint-Roch cemetery.

It was a cruel irony that the man who spent so many years of his life tending the graves of others had no grave himself. His remains were sent to a crematorium days after his death and scattered at an unknown location.

In his adopted home, however, he was decorated – posthumously awarded the *médaille de la Résistance* and the Franco-Britannique medal – and his family, friends and resistance colleagues watched as a marble plaque was unveiled in his memory on 11 July 1948.

The inscription reads: 'To the memory of Robert Armstrong, head gardener, Imperial War Graves Commission. Died in captivity at Waldheim Camp (Saxony), the 16th of December 1944, Homage from his friends in Valenciennes.'

CAPTURED

14
A Friend to Comb My Hair

'ONE DAY, INTRODUCING HER TO TWO AIRMEN, I SAID,
"SHE IS ENGLISH." SHE INTERRUPTED ME SHARPLY AND,
DRAWING HERSELF UP PROUDLY, SMALL AS SHE WAS,
SHE SAID, "I'M NOT ENGLISH, I AM IRISH!"'
NADINE ON CATHERINE CREAN

Ravensbrück Concentration Camp, February 1943: The most poignant glimpse of Irish *résistante* Catherine Crean comes to us through the eyes of her friend Andrée Dumon, or Nadine, to use her wartime alias. Both women worked in the Belgian Resistance but were betrayed and sent to Ravensbrück.

One freezing cold night in February, as she slipped into her bunk, bone-tired at the end of the day, Nadine heard a very small voice calling from a bunk next to hers. She realised that it was Catherine Crean, who like her, had been arrested and imprisoned for helping downed Allied airmen in Brussels.

'She had no strength left and all she wanted was for me to comb her hair,' Nadine recalled later. 'She handed me her comb and to my dismay I found that I could no longer hold the comb properly in my hand. Nevertheless, I strived to do my best to comb her hair as well as possible.'

The memory of seeing her friend, with her once-red long hair scattered around her pale face, moved Andrée Dumon to tears when she spoke of it in 2009, almost seven decades later.

She had known Catherine Crean when both women were helping fugitives and Allied evaders join the escape lines that would eventually bring them into neutral Spain.

Catherine Crean was a member of the Luc network, founded by Belgian Georges Leclercq. He named the organisation Luc as a sort of revenge, he said later, for his son Lucien who was killed in the early stages of the war in November 1940. It focused on sabotage and evasion and later, when it changed its name to Marc in 1942, it became one of the biggest intelligence-gathering networks in Belgium, with some 5,000 members.

We don't know when Catherine Crean joined the network, or why, but by 1942 she was helping the increasing numbers of Allied airmen being shot down over Belgium.

Nadine gave this fleeting insight into Catherine's work in her memoir, *I Haven't Forgotten You*: 'Sometimes [she] came to our house [in Brussels] to chat in English with the evaders and [she] brought them books in English. One day, introducing her to two airmen, I said, "She is English." She interrupted me sharply and, drawing herself up proudly, small as she was, she said, "I'm not English, I am Irish!"'

Like so many who led unlikely double lives it is, for obvious reasons, difficult to retrace their clandestine activity. When the people in question are ordinary civilians, albeit doing something extraordinary, the traces they leave behind are even more scant. But that does not mean Catherine Crean has vanished entirely. The details of her life, like pieces of a mosaic, are scattered and incomplete but they are retrievable in archived documents, in anecdotes and in the testimony of others.

Her entry into the world is recorded, in cursive script, on the Register of Births. She was born on 11 December 1879 to engine fitter John Crean and his wife Ellen (née Doran) of 8 Moore Street in Dublin city centre. The building is still there today, a three-storey house on a street better known for its association with the Easter Rising of 1916, whose leaders had their headquarters at number 16.

By 1916, Catherine Crean had been in Brussels for at least six years. When the war broke out, she was working as a live-in governess, or nurse, employed by the Baronne Ghislaine Empain at 1 Rue Zinner in the centre of Brussels.

She was still clearly proud of her Irishness, as Nadine's recollection shows, but perhaps of more significance was her physical description of Catherine: a woman who drew herself up to her full height, 'small as she was'.

A woman of small stature in her early sixties was the kind of person who could pass unnoticed through occupied Belgium with relative ease. She obviously did that as she went from safe house to safe house, delivering clothes and food to Allied servicemen and giving English lessons to the increasing numbers of helpers who were part of a growing network.

It is possible, even likely, that she worked with the person who set up the escape line that became known as the Comet Line. Andrée de Jongh, or Dédée, was a Belgian Red Cross volunteer of just 24 when she managed to persuade British intelligence to fund an escape line that ran from Belgium, through France and over the Pyrenees into neutral Spain.

To help a stranded serviceman make that perilous journey cost the equivalent of about €2,000 in today's terms, according to one estimate. The intelligence branch MI9, set up to help Allied servicemen trapped behind enemy lines, agreed to pay that sum for each exfiltrated man. The person who administered the funds was Airey Neave; a man with personal experience of what was involved, having escaped from Colditz, the infamous POW camp for officers, in 1942.

Dédée had the perfect cover: her appearance. She was slight, almost frail, some said, and her normal attire of floral dresses and white ankle socks belied her strength, not to mention any involvement in the Resistance. She was as strong as any man, she said later, after leading airmen on a dangerous journey over the Pyrenees.

She, and many other women in the Resistance, capitalised on the deeply ingrained idea that war was men's business. That view was prevalent among the Allies too. When an Australian sergeant pilot, Larry Birk, heard he and two other evaders were going to be guided over a dangerous mountain pass, he was expecting to meet a muscular Frenchman. He was utterly gobsmacked when Dédée introduced herself as his guide.

After she left, he looked at his fellow travellers, British gunner Jack Newton and pilot Harold Carroll, and said: 'Our lives depend on a schoolgirl.'

Catherine's friend Nadine was, in fact, a schoolgirl when she joined the Resistance. She was 18 when the first bombs fell on Belgium on 10 May 1940. This is how she recalled the moment: 'At about five o'clock in the morning, we suddenly heard a dull roar, like a thousand swarms of bees, over our heads… We watched with horror as big silver birds advanced in tight rows in a cloudless and wonderfully blue sky… One could have found it beautiful, were it not so tragic.

'Soon, we heard explosions in the distance; the first bombs were falling on our country! A great coldness came over me and I suddenly felt that the world had been turned upside down, that nothing would ever be the same again; that very dark days were ahead of us, without knowing what they would really be.'

Nadine reacted with little acts of defiance at first, cutting 'V's out of newspapers to represent Victory, and she cycled around the city distributing them everywhere. Soon, she was engaged in resistance work for real, accompanying Allied servicemen from Brussels to Paris, and travelling over the border from Belgium into France to pick up false ID papers.

On one occasion, she had a batch of false ID papers with her when she was searched at a check-point on the way back to Belgium:

'The women had to pass by the "grey mice" (as the German policewomen in their grey uniforms were called) and they did not hesitate to search you from [head] to toe, sometimes making you strip off in a room specially set aside for the purpose.

'Once, coming back from Lille, I was carrying a book in which I had hidden some blank ID cards, and, when she told me to hold my hands up, I did so still holding the book in my hand. She searched my pockets, ran her hands all over my body but ignored the book.'

It is simply not recorded if Catherine Crean faced similar ordeals or if she accompanied airmen to Paris. Given that she worked as a governess in central Brussels, it is more likely that she operated within the city. She clearly knew about the escape lines, though, and how they operated. It's likely that she knew of the network of safe houses that had been established around the city too, visiting them to give helpers lessons in English.

Being able to communicate with Allied fugitives made highly dangerous work a fraction easier. For the most part, evaders (those who were avoiding the Germans) and escapers (those who had escaped from detention) did not speak French, so they were advised to stay quiet when travelling. Many of them pretended to be deaf and/or mute. Others feigned sleep, or put a newspaper in front of their faces so that they would not be engaged in conversation while on a train.

There were other imaginative stunts too. Sometimes, they were given an orange and told to peel it messily so that juice spurted everywhere; no more effective way to deter a fellow traveller from leaning in for a chat.

Catherine Crean and her fellow *résistantes*, Nadine and Andrée, were at different ends of the age spectrum but, for a time at least, that was a source of protection because they were unlikely to draw attention to what they were doing.

The same was true of another Irish woman who lived near Catherine Crean in Brussels. Anna 'Jeannie' Duchêne née Hodges, a woman from Waterford, was 71 when she sheltered two Scottish soldiers in her home at Ixelles, a municipality in south-east Brussels.

Bobby Conville and John McCubbin, 1st Glasgow High-landers, were arrested in July 1940 and put on a train with other prisoners. As the train was passing through Boitsfort, near Brussels, they jumped off and ran for cover. They headed to Brussels where they were sheltered briefly by a woman but, when she got understandably nervous, they moved in with Anna Duchêne.

'I couldn't let the Germans take those boys again, so I said they could hide with us. We had a bed but no mattress, so [my daughter] Florrie and I ripped open our sofa pillows and made them a mattress so the poor lads would sleep easier,' she recalled.

Anna Hodges was born in Waterford in 1869 and moved to Brussels aged 18 to work as a governess. At first, she found it very difficult to adjust. 'I felt so young and strange and homesick when I first came here, but people were nice to me and I felt better after I learned their language and their ways,' she told American journalist Hal Boyle in 1954.

When she was about 30, she married Josef Duchêne, coachman to Leopold II, King of the Belgians. The couple had two children, Leopold and Florrie.

The family had struggled financially during the inter-war years, yet they were still willing to help two escapers. For 14 months, the Scots stayed with the Duchênes at their home on the rue Sans-Souci. The name of the street means 'the road without worries' and while a family harbouring fugitives could never be entirely carefree, life went along without incident for a time.

Florrie ran a milliner shop and Bobby used to help her make hats. 'That Bobby, he was such a good little boy,' Anna said of her one-time guest.

On 25 September 1941, their fragile existence came to an abrupt end when three Gestapo officers called to the house. The soldiers often spent the day elsewhere, but John McCubbin was at the rue Sans Souci when they arrived. He tried to escape, but was shot three times in the back.

Anna told Florrie to run out the back: 'It made no difference if the Germans took me as I wouldn't live long anyway. But she wouldn't leave me,' Anna said.

Mother and daughter were both arrested and put in solitary confinement in St-Gilles prison where Catherine Crean would later be interned. Anna, then in her seventies, was released after nine months. Florrie was sent to Ravensbrück and later Belsen, according to her mother.

'When she fell ill, they took her away from the other prisoners one day. I asked and asked what happened to her after that and no one will tell me. She was so good and nice ... so kind to everybody.'

Florrie Duchêne died in April 1945. Both soldiers survived the war. Andrée de Jongh helped Bobby Conville to escape along the Comet escape line while John McCubbin survived, despite his gunshot injuries, in a POW camp.

For years afterwards, the bullet hole left by the Gestapo on the Duchêne's front door became an object of curiosity; people visited it frequently after the war. Madame Duchêne became a symbol of Belgian courage and received honours from the Belgian, British and American governments.

When journalist Hal Boyle interviewed her in 1954, she was living on her own, as her son had died too. When Boyle asked her if she regretted her wartime actions, she replied: 'No, I make out. I have no regrets except that I have lost my two children. That is the worst of all.'

In the same way that Anna Duchêne asked and asked about her daughter, a friend of Catherine Crean's went looking for her when she failed to return after the war.

We might not know anything of her fate if Arthur Van de Steene of Brussels had not set out to find her. Describing himself as a friend of 35 years, he filled out a document of enquiry and sent it to a dedicated section in the Ministry of

Public Health and Family in Brussels in an effort to trace Catherine's whereabouts.

The details on the resultant response, though scant, tell us a little more about this woman who lost her life while trying to save the lives of others. She was arrested in early August 1942, just days before her friend Nadine. Their network had been betrayed to the Nazis. We know from Nadine's testimony that she was interrogated and beaten at St-Gilles prison in Brussels. It is reasonable to assume that Catherine Crean suffered similar brutality.

Although Nadine outlined the merciless interrogations, she also described the comfort of being able to talk to other prisoners by sending signals through the central-heating pipes.

'A few blows with a fork or knife on the said pipes were enough to call a neighbour; then, while kneeling in the corner of the cell speaking softly with our mouths lightly touching the pipe, we could understand each other perfectly,' she wrote.

She didn't know her friend Catherine was also in St-Gilles; their prison paths did not cross until the next year. Even though prisoners spoke, they were always careful not to mention names or to say anything specific.

As Nadine explained: 'It is a principle in captivity; we talk about the weather, if needs be about one's family, especially the women who have children, but never of any clandestine activities. We all knew that there could be "sheep" among us, false prisoners put here and there by the Germans in the hope of gathering information. One does not stay a year in prison without knowing that one must be wary of everybody.'

Nadine was able to receive parcels from her family. Catherine never married, but perhaps her friend Arthur Van de Steene and others she met during her many decades in Brussels sent her parcels of food and clean clothes.

When she was sent to Ravensbrück on 31 July 1943, a month before Nadine, she was out of reach. The Red Cross was able to say that it had been in touch with her more than a year later, in December 1944, but the surviving document doesn't say any more than that.

There's another note in her file that suggests Catherine Crean was not entirely on her own, though. The leader of the Comet escape line, Andrée de Jongh, was also betrayed and sent to the notorious camp, remaining in Ravensbrück until it was liberated in 1945. The two women seem to have been in contact. A single handwritten document in the State Archives of Belgium suggests that was the case.

That small fragment of paper also tells us Andrée was the one who confirmed the news that Catherine Crean, governess and little-known Irish *résistante*, died of dysentery on 3 April 1945, aged 65.

Catherine Crean might not be well-known, but she was never forgotten. The two women she worked with, both named Andrée, made sure of that. Andrée de Jongh reported her cause of death while Andrée Dumon, aka Nadine, was adamant that her memory be kept alive. Another camp companion, Soeur (Sr) Marie Pascale, also gave evidence of her death.

The airmen she sent shuttling down the Comet Line, so named because it moved people along at such speed, likely also recalled this woman who took such risks to help them.

The search by her long-time friend Arthur Van de Steene means there is an archival trace of her too. And a single surviving photograph. Maybe he took it. It shows Catherine

Crean on a balcony; her hair is tucked up under a hat and she's wearing a smart coat over a floral dress. She looks like a woman ready to go out.

We can only imagine how Arthur Van de Steene felt when he discovered that she was never coming home.

15
The Extraordinary Resilience of Two Marys

'I KEPT GOING BY SHEER WILL-POWER. I CAN'T EXPLAIN
HOW I DID IT, BUT I INTENDED TO LEAVE THAT CAMP ALIVE.'
MARY O'SHAUGHNESSY

'I JUST SAID, "INTO THY HANDS, LORD, I COMMEND MY
SPIRIT".'
MARY CUMMINS

Brussels 1941: Mary Cummins woke with a start to find a
member of the Gestapo shaking her. Her landlady had given
him the key. The chief of Mary's resistance network had been
arrested and his papers seized. Among them, his captors found
a list of the names and addresses of some 40 members of the
group. The Germans swooped on every one of them in a series
of early morning raids.

Mary was taken to Brussels for questioning and then put
on a train to Hamburg: 'We were packed like sardines. [There
was] practically no air,' she said later, recalling the stop-start
journey that took two-and-a-half days as the train juddered
regularly into sidings to avoid the Allied planes that Mary
could see through the bars overhead.

When she got to Berlin, she was sentenced to death and
imprisoned. She would spend the next 'four years of a living
death' in captivity in several camps and prisons while Irish
diplomats tried to broker a release.

When she was in her eighties, she spoke about her existence in those 'dark precincts of terror'; prisons and camps where people were routinely beaten, brutalised, starved, humiliated and murdered.

'The Germans were perpetually thinking of ways and means of torturing people,' she said in an aptly named documentary, *In the Shadow of Death*, in 1993. 'I was beaten. I had my hands in a vice. I had very often a revolver on my back. I was under continual threats of being sent to Auschwitz concentration camp to be done away with.

'There was no end, absolutely no end, to the torture. I can hardly describe what it was like… I often fainted from hunger and because of the stress of it. The last two years I was there, I was dying little by little, bit by bit. I was beginning to lose my memory, fainting and vomiting, dysentery… and felt really that I was going down.'

Mary Cummins survived her ordeal in a display of extraordinary endurance. So, too, did three other Irishwomen who found themselves at Ravensbrück – as Cummins ultimately did – a place of unimaginable depravity.

An estimated 130,000 people passed through its electric-fenced enclosure on a site near a lake and a forest about 50 miles north of Berlin. The death toll is still not known, although it is estimated to be between 30,000 and 90,000. The wide variation in figures illustrates just how difficult it was to trace missing people after the war due, in part, to the fact that the SS destroyed all prisoner files before the camp was liberated in 1945.

Sr Katherine Anne McCarthy (see Roll of Honour), a nursing sister from Cork who joined one of the first resistance movements, ended up there. On four separate occasions, she managed to avoid being picked out of a parade of women destined for the gas chambers. She hid or was hidden and, once, jumped out of a window. She weighed just four stone when she was released in 1945.

Agnes Flanagan (see Roll of Honour) from Offaly also spent time in the camp and she, too, narrowly escaped the gas chamber. She was emaciated on her return home to Belgium and engaged in a bureaucratic battle before she received a pension.

Many never spoke of the horrors they endured. It was enough to try to recover their health – or at least to deal with the lasting after-effects – while trying to build a new life. For others, such as Mary Cummins and Mary O'Shaughnessy, it was important to bear witness and seek some sort of justice.

─── ──

When Mary Cummins was first approached by members of the Belgian Resistance, she was warned that it would be very dangerous work. She was in Brussels when the Germans swept through the low countries in May 1940. Like so many others who joined the Resistance, she had a gift for languages.

Her flair for French, in particular, was evident from her school days in Dublin. She came into the world on 24 April 1905, one of ten children born to Ellen Black and Thomas Cummins of Richmond Road in Dublin. She went to Fairview National School and later the Dominican College in Eccles Street, where her remarkable aptitude for languages was encouraged. The school's reverend mother suggested she spend time in Belgium to develop her knowledge of French.

In Brussels, she found work as an English teacher and later worked as a translator at the Canadian embassy. She was also an Irish passport holder. '*Ça, c'est bien*,' (that's good), her Belgian friends said when they invited her to have a chat about the possibility of joining the Resistance.

'They won't suspect you. You'll be wonderful for the Resistance,' they said.

Mary later said she was intrigued by the prospect, but a bit nervous. They had warned her of the considerable risks, but she felt they were relying on her. She put aside her thoughts of returning to Ireland because now she felt she had an obligation as the only English-speaker in a group of some 40 *résistants*.

Her network transmitted intelligence on troop movements to General de Gaulle in London and to British Intelligence. Mary worked as a translator and a courier, transporting weapons from place to place. She recalled visiting various cities in Belgium – Charleroi, Liège, Ostend and Le Mons – picking up two or three revolvers at a time and then bringing them back to Brussels.

The Belgian Resistance, like so many movements in other countries, grew from the bottom up, often coalescing around groups that existed before the war such as sports clubs. Historians estimate that about 150,000 people took part in some kind of resistance activity. Some 40,000 of that number were arrested and, of those, an estimated 15,000 people died, either in prison, by execution or in action.

While most of the arrests took place in 1944, Mary Cummins and her group were betrayed much earlier, around 1941. It meant that Mary had several years of prison and camp life ahead of her. Many of her fellow resistors were executed or died.

'The whole stay in Germany was torture from beginning to end,' she said. 'The torture of hunger. The torture of thirst. The torture of humiliation.'

She was held in about 20 different prisons and camps from Bremen and Essen to the worst, Ravensbrück. In some ways, she said, the prisons were better because you were isolated from large crowds of people, which meant that you were not as vulnerable to the diseases – typhoid, dysentery, tuberculosis – that took so many lives in the camps.

In one prison Mary remembers being brought a big sack full of the gloves of shot-down aviators. She had to wash away the mud and blood and knit new fingers where they were missing. 'That was another humiliation,' she said.

There were many others. She was kept in solitary confinement, not knowing the day, or even the month. She was stripped, put on an apparatus where every orifice was searched. She was so thirsty at times that she had to drink her own urine and she felt her eyes and mouth completely drying up. She saw people being tortured and men being put in baths of near-boiling water and then plunged into ice-cold water. She saw people go crazy with hunger and heard the screams of the dying and the tortured.

'At times,' she said, 'there was no sound at all. That was even worse.'

Yet, she kept going, saying often: 'Into thy hands, Lord, I commend my spirit.'

Meanwhile, the Irish diplomatic representative in Berlin, William Warnock, followed by his successor, Con Cremin, were trying to establish why an Irish citizen had been sentenced to death.

At first, the German authorities said they did not give details of espionage cases but they did venture the information that Mary Cummins had apparently admitted her own guilt. After repeated pleas, Con Cremin managed to visit her in Cottbus prison in September 1944.

'She does not look strong to me,' he wrote. 'She says however her health is generally speaking good but that she does not get enough to eat and is consequently somewhat weak. It is not permitted to send such prisoners food or clothing but I propose to raise the question with the foreign office.'

Cremin made representations to the German foreign office and secured an improved clothing allowance for her. He also continued the campaign to have her released and, after much back and forth, finally succeeded.

Mary Cummins was released from prison on 17 January 1945 and went to stay with Con Cremin and his family not far from Berlin.

'Cummins is now much stronger and quite well,' Cremin wrote in a letter to Dublin. 'She admits being guilty of charge... She says that she belonged to an organisation financed from London and working in co-operation with Brit Intel [British Intelligence] Service and French 2nd Bureau [French Intelligence] and that her motives for so acting were fundamentally charitable and to some extent financial. I intend to take her with us [to Switzerland] if possible.'

Mary Cummins later described the 'paradise' of arriving in Switzerland after the war, though her account suggests that she was liberated directly from Ravensbrück camp in April 1945.

Wartime accounts – of escapes, imprisonment and release – often contain inconsistencies even when the general outlines concur. In this case, there are differing accounts of the date of release but there is no doubt about Mary Cummins's wartime ordeal, much less the indomitable spirit she showed in surviving several years of imprisonment.

Those years had a lasting effect on her health. She had heart and lung difficulties and decalcification of the spine which meant she had to wear what she described as 'a plaster jacket' for six months after her release.

In 1946, she was decorated by King Leopold of the Belgians and General Eisenhower. In the same year, she travelled to Brussels for a compensation assessment and met Count Guy O'Kelly de Galway, a barrister with Irish descendants. They married in 1949 and moved back to Ireland. Mary Cummins, or Countess O'Kelly de Galway as she became, put the war behind her.

Then, fifteen years into what she described as a happy marriage, she had to deal with another shock. On 20 July 1964, she waved goodbye to her husband at Dublin airport. He was going to England on a business trip, a journey he made often. When he failed to return, Mary made several attempts to trace him, but all without success. She never saw her husband again.

For a second time, she got on with her life, making the most of each day. She never lost her appreciation for the simple joys of life – the smell of freshly mown grass, clean drinking water, the moon and the stars – which, she said, was sharpened after spending so many years behind bars.

A week before she died, aged 94 on 20 June 1999, she was still taking regular walks, having her hair done and going to parties. 'Aren't I marvellous for my age,' she used to say. 'They'll have to shoot me.'

Mary Cummins's extraordinary resilience is the first thing that comes to mind when Dorothy Seagrave recalls her great-aunt: 'She was a real go-getter and she had a bucket list before anyone else had such a thing. She always wanted to do things; she travelled on Concorde, for example.'

Given what she had endured, she wanted to make the most of her life. That was why she stopped smoking later in life. 'After all she had been through, she said she wasn't going to let a weed get her,' Dorothy said.

For the most part, Mary's hellish experiences stayed in the background but, at times, something would trigger a bad memory. At one family get-together, there weren't enough chairs to go around. When two sisters shared a chair, Mary (or 'Bunny', as she was known) told them that it brought back the awful memory that the Nazis used to force two women to sit on the toilet together.

She got on with life, though, and was very happy to return to Belgium where she was always treated very well. The country, unlike Ireland, had given her a pension and one of several medals she received for her resistance work. The medals were heavy, though, and she was a very slight woman so she had them melted down and recast as miniatures which she wore with pride, her grand-niece recalled.

If the war left one enduring scar, it was a fear of fanatics. They were unpredictable and dangerous when in power, she said. She was somehow able to come to terms with the cruelty meted out to her by the people under their control, but she always warned against extremists.

In her personal life, she found her husband's unexplained departure very difficult to accept. She never understood why and although she made contact with his family, they never told her where he was. And yet, she made the most of each day.

At the time of her death, it was reported that she had been the only Irish person in the Belgian Resistance. But there were others: Catherine Crean, Agnes Flanagan and Anna Duchêne, even if their names and their courageous deeds were forgotten.

——— ——

Another inmate of Ravensbrück concentration camp, Mary O'Shaughnessy, was determined that the world would not be allowed to forget what happened to hundreds of thousands of women at the hands of their captors. She told the press about her unimaginable ordeals and, when asked by the British War Office, agreed to give evidence at the war crime trials against 16 Ravensbrück personnel in Hamburg in December 1946.

The *Liverpool Evening Express* captured Mary's determination to bear witness with its headline: 'Miss Mary (late of gas camp) will have her say now.'

When she took the witness stand in Hamburg on 11 December 1946, her voice faltered at first. But she continued to speak and, when questioned by Maj. Stewart, she outlined the torture she endured, the murders she witnessed and years of unthinkable daily cruelties.

Her harrowing testimony was reported in several papers in Ireland and Britain, each one highlighting a different atrocity. One focused on the SS woman guard who smashed her teeth and broke her nose but later said she had mistaken Mary for someone else.

Another focused on the heart-rending story of two French sisters, Germaine and Madeleine Tambour: one of them was singled out to be gassed, but the other sister ran across the square and joined her in the death squad, refusing to be parted.

Yet another claimed that Mary O'Shaughnessy herself would be sent to the gas chamber if the camp authorities discovered her artificial arm. She had been born with a fore-shortened left arm. At school, she had been bullied because of it. Despite this claim, when her prosthetic limb was discovered in the camp, it did not initially single her out for death, but it did mean she suffered regular beatings – 'with sticks, whips and fists', she said.

And yet Mary O'Shaughnessy endured. 'I kept going by sheer will-power. I can't explain how I did it, but I intended to leave that camp alive,' she told the trial.

Another newspaper, the *Cork Examiner* of 12 December 1946, headlined its article, 'Irish Governess Gives Evidence', and began with Mary's account of those she saw die in the camp of horrors.

'Her voice trembling with emotion, an Irish governess, Miss Mary O'Shaughnessy, said to be residing at Reading, England, told the Military Court trying the Ravensbruck Camp staff in Hamburg yesterday how heroic British and French women died in the camp. Among the six or seven who were shot or gassed were a WAAF officer, Mary Ellen Young and Cecily Lefort, an English girl married to a French editor,' it said.

Cecily Lefort, a woman of Irish descent and a regular visitor to Ireland, was in fact married to a French doctor, Dr Alix Lefort. The couple had a villa in Brittany with its own bay. In 1943, Cecily gave a fellow agent an antique Irish ring to give to the villa's caretaker as a sign that he had her permission to use the bay as a safe place to land. She landed in France herself in June of that year and was arrested by the Gestapo in September 1943.

She was sent to Ravensbrück and shortly afterwards her husband sent her a message via the Red Cross asking for a divorce. He said he was 'suffering profoundly' because she had abandoned their home and it was unreasonable to expect him to cope on his own.

She, meanwhile, had undergone Gestapo interrogation, imprisonment and, unusually, an operation for suspected cancer of the stomach. Her health seemed to improve at first but then, when she became increasingly ill, she was singled out for the gas chamber. Her camp friends later said that she had written her husband out of her will after getting his message.

Mary O'Shaughnessy didn't mention that detail, but she was one of the last people to see Cecily Lefort alive. She nearly suffered the same fate herself because she, too, had been transferred to another camp *Jugendlager* (literally, youth camp) where conditions were supposed to be easier. In fact, most of the people sent there faced imminent death.

Many of them had been issued with pink cards. At first, the slips of paper were seen as some kind of dispensation from heavy work for those who were ill or too old, but it soon became clear that the holders were going to be murdered. Those who were transferred to the death camp rarely made it out again, but somehow Mary was transferred back to the main camp after six weeks and survived until she was liberated in April 1945.

When she arrived back in England, she stayed with her sister. She 'was more dead than alive', one newspaper reported. Like so many other women who survived Ravensbrück, she was a shell of her former self and had a series of health issues.

She gave a long interview to *The Journal*, an English newspaper, on 12 October 1945. It outlined her arrest in Lyon on 14 March 1944, after being betrayed, and the torture she first endured at the hands of her Nazi interrogators. If Mary Cummins had witnessed men being tortured by immersion in scalding baths, Mary O'Shaughnessy had personal experience of it. She was doused in water which was near boiling point and then plunged into ice-cold water, a total of 13 times. She had counted them, she said, but she never gave any information to her interrogators.

At one point, the Germans asked her what a woman with an Irish surname like O'Shaughnessy was doing working for the British Secret Service. She said she was neither Irish nor in the employ of the British. Mary was later referred to as an Irish governess – in the Irish newspapers at least – and she did come from an Irish family, but was born in Ashton-in-Makerfield, near Wigan, in England, on 12 March 1898 to Irish-immigrant couple Mary O'Shaughnessy (née O'Connor) and her coal-miner husband Dennis.

When World War II broke out, she was working as a governess to three children in Angers in the west of France. She made use of her ancestry and applied for a neutral Irish passport. She might have thought about returning home but that was not straightforward, due to an event from her past.

On 31 March 1920, she had given birth to a baby boy, whom she named Patrick Dennis O'Shaughnessy. There was no father's name on the birth certificate and in an Irish community – indeed, any community in the early twentieth century – it was difficult to be a single mother.

She had been working as a domestic servant at the time and there was speculation the pregnancy was the result of rape. There was a whisper, too, that the father might have been a prominent man in the town, but the end result was that Mary went – or was sent – to join her sister Hetty, who was living in Paris. Her son ultimately stayed with her parents and was brought up as their son. Although almost two decades had passed – and her son was now old enough to enlist himself – it may still have been socially awkward for her to return. So she stayed.

As for her son, Patrick Dennis O'Shaughnessy ended up in a POW camp during the war. Mary, however, did not know of his wartime fate when she began to work for the Resistance.

Her involvement came about by chance. A doctor she knew asked her to visit wounded servicemen in one of the city's hospitals. During one of those visits, she met RAF sergeant, E.G. Hillyard, who had been shot down near Chartres in France on 14 June 1940. He had been taken by French ambulance to Le Mans and then hospitalised in Angers where he had his right arm amputated. There is something very poignant in knowing that a woman who had lived all of her life without her left arm visited a man who had just lost one of his, although we do not know if they ever spoke of it.

Sgt Hillyard did, however, recall Mary's visits in his post-war deposition: 'An Irish governess, living in Angers, Miss O., [Mary O'Shaughnessy] who from August visited me in the hospital every Sunday, and a Scottish governess, Miss S. who accompanied her, brought me civilian clothes. During the 1st month of my stay at the hospital I was allowed out in the town on parole, for which I was provided with a pass, duly stamped with the date of leave.'

A few months later, when Sgt Hillyard was told that he was fit enough to go to a German POW camp, he decided to try to escape.

'I decided to get away as soon as possible,' he told his superiors later. 'I altered the date on the pass and so avoided, technically, breaking my parole. On the 21st October (1940), I walked out of the hospital in civilian clothes and met the Irish governess at a rendez-vous in the town. That evening I took the bus to B. where Miss S. lived and with whom I stayed until the morning of the 23rd October, when I returned to Angers.

'Miss O. [O'Shaughnessy] then hid me in the attic of her employers' house for a week. The latter were quite unaware of what was going on, and were on the best of terms with the Germans.'

Another document suggests that Mary's employers' house had been requisitioned by the Gestapo as their headquarters, but the address given is unclear. It is not beyond the bounds of belief that Mary hid the escaping sergeant right under the Germans' noses. In any event, it was a huge risk to hide him at her then address, number 8 bis Boulevard Foch.

Sgt Hillyard got out of Angers a week later, on 31 October 1940, and drew on several other resistance helpers to make his way to Marseille, then Madrid and eventually back to England through Gibraltar.

Mary went on to help many other servicemen, she said after the war. In fact, through the columns of a newspaper she appealed to those men, who had known her as 'Miss Mary', to come forward and offer proof of the work she had done. She had made contact with one of them in Reading, but hoped to hear from more.

Their testimony might help her to secure a better pension, she said. Her disability pension of 8 shillings a week did not go very far and she had no savings, having spent all of them buying food and clothes for servicemen from England, France and Poland.

She wasn't able to work either and didn't do so for at least eight years. As for her son, he survived the war and Mary met him a few times, though they didn't form a lasting relationship. He died in the 1970s in a work accident.

After those eight years of unemployment, her life took a turn in another direction. She got another job as a family governess and moved with her employers to Kenya in 1953 while the Mau Mau revolt against the British authorities was gathering pace.

Despite the political unrest, Mary stayed on and did several jobs in Nairobi – school assistant, housekeeper, matron – but still kept up her fight for some kind of compensation.

In 1964, British Labour MP Barbara Castle wrote to Duncan Sandys, secretary of state for the Colonies, saying that Mary O'Shaughnessy felt she was entitled to compensation from the German government for injuries suffered at the hands of the Nazis.

Another document outlined what Mary had lost – 'everything that she possessed in France, all clothing, books, personal effects, the jewellery left to her by her mother'. It also said that she had used all her money – a sum of about £1,000 – paying bribes to Frenchmen to help her escapees.

Her health never recovered either. She had a lifetime of back trouble from the beatings. She had several operations on her nose after it was broken so many years before. There were big dental bills too, the result of losing so many teeth.

By then, she had settled into a relatively happy retirement when she went to work with (or for – it was never really clear) Anne Spoerry, a French 'flying doctor' who flew all over Kenya delivering medical aid to over one million patients.

Anne, like Mary, had been in the Resistance in France and was later imprisoned in Ravensbrück. She, however, hid a much darker past. While in the camp, she was assigned to work with TB patients and 'lunatics' at Block 10 and was later accused of being complicit in war crimes.

The two women never broached the subject of the war or the camp and seem to have spent a happy seven years in one another's company. Mary, if she was remembered at all in Africa, was described as a woman who preferred to fade into the background. 'This fastidiously dressed woman spoke with precision, husbanding words, economizing emotions, easy with silence,' John Heminway wrote of her in his biography of Anne Spoerry.

Yet Mary O'Shaughnessy continued to be proud of her own resistance work. When a reunion of Ravensbrück survivors was organised in London in 1973, she went. Anne Spoerry paid for her ticket. While there, she took ill suddenly and died on 11 September, surrounded by the women who knew exactly what she had suffered.

As one of them said: 'Ravensbrück made us passive beasts, corpses or it made us superhuman.'

Mary O'Shaughnessy's work and extraordinary resilience were not forgotten. The Royal Air Forces Escaping Society enrolled her as an honorary member. Her nephew Denis O'Shaughnessy, who had arranged her funeral when she died in 1973, wrote a tribute to her in 2003. It was posted on the BBC's archive of war memories. 'I consider [her] to be one of the many unsung heroines of World War Two,' he wrote.

In turn, his son Jamie O'Shaughnessy has continued to gather information and speak about his great-aunt's courage. 'I feel proud to have had a civilian family member who helped with the Resistance. More so, to have survived the horrors of a concentration camp. And as a woman. For such a normal person to do this, it's heroic. I do think it's important for people to hear these stories. Many sacrificed a lot for us all to be where we are. Perhaps if we were more mindful of how we got here, the actions people took and sacrifices, maybe we'd have a better world and behave better to each other,' he said.

Babs Hennessy, a retired government officer from Ashton, founded the Mary O'Shaughnessy Society after she began researching Mary's life. A bench in Mary's honour was unveiled at Ashton's Jubilee Park in 2022.

Mary O'Shaughnessy leaves behind a considerable legacy, not least for the descendants of those servicemen she helped to save. Her testimony at the Hamburg Ravensbrück war crimes trial helped lead to the conviction of all 16 camp personnel on charges of killing and ill-treating Allied nationals. One of the accused died during the trial and the other 15 were sentenced to death and were later executed.

After the war, Mary O'Shaughnessy wanted to write a book about her experiences, but the public was weary of war stories. They wanted good news and upbeat tales to help them forget. A Fleet Street journalist told Mary as much and she abandoned the idea.

She might never have written down her story in book form, but her testimony lives on – and it continues to shed light on the fate of other forgotten women. There is one overlooked line in her war-crime trial transcript that reveals a little more information about the fate of an Irishwoman and fellow *résistante*.

Mary told the war trial in Hamburg about six or seven women who had died or were murdered in the camps, but she gave this description of a death that went unreported at the time. She said: 'One that I saw myself died through illness. She was an Irish governess that had been taken in Brussels.'

Mary O'Shaughnessy was referring to Catherine Crean. Mary witnessed the Dublin woman's death but her reference to it is coming to light only now, almost eight decades later. It's another tiny piece of evidence that helps build a more complete picture of the forgotten women of Ravensbrück.

IN THEIR FOOTSTEPS

16

Pugna Quin Percutias
(To fight without weapons)

'THE GUIDE WAS NERVOUS AND ILL AT EASE. HE REPEAT-
EDLY HISSED AT US TO BE SILENT OR TO HURRY.'
GEORGE MILLAR.

The Pyrenees, June 2023: It feels as if the whole world has contracted to this single stretch of mountain path: the scree underfoot, the guide up ahead, the hiking pole held in an ever-tightening fist. It's not yet dark and it's early summer, yet the going is challenging. Each step demands concentration. And effort.

In truth, the stakes are very low. There might be a twisted ankle. Or an unscheduled stop to sip from a water bottle in our well-stocked backpacks. Maybe someone will lag behind to sneak a selfie against the magnificent view. This, after all, is a recreational trek, even if we are commemorating those who passed this way before us during World War II. Their experience could not have been more different: they were, literally, fleeing for their lives.

They were Allied servicemen, Jewish people, anti-fascists and persecuted civilians, many of them already exhausted after spending weeks, more likely months, on the run. They had the wrong clothes and the wrong shoes as they stumbled, in the dark, through raging rivers and over rocks on treacherous mountain paths.

They were often cold and hungry and in constant danger of injury, arrest or betrayal. Many of them didn't make it.

Some spoke of the unimaginable difficulty of leaving behind comrades too ill or too weary to go on. To slow down would put the entire party at risk.

George Millar, a British soldier and journalist, was making his third, and ultimately successful, attempt to cross the Pyrenees into Spain when an American airman he had nicknamed Gable – after the film star Clark Gable – collapsed from exhaustion.

They tried everything they could think of to revive him: '... praise, vilification, encouragement, massage, wine from the Spaniard's skin, alcohol from Fritz's little bottle. The big man would not move. Tears oozed from his eyes,' Millar later wrote in his memoir *Horned Pigeon*.

'The guide was nervous and ill at ease. He repeatedly hissed at us to be silent or to hurry,' Millar continued, giving a sense of the urgency to press on before being discovered on the secret escape route.

A gallant Gable said he would stay behind and continue when his legs recovered. He did stay behind but another American stayed with him. Both of them eventually made it to safety. That was the exception rather than the rule.

There are no words to describe the range of emotions those men must have experienced. That thought was in our minds as we headed out from St-Jean-de-Luz in the French Basque Country to cross the border to Bera in Navarre in northern Spain.

We recalled the Irish airmen who made this journey too.

Many of them had already been through terrible ordeals before they even got this far.

Edward Kinsella (b. 1917), an RAF radio operator and machine gunner from Arklow, Co. Wicklow, was shot down over France on 16 August 1943. The plane landed in a field of wheat at Campagne-lès-Hesdin, in north-west France, and burst into flames. As he made his way towards the wreckage to help the fellow members of Bomber Command 88 Squadron, he saw Germans coming in his direction. He took off as fast as he could in the direction of a wood.

When they opened fire, he shot back with a revolver but kept running. As soon as he reached the wood, he climbed into the first tree he saw.

Five minutes later, the Germans passed beneath his hiding place, but they did not see him. When they had gone, Kinsella released a pigeon he had with him, but without a message. RAF bombers routinely brought carrier pigeons with them. They acted as an early form of GPS. In some cases, when a pigeon returned to England, even without a message, it prompted the RAF to initiate rescue operations.

Two of Kinsella's colleagues were killed and one was captured. He was injured, but kept going. He found a place to sleep near a farm and when he woke up an old man was beside him. The man not only helped him but put him in touch with other people willing to help.

His injuries – to the head, hand and leg – were bandaged. He was given civilian clothes, false identity papers and 'plenty of tobacco and cognac'. He was hidden and fed and transported – by covered cart, bicycle, tram and train – by members of the Comet escape line.

It took him five weeks to make his way through France, from Paris to Bordeaux, then to Bayonne and lastly St-Jean-de-Luz before he finally crossed the Pyrenees. The journey took 10 hours due to heavy rain. He made his way to San Sebastian, Madrid and Gibraltar. He left for England on 5 October 1943.

Other Irish airmen made it to St-Jean-de-Luz, the starting point for so many evaders, under similarly dangerous conditions.

Alfred Martin's plane also burst into flames after it was shot down over France a few months before, in April 1943. He was returning from a mission in the then Czechoslovakia with Bomber Command 102 Squadron. He walked for hours and then fell asleep under a bush. He was woken by a cow and then met a boy who recognised his uniform.

The boy brought the RAF bomber from Belfast home. His parents fed him and gave him clothes. He escaped over the Pyrenees on 5 June 1943.

Sgt Richard Irwin (22), an RAF machine gunner from Cork city, was the only one of his crew to escape when his plane was shot down on the night of 12 June 1944 during a mission to attack rail installations at Cambrai in northern France.

Dozens of people lodged and fed him and helped him to make his way along the Comet Line to safety. The same was true for Robert 'Bob' Clarke, an RAF gunner from Derry, and John Patrick Finn, a gunner with Bomber Command 466 Squadron, who were both helped by the Comet Line.

Each man's story is different but they all had one thing in common – none of them would have made it to freedom without the helpers of the escape lines.

It's a point made in *Unspoken*, a book by Tom McGrath, whose father would not be alive without them. Tom McGrath

Senior, a British Army conscript from Waterford, passed through St-Jean-de-Luz in 1942 on the last leg of a perilous journey after his escape from Stalag XXA POW camp in Poland. It took him nine months to travel through Germany and France before he arrived at the foot of the Pyrenees.

When the story came to light many decades later, the newspapers labelled Tom Snr a war hero. It's an accolade that probably would have embarrassed him, Tom Jr said in 2023, as he retraced his father's journey through the Pyrenees.

'If he were here with us this evening, I think he would be shuffling somewhat uncomfortably and he might put up his hand and say, "I was just a young man caught up in a war not of my making. All I was trying to do was to get home to see my family. I am not the hero, the heroes are those brave men and women of the SOE and the Resistance who put their lives and their families' lives on the line every day to help people like me. Starting with that old Polish man who I came across in the woods in Poland, who hid me in his attic, to people like Florentino and Martin from Hernani, who led so many to safety over the Pyrenees. They are the real heroes."'

Florentino Goikoetxea was a legendary Basque guide who led hundreds of evaders over the mountains in all weathers.

As we stood at the Loidi monument to local wartime escape line guides near Hernani, his great-grand niece, 16-year-old Enara (Aierbe) had this to say of him: 'My great grand-uncle was born 200 metres from here at Altzueta farmhouse. Everyone who knew him emphasised his loyalty and honesty. With his help, a total of 227 airmen crossed the Bidasoa river.'

As we walked towards Ibardin Pass and down towards Bera in Navarre, the beauty of the scenery, with its magnificent trees and furze bushes grabbed our attention. It was almost impossible to imagine walking here in the dark and in single file as evaders were ordered to do.

'Can you imagine how tiring and frightening it must have been to constantly look over your shoulder and watch out for German patrols or wild animals?' as Tom McGrath's grandson Eric put it on a trip here in 2018. 'The cold, the ice, the lack of appropriate clothing, the shrapnel wound on his leg and, worst of all, the emotional drain of not being able to mentally switch off. Always thinking of what ditch to jump into if needed, or what fields to cross without farmers noticing.'

It is hard to imagine, too, that this escape line was co-founded by a 24-year-old Belgium woman, Andrée 'Dedée' de Jongh, who made the journey over the Pyrenees several times herself. The Comet Line helped more Allied airmen to escape than any other. It is estimated it brought in excess of 800 people to safety.

For each person saved, several people's lives were put at risk. There were about 1,000 helpers along the route which started in Belgium and sent 'packages', as they called evaders and escapers, down the escape line through France and onto Spain. According to one estimate, after joining the network, helpers were usually arrested within three months.

Andrée de Jongh was arrested as she made her 33rd crossing into Spain with downed airmen. She was sent to a concentration camp where, we now know, she had contact with Irish résistante Catherine Crean.

In 2009, Andrée Dumon (alias Nadine) retraced the footsteps of the many airmen she helped to guide to safety from her base in Brussels. She worked with her namesake, Andrée de Jongh. She was determined to speak of another former colleague who was not so well known: Catherine Crean.

She should never be forgotten, she said.

As she sat in the Hôtel de La Poste in St-Jean-de-Luz, she was overcome with emotion as she recalled the woman she later saw close to death at Ravensbrück concentration camp.

The Comet Line helpers, she said, were more than soldiers. They had not formally enlisted and they were not paid, but they chose to extend the hand of friendship to another human being in danger. And they did so without violence. The escape line's motto was *Pugna Quin Percutias* (fight without weapons).

She had not forgotten Catherine Crean, she said, as if she were passing on the baton of remembrance to other *footsteps-travellers*, to coin a phrase, walking the freedom trails.

The encounter was the genesis of this book. It also inspired the formation of the Basque Pyrenees Freedom Trails' Association in 2015, a not-for-profit organisation dedicated to recovering the memory of all Basque escape lines on both sides of the Pyrenees.

The organisation remembers the rescue of evaders, but also the price paid by members of escape lines, many of whom died or were imprisoned in concentration camps.

A Travelling Companion

September 2023: It was time to set out for the Basque Country again, but this time we had company.

We had known of our travelling companion for some time, but we didn't know her well. It was going to be a privilege to spend time with her in a place where she had such an influence. We settled into our seats for take-off. Our fellow traveller had a loftier perch in the compartment overhead. Catherine Crean, the courageous helper on the Comet Line who lost her life in Ravensbrück in 1945, was accompanying us in the form of a photograph.

To the best of our knowledge, Catherine had never travelled from her wartime base in Brussels down through France to the Basque Pyrenees as so many of the aviators she helped had done.

We were heading to the Basque Country to pay tribute to those who risked their lives to rescue evaders, among them the Comet Line helpers, including Catherine.

She had proved elusive for so long. A search for her image proved fruitless for many years but then we discovered one in an archive in Belgium. It was attached to a wartime identity card. We now had details of where and when Catherine Crean was born in Dublin.

The photo showed a woman with a kind face and warm but determined eyes. Why had she left Moore Street to work in Brussels? To find a better life, like so many emigrants, we supposed.

Why, then, had she decided to take part in resistance against the Nazis during the war? She must have known the dangers. That was a much harder question to answer. Whatever the reason, she paid the ultimate price.

What would she have thought of the Basque Pyrenees, so cold and unforgiving during the winters of World War II, and now so welcoming and emblematic of freedom?

She hadn't lived to witness their beauty, but at least now she would cross the Pyrenees with us, walking in the footsteps of all the evaders whose freedom she had secured.

They say you die twice. The first time when you stop breathing, and a second time when somebody says your name for the last time. We will say the name Catherine Crean for a long time to come. And we hope that her name, and the names of all the Irish people who joined the Resistance in World War II, will live on through you, the readers of this book.

Roll of Honour

Irish people in the Resistance during World War II risked, and in some cases lost, their lives for freedom. They worked in the shadows – necessarily – which means that, very often, they left little trace of their work. The preceding chapters tell the stories of lesser-known *résistants* whose astonishing achievements were pieced together from their own accounts, those of others and archived documents, some of them recently declassified.

There were others who have already been written about in detail, and many more still whose actions are part-revealed in the fragmentary available sources. This Roll of Honour is designed to recognise all of those people – those with big profiles and those with none. It is also a call-out to people everywhere to record the stories of the unassuming war heroes in their wider families before it is too late.

Helping Allied Soldiers

BRIDGET BOLGER

Wexford-born Bridget Chevallier (née Bolger) paid a very heavy price for helping British airman Olaf/Fred Hansen as he passed through Paris before making it safely back to England along the Shelburn escape line in Brittany. All she had done was give the man some food as he laid low in an apartment upstairs from hers at 15 rue Montrosier in Neuilly-sur-Seine just outside Paris.

Her neighbour Marie Mazillier, a general's widow, had taken an enormous risk in sheltering the RAF man in her flat on the fourth floor, but it would prove to be just as dangerous to give food to the evader over a number of weeks from December 1943 to January 1944.

By then, Bridget Bolger had already been in Paris for several decades. Born in Ballyroe, Co. Wexford, on 27 February 1889, Bridget (Bride or Bid) worked in England as a servant in her twenties before moving to Paris. There, she met Frenchman Jean Chevallier and married him in February 1913. Just before World War II, they were both working in hotels: Jean (possibly as a porter) at the five-star Prince des Galles on Ave George V, off the Champs-Élysées, and Bridget as a massage therapist at the upmarket hotel and spa, Le Mathurin, on the rue des Mathurins in the eighth arrondissement. Both hotels are still there today.

It is not clear how Bridget, or Brigitte (she adopted the French spelling of her name), and her husband got involved in resistance activity, but it appears it was through her neighbour, Mme Mazillier, who regularly helped airmen. Mme Mazillier was arrested by the Gestapo at Dijon in February 1944 while helping another aviator to escape. Three weeks after Hansen left their Paris apartment block, the Germans also arrested Bridget and her husband. She was released two days later, but her husband was deported to a concentration camp in Germany and died there in 1945.

We know of the couple's bravery because Brigitte was later compensated by the American and British governments. In February 1946, Capt. Mayeaux, of the American office in Paris, wrote to say that she was to receive compensation of £500 (worth about €20,000 today) 'in recognition of the great service rendered to the Allied cause by M Chevalier, a generous act for which he paid the supreme sacrifice'.

The couple were also awarded Eisenhower certificates by the American government 'to express… the gratitude and appreciation of the American people for gallant service in assisting the escape of Allied soldiers from the enemy'.

The next official reference to Brigitte Chevalier is her death certificate, unearthed by her Dublin-based grand-nephew, Thomas Bolger. It says that she died on 19 April 1952. She was still living at the same address but, as her grand-nephew poignantly points out, the fact that the exact time of her death was not known suggests she was probably on her own. The couple didn't have any children.

OLGA BAUDOT DE ROUVILLE

Olga Baudot de Rouville, teacher, Red Cross nurse and *résistante*, spoke English with such a strong Irish accent that people thought she was from Ireland. She was, in fact, born in France in 1891, but to an Irish mother, Susan Walters from Newport, Tipperary. Her mother's influence meant her command of English was 'particularly distinguished', a vital skill for clandestine work.

She worked as a Red Cross nurse in World War I and nursed British troops in Lille after the Dunkirk evacuation. In 1941, she joined the Resistance, working as a courier for the Pat O'Leary evasion network. She held the rank 'lieutenant' (codename Thérèse Martin) and was second in command of the network in northern France. When she became aware that she was under Gestapo observation, she fled south.

From a new base in Marseille, she helped at least 30 British soldiers get to safety. When that network was blown, she moved to Toulouse to continue her resistance work.

She received the Croix de Guerre with bronze star for her courage. In its citation, the French Ministry of Defence described Olga as 'an ardent patriot' who was active from 4 June 1940 to July 1944.

After the war, she moved to Cumbria and, in 1947, to Ireland. According to her papers, she left 'on family business', but she was still here in the 1950s because her name appears in a court case she took in connection with land in Tipperary. She moved to Brittany at some point after that and died there, aged 87, in 1979.

AGNES FLANAGAN

We might not know of Agnes Flanagan's resistance work had she not applied for a badly needed pension after the war.

For many years, the woman born in Birr, Co. Offaly in 1909, denied she had done anything to help Allied servicemen during her time as a nursing sister with the Congregation of the Sisters of Saint Augustine at Tournai, some 90km south-west of Brussels in Belgium.

Yet, she was arrested on a charge of hiding a British POW and spent time in a Belgium prison in 1941. She was released on health grounds. The following year she was arrested again on a charge of having resistance documents. This time, she stood trial in Essen and was sent to Ravensbrück in December 1942.

She was there until the end of the war and later recalled the awful last days when she thought she was going to be sent to the gas chambers. In a letter to a family member at Easter 1946, she wrote: 'It is a dreadful time for me this Holy Week… On that Thursday last year, I was destined for the gas chamber on Good Friday morning.'

Instead, she was rescued by the Swedish Red Cross and taken to Sweden. An official at the British embassy in Stockholm noted that she was very nervous, but added: 'her fellow prisoners speak of her with greatest admiration as being one of the bravest women in the camp.'

Agnes Flanagan first moved to Belgium when she was 21. She worked as a maid in Namur and later in Tournai before joining the convent in 1934. She left the convent in 1947 and married Belgian Emile Depret. The couple had one child, Rose, who died in infancy.

It was only in 1952, when Agnes was in desperate need of money, that she wrote to the State Commission on Pensions to say that she had, in fact, helped a British escapee by giving him clothes, money and a French-English dictionary. She also recalled how, in 1941, she snatched a letter from a member of the Gestapo searching her room. She tore it into little pieces.

At the time, she claimed the letter contained private details relating to a nun's moral life but later she said it contained a list of Belgian traitors which she was to send to the Allies. Her room, it was noted, was decorated with photos of Free-French leader Charles de Gaulle and British Prime Minister Winston Churchill, clearly showing where her sympathies lay.

In May 1952, Agnes Flanagan was awarded a pension from the Belgian government.

UNA GIONCADA (NÉE HALDENE)

'God inspire me to help them,' Una Gioncada (née Haldene) wrote in her diary on 27 September 1943 after meeting a group of escaped British servicemen in hiding near Milan in Italy.

'We passed the whole afternoon with the boys and I could hardly drag myself away from them. All the time in the train this morning my head was busy planning escape for them. I must do something!' she wrote.

Born in Benburb, Co. Tyrone, in 1892, Una moved to Milan after she married Italian lawyer Mario Gioncada. She recorded her reflections on the war – and the couple's dangerous work helping servicemen who had escaped from POW camps – in a diary she kept from 1941 to 1944.

On 6 November 1943, she wrote: 'We haven't gone into this business [of helping servicemen] lightly. We know it's a tremendous responsibility we're facing, but I don't see how I can risk less than the Italians who are doing so much for my countrymen [...]

'My mind was a blank with worry when suddenly I remembered an old Irishwoman who told me once when I was a child that God didn't approve of much praying, so much that once, while she was praying fervently for guidance, God said to her quite crossly, "For God's sake woman, quit praying and do it!" A clear though Irish answer.'

She went on to describe the logistical difficulties, the terror, and the excitement of helping the men get into neutral Switzerland. 'I hope you never have to organise an escape from danger – it can be thrilling, but what head work. What details have to be gone into – what possibilities to be thought out […]

'I have prepared the exact sum of money for each man for the tram […] I have studied the Milan, Como trains towards evening so that we can leave when it isn't too dark and arrive when dark. The boys have found second mothers in the women who feed, wash for them and even nurse them through serious illnesses, risking their lives every minute of the day and night in doing so.'

After the war, she spoke of her experiences on BBC radio. Her words now form part of a Dear Diary exhibition, a community outreach programme undertaken at the Public Record Office of Northern Ireland (PRONI) in 2020.

FR PATRICK KELLY

When Patrick Kelly, an Irish curate at Agen cathedral in south-west France, called to Jean Thibaut's house in May 1943, he rang the doorbell with the agreed signal. Shortly before, a man had arrived at Thibaut's house on a bicycle saying he was American Lieutenant Harry E. Roach, the navigator of a B-17 which had been shot down a week earlier.

Jean Thibaut had exhausted his English finding out that much. He needed Fr Kelly to help him establish the man's credentials before making contact with members of an escape network which brought aviators over the Pyrenees into neutral Spain.

Fr Kelly spent an hour interviewing Harry Roach and was confident that the airman was who he said he was, and not an infiltrator. The priest later told the airman's son, also named Harry Roach, that he then got in contact with his primary contact in the Resistance, a Madame Larrieu, who worked in the local post office.

By 1943, getting across the Pyrenees was much more difficult than before. As Fr Kelly later explained: 'The frontier near St Jean de Luz [was] a sieve until the Gestapo began rolling up the networks and placing men at the crossings. Up until then we had only minor difficulties in getting rid of our friends in trouble.'

Three weeks later, Lt Harry Roach made it safely across the Pyrenees. He was the forty-fourth airman to escape from France. All Fr Kelly knew about it was what he heard in the confessional after early mass one morning. He pulled open the grille to find Madame Thibaut on the other side. 'He's gone,' she said.

Lt Roach stayed on in the air force after the war, but died in an air crash in 1954 while approaching a runway in Iowa. His son later traced his last journey during World War II, making contact with Fr Kelly in 1983, who was then living at a retirement home in Banbridge, Co. Down, after a 40-year career in France.

'[Fr Kelly] was not a direct link in the escape network,' Harry Roach Jnr wrote later, 'but was instead something like a tributary creek flowing into a river, directing escapees into the mainstream when they came his way.'

Although Fr Kelly's work helping escapees didn't emerge until much later, the Irish priest found himself in the limelight in 1960 when he discovered a painting hidden behind a wardrobe in the presbytery in Mas-d'Agenais, where he was then parish priest. He moved it to the local church and became something of a celebrity when the painting was later authenticated as a lost Rembrandt.

SR KATHERINE ANNE MCCARTHY

In recent years, there have been increasing calls to honour Sr Katherine Anne McCarthy's resistance activity with a Hollywood film, a statue or some other, more sober, tribute. As a result, her work helping up to 200 Allied servicemen to get out of occupied France is widely known.

Born in Drimoleague in Co. Cork in 1895, she was 18 when she joined the Franciscan order in Cork. She took the name Sister Marie-Laurence and was transferred to Béthune, in France, where she nursed wounded soldiers during World War I.

When World War II broke out, she visited and treated Allied soldiers in POW camps and saw the need to help them further. She joined forces with two local women, mechanic Sylvette Leleu and café owner Angèle Tardiveau, to hide servicemen before their escape.

Later, they joined forces with the Musée de l'Homme, one of the earliest resistance networks established in France. Sr Kate is thought to have helped up to 200 Allied servicemen get out of occupied France.

She was arrested on 18 June 1941 and endured 'five very difficult interrogations with the Gestapo', according to her witness statement. After a year in solitary confinement, she was taken to a series of camps and prisons, according to writer Catherine Fleming. It was part of Hitler's *Nacht und Nebel* decree (Night and Fog) on 7 December of that year, which targeted the Resistance.

In some of the camps, she was reunited with friends from Béthune; the camaraderie helped all of them get through day after torturous day. The last days of captivity in Ravensbrück were particularly hellish, though, and Sr Kate was in constant fear of being sent to her death in the gas chamber. She managed to avoid selection for the gas chambers at least four times, by hiding and, on one occasion, by climbing out of a window.

'It was immensely lonely,' says Fleming. 'She had to fight with all the moral and physical strength she had left.'

When she was released in 1945, she weighed little more than four stone after years of deprivation, but she went on to make a full recovery.

After the war, France awarded her the Médaille de la Résistance and she was decorated by Britain. She moved back to Cork and went on to become mother superior at the Honan Convent in Cork. She died in 1971.

If her courage has been recognised in Ireland only in recent years, she was celebrated in France as early as 1946. As Jean Prévost wrote: 'Sr Marie-Laurence! It's a name that many in Béthune know but one that has travelled further because of her heroism. And it's a name that we say with respect mixed with admiration.'

ROME ESCAPE LINE

Monsignor Hugh O'Flaherty was the well-known linchpin of the Rome Escape Line, a network that saved the lives of some

6,500 Allied servicemen, Jewish people and fugitives in a city under German occupation from September 1943 to June 1944.

The line could not have functioned without the involvement of hundreds of people willing to hide, feed, clothe and, in some cases, nurse the fugitives.

The chapter on Delia Murphy Kiernan mentions a number of the Irish priests involved, but there were others. Fr John Claffey, from Westmeath, and Fr Vincent Treacy from Galway, were both members of the Congregation of the Priests of St Mary; new escapees often passed through their living quarters before being moved elsewhere.

When Augustinian priest Fr Kenneth Madden first asked Monsignor O'Flaherty to help an escaped British POW, he had no idea of the work the monsignor was doing. He soon got involved, as did Fr Lenan and Fr Ben Forsythe from Fermoy.

Irish nuns were involved in the network too. Sr Noreen Dennehy from Kerry worked as a courier for the Rome Escape Line, delivering messages for the Monsignor. She and her fellow Irish Franciscan Missionary Sisters also hid, fed and clothed hundreds of Jewish women and children, keeping about 30 or 40 at a time. A notice on the convent door said the nuns were neutral and, remarkably, they were left alone.

Helping Jews

HUBERT BUTLER

In 1938, essayist and humanitarian Hubert Butler and his wife Peggy Guthrie travelled to Vienna in Austria to see how they could personally help the Jewish population at risk from Nazi persecution. Butler had been to the Evian Conference in

France that year and realised, with horror, how little action the delegates gathered from 32 countries were taking to ease the unfolding refugee crisis. He was particularly critical of his own country, Ireland, which, during the course of the Nazi period, admitted very few refugees.

Even Robert Briscoe – a man who had fought in the Irish War of Independence and was an elected Fianna Fáil TD – was unable to persuade official Ireland to admit his Jewish aunt and her family. His aunt Hedwig Kudesch-Salomon and her husband, Adolph, were later murdered in Auschwitz.

Hubert Butler, however, acted on his own initiative and worked with the American Quakers in Vienna to secure exit visas for those at risk. Some of them stayed briefly in Ireland, but they were very often forced to seek shelter in other countries. During his time working with the Quaker International Centre, over 2,400 Jews got visas to leave Austria.

Among those were Erwin Strunz, his Jewish wife, Lisl, and their two sons, Peter and George. Thanks to Butler and his wife, they spent three months at her home place in Annaghmakerrig, Co. Monaghan (now the Tyrone Guthrie Centre) before staying for a time in Ardmore, Waterford, with other refugees.

'It saved our lives that we had the good fortune to meet Hubert Butler, the Kilkenny writer, in the International Quaker Centre in Vienna,' Erwin Strunz later said.

An order had been issued for Strunz's deportation and he was brought to safety with just hours to spare. The couple later opened the Unicorn restaurant in Dublin in 1941, and Lisl wrote a Viennese cooking column for the *Cork Examiner*. Many years later, a letter writer to *The Irish Times*, D.K. Henderson, described how Erwin had been 'incandescent with rage' when the German ambassador to Ireland, Edouard Hempel, and people from the German legation visited the restaurant.

As Henderson wrote: 'Erwin sprinkled salt liberally over all the meals. Hempel took one mouthful, and nearly choked. As one, the party of Germans got up and walked out... In those days of worldwide political uncertainty, I think it was an incredibly brave act of defiance on the part of Erwin Strunz.'

MARY ELMES

A pencil-written document describes how Mary Elmes, a Cork-born scholar and aid worker, 'spirited away' nine children when some 400 Jewish people were being loaded onto the first convoy leaving Rivesaltes holding camp in south-west France en route to Auschwitz on 11 August 1942.

With camp commander, David-Gustave Humbert, Mary managed to save as many as 34 children, Lindsley Noble, the Quaker director in France, wrote in a private wire communication sent securely from Vichy to the US. At the time, Mary Elmes was head of the Quaker delegation in Perpignan where she worked in the camp-villages first built to house refugees from the Spanish Civil War.

After World War II broke out, those camps began to fill with Jewish refugees. When it became clear in autumn 1942 that children and adults were being deported to Nazi concentration camps, Mary bundled a number of children into her car and drove them to safety. She had established children's homes – or colonies, as they were known – to provide temporary respite from the camp's harsh conditions. They acted as safe houses now.

As deportations continued between August and October

1942, Mary and her fellow volunteers at Rivesaltes camp saved an estimated 427 children from deportation. She also hid a Jewish family in her apartment in Perpignan.

Her work brought her to the attention of the Germans and she was arrested in 1943. She was charged with espionage, secret border crossings and disseminating propaganda against the Reich. She was sent to jail in Toulouse and then to Fresnes prison, outside Paris. The Quakers, the Red Cross and her mother in Cork mounted a relentless letter-writing campaign to have her released.

When she got out of jail six months later, she went straight back to work, and later said of her experience: 'Oh, we all had to suffer some inconveniences in those days.'

Nearly a decade after she died, aged 93 in March 2002, one of the children she saved, Professor Ronald Friend, nominated her for Israel's highest award. In 2013, she was named Righteous Among the Nations.

Another Irish woman also played a role in helping Ronald Friend and his brother Michael get to safety. Like Mary, Dubliner Una Mortished worked for the US Quakers, or the American Friends Service Committee, but in Marseille. She worked with refugees in camps, but also helped to secure travel documents. Letters in the Quaker archive show that she was also involved in the Friend case.

MARGARET KEARNEY TAYLOR

Her friends knew her as the elegant, genteel Irish lady who ran the chic Embassy Tearoom in Madrid, but Margaret Kearney Taylor's café also operated as a front to help thousands of Allied servicemen and Jewish people escape to safety.

She went to her grave without speaking of it, but details of how her café operated as a safe house for thousands of evaders came to light in 2003 when Spanish author Patricia Martínez De Vicente discovered her father Dr Eduardo Martínez Alonso's papers after his death. They revealed his part in a British intelligence-backed operation and the role Margaret's café played as the unlikely centre of an escape route operating within a stone's throw of the German embassy.

Margaret Kearney Taylor was born in a workhouse in England in the 1890s to a single parent, Ellen Taylor, who, in turn, had been born in a workhouse in Kanturk, Co. Cork, two decades before. Margaret, or Margarita as she was known, went on to become a single parent herself when her only child, Consuelo, was born in 1924. She took a successful paternity case again the father, a Spanish diplomat, so that her daughter could take his name. It was a brave and very unusual thing to do in the 1920s.

As Richard Fitzpatrick, who uncovered evidence of the case, put it: 'The legal battle was an important clue to Taylor's character and motivations.'

In 1931, she set up the Embassy Tearoom on the stylish Paseo de la Castellana in Madrid. It soon became a meeting place for diplomats and the Spanish elite, the kind of place that would never be suspected as a cover for an escape-line operation. During the war, Nazi sympathisers rubbed shoulders while taking tea in the café downstairs while servicemen and Jewish people hid in an apartment upstairs, waiting for forged papers and safe passage through Gibraltar or Lisbon.

Although born in England, Margaret's Irish roots were very important to her and she was considered Irish in her adopted home. Writer Jimmy Burns said he remembered a 'quite small, delicately framed lady with beginning- to-be-bleached hair, with very Celtic, blueish eyes' when he visited the café as a child.

'She was a mixture of reserved and focused. She ran her establishment with great discipline, great panache, in the sense that she always made her clients feel very welcome. I wouldn't say she was a snob – luckily, she had too much Irish in her for that – but she clearly had a way with the Spanish aristocracy,' he said.

It's not clear how many people Margaret Kearney helped – some estimates say thousands – but one of them, Benjamin Hirsch, later described how it felt to be free, and safe, for the first time after three years on the run:

'One afternoon, I was walking along the beach of Lisbon (and Lisbon is just one long beach...) and all of a sudden I had this shoulder-shrugging experience... And I realised that... I was walking along the beach with nobody else. No need, no feeling of a need to look at either side of me. I felt I just didn't need that. I was free for the first time in my life. I felt freedom from fear.'

SR AGNES WALSH

Sr Agnes Walsh, a religious sister with the Daughters of Charity, was holding an Irish passport when she helped to save a Jewish family from deportation during the war.

Born Ada Vallinda Walsh in Hull, England, she acquired an Irish passport while serving in a convent in Ireland and kept it when she moved to the Saint Vincent-de-Paul convent at Cadouin, in the Dordogne region of France.

In December 1943, a Jewish man Pierre Cremieux asked the nuns to shelter him and his family. Sr Agnes pleaded with her superior, Sr Louise, to hide the man, his wife, infant twins and seven-year-old son, Alain.

The family were introduced as relatives of the mother superior and stayed in the convent until the country was liberated. After the war, the children kept in touch with Sister Agnes. Testimony from the twins, Jean-Pierre and Collette Cremieux, led to her being named Righteous Among the Nations in 1990, Israel's highest award given to non-Jews who risked their lives to save Jewish people during World War II. She died three years later, aged 93.

Special Agents

WILLIAM CUNNINGHAM/PAUL DE BONO

William Cunningham was born in 1911 in Kimmage, Dublin, to Mary and Thaddeus Cunningham. He worked as a journalist in Paris in the 1930s until he joined the French Foreign Legion in 1933. He was stranded in Dunkirk in 1940, but was evacuated to England where he was recruited by the SOE.

He was parachuted back into France to work as a saboteur under the codename Paul de Bono. On 18 August 1943, he and two other agents were dropped west of Toulouse to sabotage a number of tanneries in Mazamat. Dressmaker, as the mission was called, was a disaster. The targeted factories were no longer operating and the agents eventually made their way into Spain and back to Britain.

The team leader, SOE agent J.G. Larcher, later said the three men had landed without Tommy cookers. It meant they couldn't make tea or boil water and they were violently ill after drinking bad water. That was the least of it. Larcher said the team should have been given aerial photographs and up-to-date information about the targets.

His superiors, however, were less than impressed. This harsh assessment was written in pencil under the report: 'A thoroughly unconvincing report. No effort was made to do the job. We must get rid of Larcher at once. Criticism, sheer nonsense.'

There was no mention of William Cunningham or whether he completed another mission. After the war, he went to live in Britain, according to historian David Murphy.

CAPT. CONAL O'DONNELL

Conal O'Donnell, from Gurteen, Co. Sligo, was parachuted into occupied Greece in October 1943 to help build airstrips to land weapons and supplies for use by the Greek Resistance.

A captain with the Royal Engineers, the 28 year old was a British Liaison Officer with the SOE Middle East branch, known as Force 133.

'His mission,' his son Conal O'Donnell recalls, 'was to discover and construct isolated mountain airstrips which could be used to receive arms supplies for the Greek Resistance in the Peloponnese. It was also intended to build landing grounds from which Allied fighter bombers could harry the Germans once the invasion was underway.'

Capt. O'Donnell had hardly begun his work when he got caught up in the German army's brutal reprisal for the execution of 78 German soldiers by Greek resistance fighters some months earlier. On 13 December 1943, the Germans massacred the entire male population – 496 men and boys – of Kalavryta, a mountainous town in the Peloponnese.

Capt. O'Donnell and his party heard the gunfire as they made their way to Helmos mountain, some ten hours away. The captain managed to send this message to the SOE headquarters in Cairo: 'Kalavryta occupied by Germans burned... Guides were forced to bury remains afterwards shot. Population desolate no clothes or houses for winter.'

He later went to the town and helped the survivors. 'The wailing of women was unbearable,' was all he said of an atrocity that stayed with him for the rest of his life. He suggested to his superiors that relief drops to Kalavryta should take priority over the supplies of arms.

Over the following months, Capt. O'Donnell continued to work with a radio operator, an interpreter and, sometimes, armed partisan guards trying to find suitable locations for airstrips. It was hard, frustrating and dangerous work. At one point, he was abducted by Greek Communist guerrillas, but managed to escape. He succeeded in setting up a number of airstrips before being withdrawn in June 1944.

After 'four months continuous march, irregular meals and often the lack of them, I had scabies, boils, discharging ears and indigestion,' he wrote in a debriefing report. He had a few months to recover before he was parachuted back into Greece on 19 September to prepare for Operation Manna, a British operation to retake the country, in early October. 'I consider myself one of the luckiest of the mission officers as I had a front seat from beginning to end of the liberation of good old Greece, which we all so loved to moan about,' he wrote.

Air power was the major factor in harrying the Germans out of Greece. In 1945, Capt. O' Donnell was awarded the

MBE. The citation mentioned his 'outstanding initiative and ingenuity in preparing airfields', going on to conclude that 'the speed with which the RAF was able to establish itself [in Greece] was entirely due to his untiring efforts'.

When Conal O'Donnell died in 1996, his family discovered that every year, on the anniversary of the Kalavryta massacre in December, he paid for a Requiem Mass to be said for the town's people.

'He felt strongly that Kalavryta, and the suffering of the Greeks generally, wasn't widely enough recognised outside Greece,' his son, also Conal O'Donnell, said. His son hopes that by telling his father's story it will highlight the contribution made by the tens of thousands of Catholic Irishmen who volunteered to fight, even though their country was neutral.

ERICA O'DONNELL

Erica O'Donnell had the kind of education that gave her perfect credentials for intelligence work. She was born in Dublin in 1920 to Mary Mabel Elizabeth (née Dunbar) of Cork and Ceylon (now Sri Lanka) and Eric Hugh O'Donnell, of Dublin and Limerick, and went on to study art history in Paris and Salzburg. She also travelled around Germany. That not only honed her command of French and German, but gave her a good knowledge of Europe.

When war broke out, she returned to Britain and got a job with the BBC's overseas service in England. She was recruited by the SOE in 1942 and completed an officer's course. When she was in line for promotion, one of her superiors noted: 'She shows confidence. Is inclined to be headstrong and knows it. Her initiative needs controlling.'

It was acknowledged, however, that she was already carrying out much useful work and had the capabilities for further training.

She worked in the SOE's Czech section, overseeing the training of Czech agents. Later, she was transferred to F Section where she worked at the headquarters of the French Forces of the Interior in Paris as the country was being liberated.

Her personnel file does not contain a photograph, but it has this description: 'She was 5ft 3, had red hair, green eyes and a fair complexion.'

Erica O'Donnell left the service in 1945 to take up a post with the Red Cross, helping concentration camp survivors. She returned to her first love, the history of art, and set up the Study Centre for the History of the Fine and Decorative Arts in 1964 in London. In 1990, she was awarded an MBE for services to the decorative arts.

MICHAEL TROTOBAS

Michael Trotobas was born on 20 May 1914, in the UK, to a French father and an Irish mother, Agnes Whelan. In 1926, Michael moved to Dublin to attend school for two years at the Catholic University School on Leeson Street. During that time, he stayed with his mother's family.

He joined the British Army in 1933 and in 1939 he was sent to France with the British Expeditionary Force. He was wounded during the evacuation from Dunkirk and was commended for bravery.

He displayed leadership qualities and, with his French-language skills, he joined the SOE in 1941.

He set up and led the SOE Farmer network in northern

France. The network's activities included sabotage, intelligence gathering, escape-line activities and operating several parachute landing grounds. He was also in charge of over 800 *résistants*.

He was described as 'an accomplished organiser, an audacious saboteur, and an inspirational leader'.

In November 1943, aged 29, he was betrayed by a member of his group and was killed in a gun battle with Nazi forces near Lille in France.

Radio Operator

ROBERT VERNON

Robert Vernon was born in Dublin in 1912 to Edward Kingston Vernon, the last of the line of Vernons associated with Clontarf and its castle. The eldest and only son, Robert Edward Kingston Vernon, to give him his full title, was a painter living in southern France when the war broke out. He trained as a radio operator with a resistance movement called Alliance in Marseille and worked throughout the region.

He was arrested in February 1943, imprisoned in France and later deported to a concentration camp that was so brutal the prisoners called it the 'torture hell of Sonnenberg'.

There was some hope for Robert Vernon, though. In 1944, the Irish minister to Berlin, Con Cremin, succeeded in delaying his death sentence. There were also tentative discussions between Dublin and Berlin about a prisoner exchange. Under its terms, Vernon and two other Irish prisoners, Robert Armstrong and Mary Cummins, were to be released in exchange for German political prisoners held in Ireland. But the talks came to nothing.

Robert Vernon might have survived the war had it not been for the massacre of 30 January 1945 when an SS execution committee murdered over 800 prisoners in Sonnenberg prison, including him. There were only four survivors, who were liberated by the Russian army just two days later

Codebreakers

(CONEL) HUGH (O'DONEL) ALEXANDER

The significance of (Conel) Hugh (O'Donel) Alexander's contribution to codebreaking during World War II is captured in this succinct summary once displayed in the 'Hall of Fame' at the Bletchley Park mansion:

'Hugh Alexander was an outstanding chess-player, and he was also amongst the greatest of British cryptographers. When he arrived at Bletchley Park in early 1940 he had no previous experience at codebreaking, but in Hut 6, and then Hut 8, he soon became adept at using both traditional and machine-based methods for breaking Enigma. He led the Naval Enigma team in Hut 8 from 1942, and ended the war on Japanese codes.'

The man who went on to become one of the greatest cryptographers in Britain was born in Cork on 19 April 1909 to Hilda Barbara Bennett and Conel William Long Alexander. His father, originally from Donegal, was a professor of engineering at University College Cork. When Hugh was 11 his father died and the family moved back to his mother's native Birmingham.

There, he went to King Edward's School and, like so many other codebreaking recruits, had a distinguished academic career. He won a scholarship to study mathematics at King's College in Cambridge and graduated with first-class honours in 1931.

A friend recruited him to Bletchley Park, where he would go on to become deputy to Alan Turing at Hut 8. He became acting head in November 1942 when Turing left on a visit to the United States.

'If the theoretical ideas for breaking Naval Enigma largely stemmed from Turing, it was Alexander who led the team to practical success, in particular in breaking the German Atlantic key, Dolphin, in the summer of 1941 and by breaking the U-boat key, Shark, in December 1942,' his Bletchley Park biography notes. (Naval Enigma signals used different ciphers, each with its own daily key.)

He was remembered there as an inspiring, popular leader with his endless enthusiasm and energy: 'He certainly ran one of the best organised and productive teams at Bletchley Park, despite his own untidy ways. He had phenomenal powers of concentration, and habitually worked very long hours,' according to his entry on the 'Hall of Fame'.

After the war, he continued to work in cryptanalysis at GCHQ until 1971. He then joined the British diplomatic service. He continued to play chess, too, taking on some of the world's best players and earning the title of international master.

JOHN JAMES DOHERTY

John James Doherty was born in Letterkenny, Co. Donegal, and was recruited as a cryptanalyst and linguist after qualifying from the University of Birmingham.

His son, Dr John Doherty, believes he may have been the only recruit from an Irish-speaking family, and noted wryly: 'While his German, French, Italian, Spanish, Polish, Russian,

Latin and Greek were fully utilised, my father never disclosed whether his knowledge of Irish helped in Hitler's defeat.'

SHEILA DUNLOP / LADY KILLANIN

In 1940, Sheila Dunlop, of India and Galway, went to work at Hut 6 at Bletchley Park, where cryptanalysts worked to decode German army and air force ciphers. Like so many others, she never spoke about her work other than to say that she worked in the post room. She was, in fact, head of the registration room where incoming messages were sorted. She was later awarded an MBE for her work.

'A colleague remembers Lady Killanin [she later married Michael Morris, 3rd Baron Killanin in 1945] as very efficient, coping calmly with every crisis; her desk was never untidy and despite the war shortages, she was "always so elegant",' her obituary in 2007 noted.

In later life, she was vice chair and a two-time president of the Irish Society for the Prevention of Cruelty to Children.

KATHLEEN FERGUSON (CUTHBERT)

Kathleen Ferguson was asked to join the staff at Bletchley Park after she graduated with a degree in French and German from Queen's University Belfast in 1942. She was assigned to work as a translator in the naval section and, during her year at the war station, took a course in Japanese.

Born in 1920 to Sara (née Foster) and James Ferguson at Ballyvoy near Doagh in Co. Antrim, she excelled at Londonderry High School for Girls and won a double scholarship to study at Queen's University. There, she won a number of prizes and later completed a Master's degree on the maritime vocabulary in a German poem – subjects influenced, perhaps, by her time at Bletchley Park.

She married Norman Cuthbert in 1943 and moved back to Northern Ireland. She returned to her alma mater to work as a tutor in the French department and maintained her interest in languages. She took classes in Irish later in life and took an interest in the local languages of the 40-plus countries she visited. In her seventies, she qualified as an Advanced Motorist and took part as navigator in the 'Monte Carlo Dash', a women-only rally driving race.

She never spoke of her time at Bletchley Park, but her contribution was acknowledged in 2016 when she was awarded a medal and certificate by Prime Minister David Cameron.

'Extraordinary, clever, talented and game to the last,' her grandson James Caundle King wrote in an appreciation.

EILEEN (LESLIE) GREER

Eileen Greer (née Tyrrell) graduated with a first-class degree in German from Trinity College Dublin and was lecturing in the subject at Queen's University in Belfast when the war broke out.

'It occurred to me that there was the war going on and it seemed to me that the war was more serious than teaching German,' she said later, explaining her decision to put her linguistic expertise at the disposal of the British government.

She was assigned to Hut 3 at Bletchley Park where she worked as 'temporary senior assistant officer', using her linguistic skills to decrypt German army and air force signals.

'The work was, on the whole, boring,' she said in her nineties. 'Some of the information was unimportant. But some was very important. We had one or two things come in that really got us all on our seats, [for instance] when something happened that showed the Germans were deciding to start something with Russia, everybody got excited.'

After the war, she continued to work with the Foreign Office and travelled extensively (working in Germany, Spain, Uruguay and Brazil) and was awarded an MBE for her work. Aged 98, her contribution to the codebreaking work at Bletchley Park was acknowledged when she was presented with a medal, a Bletchley Park commemorative badge and certificate at a nursing home in Dublin.

Her relatives recalled 'a woman of remarkable wit and intelligence' when she died shortly afterwards in 2016.

RICHARD HAYES

Richard Hayes was born in 1902 in Abbeyfeale, Co. Limerick and grew up in Mayo. He won an academic scholarship to Trinity College Dublin in 1920.

He was appointed Assistant Librarian to the National Library of Ireland in 1924, eventually becoming the fifth director of the National Library in 1940, and the youngest person appointed to the post since the library's foundation in 1877.

In 1941, Colonel Dan Bryan, who would become Head of Irish Military Intelligence, G2, asked Dr Hayes to lead a unit to attempt to break coded messages being transmitted by Nazi agents in Ireland, including messages from a transmitter at the German Legation on Northumberland Road in Dublin.

Dr Hayes was assigned a small team to help him. Based at Beggars Bush barracks, Dr Hayes and his team were successful in breaking Nazi coded messages. Specifically, Dr Hayes was the first person in the world to break the German microdot encryption method.

His team also monitored the activities of Nazi spies in Ireland during the war, leading to their arrest. Thanks to Dr Hayes's codebreaking work, G2 had considerable success in its work against German agents.

Dr Hayes was fully aware of the cooperation between Ireland and the Allies during World War II and later wrote in an anonymous letter to *The Irish Times*, printed in November 1961:

'During the war Irish neutrality was constantly misrepresented in the Allied press. Security reasons prevented the actual facts and the measures taken to prevent espionage from being published to counteract this frequently vicious propaganda. It is about time that some of the truth should be released to set the record straight. The Irish government had the situation under complete control throughout the war, and contrary to the popular belief in the English-speaking world this country was not permitted to be used as a centre for espionage. When the full story is told, this will be clearer still.'

He went on to say that the effectiveness of Irish security controls was evidenced by the fact that all German spies to Ireland were arrested. Dr Hayes and his colleagues worked diligently, quietly and successfully to protect Ireland from potential invasion during World War II.

In his book, *Codebreaker*, Marc McMenamin wrote: 'Sometimes heroes aren't statesman, they aren't soldiers, they aren't carved into marble statues on city streets. Very often it is those who work quietly in the shadows to whom we owe the greatest debt of gratitude.'

JOHN HERIVEL

John Herivel, from Belfast, played a key role in Bletchley Park's efforts to decrypt the Enigma code. In 1940, he came up with a system to break ciphers that was known as the 'Herivel Tip' or 'Herivelismus'. The Herivel Tip was based on an assumption that German code operators would fail to change some Enigma settings at the start of their shift.

He later described how he came up with the idea at his digs: 'One evening, I remember vividly, suddenly, finding myself thinking about the other end of the story, the German operators, what they were doing and inevitably then I thought of them starting off the day. Then I had the thought, suppose he was a lazy fellow and he were to leave the wheels untouched in the machine and bang the top down and look at the windows, see what letters were showing and just use them.'

Herivel's hunch that a careless operator would not change the code, coupled with the German's belief that the Enigma code was unbreakable, led to a breakthrough. His tip started to work from May 1940, which meant the number of possibilities for each letter was reduced from some 17,000 to just 20.

John Herivel was born in Belfast on 29 August 1918 to Josephine Allison Moat and John Jamieson Herivel. He went to the Methodist College and won a scholarship to study at Sidney Sussex College, Cambridge, in 1937. He was studying mathematics when he was recruited to work at Bletchley Park in January 1940.

His future wife, Elizabeth Jones, also worked at the war station but they did not talk to one another until they met again after the war. When the war was over, he lectured in maths and later the history and philosophy of science at Queen's University Belfast.

In 2022, an Ulster History Circle blue plaque commemorating his codebreaking work was unveiled at his former school, the Methodist College Belfast.

Counterfeiter

ELIZABETH FRIEDLANDER

Elizabeth Friedlander (1903–1984) of Germany, London and Cork, fled Berlin in 1936 amid a climate of heightening racial persecution in Hitler's Nazi Germany. She was already an accomplished designer, with a qualification from the Berlin Academy and experience at German women's fashion journal *Die Dame* (*The Lady*) under her belt.

She had even invented a typeface for the Bauer type foundry, something few female designers had done. She called it 'Elizabeth' because her Jewish surname 'Friedlander' would draw too much attention.

When she arrived in London, she soon got editorial commissions and, given her skill-set, was quickly introduced to the PWE, the secret intelligence organisation that produced propaganda designed to undermine German morale. She had form too, having produced books and newspapers for Italian and German POWs.

British author Ellic Howe hired her to forge German ration books, *Wehrmacht* and Nazi rubber stamps and identity papers. She was later appointed head of design and was in charge of designing and distributing black propaganda.

After the war, she stayed in London and worked at Penguin, designing book covers. She was also employed as calligrapher to the Royal Military College at Sandhurst where she inscribed the names of those killed during World War II on a Roll of Honour. She moved to Kinsale in Co. Cork, Ireland, in 1961 where she continued to work in design. She died there in 1984. Her papers are kept at University College Cork.

Courier

MARY GIORGI (NÉE DEWAN)

Mary Dewan from Kildare was expecting her fourth child in 1942 when she was working as a courier for a resistance network in North Africa.

Born in Newbridge, Co. Kildare, in 1898, she married a commandant in the gendarmerie, Louis Joseph Giorgi. They were living in Oran, a coastal city in Algeria, when the war broke out. Both of them were involved in resistance activity in a group set up by the Free Polish Forces.

The network PSW-AFR (an abbreviation for Polska Służba Wywiadowcza Africa, which translates as 'Polish Intelligence Service Africa') had members from a range of countries: Poland, France, Italy, Algeria – and Ireland. It was particularly active in the run-up to Operation Torch when tens of thousands of Allied troops landed on the French North African coast.

Mary carried intelligence about enemy troops, which was copied, photographed, miniaturised and sent to London. She gave birth to her fourth child, Charles Giorgi, on 20 March 1942, but did some further courier work after the Allied Landings in November 1942.

Intelligence-gathering

DANIEL O'CONNELL'S DESCENDANTS IN VIETNAM

The Irish-French O'Connell family, descended from the famous Irish liberator, Daniel O'Connell (1775–1847), moved to Vietnam at the end of the nineteenth century, settling in Tây Ninh province, at the Plantation O'Connell. Many of the family members joined the intelligence-gathering network, Plasson, from 1941.

Daniel O'Connell, his younger sister, Marie Madeleine O'Connell, and son, Patrick O'Connell, all served in the network, helping to locate POWs being held by the Japanese.

Coincidentally, another member of the O'Connell family, Guy – Daniel's younger brother – joined the Hector network in Paris.

JOHN PILKINGTON

John Pilkington, born in Dun Laoghaire, Co. Dublin, in 1905, was active in the Resistance in Paris between 1940 and 1944. Described as an *homme de lettres* (a literary man), he joined the reserve infantry regiment of the French army in 1940. That year, he was arrested and interrogated by the Germans, who broke his teeth. He was released in November and exchanged his British passport for an Irish one.

He was active in the liberation of Paris, fighting from 19 to 25 August. The battle claimed the lives of 1,000 resisters, over 500 civilians, 156 soldiers from the French 2nd Division and more than 3,000 Germans and members of the French militia fighting with them.

Maquis (underground fighters)

SAM MURPHY

Electrician Sam Murphy from Belfast got the idea of joining the Resistance when he was walking past an unguarded vehicle in Toulouse: he realised that he could sabotage and disable it very quickly.

He joined the *Maquis* (underground) group, Veny, in October 1942 and specialised in sabotage and stealing vehicles for the Resistance. The network operated over a vast area of France, taking in the Lot-et-Garonne and the Hautes-Pyrenées. Murphy stayed with Veny until the region was liberated in 1944, and then joined the Free French Forces led by General de Gaulle.

Bibliographical Notes

Archives

Service Historique de la Défense (SHD), Vincennes, France

Archives Nationales (National Archives), France

National Archives, Ireland

The Special Operations Executive archives at the National Archives,
Kew, London

American Friends Service Committee archive, Pennsylvania,
United States.

National Archives and Records Administration (NARA), United States

State Archives, Belgium

Freedom Museum Archives, Copenhagen, Denmark

Public Record Office of Northern Ireland

The documents consulted and their archival references are quoted in
individual chapters.

Newspapers

Several newspaper articles are quoted throughout the text. Each one
is credited in the endnotes relating to each chapter.

A note on the word 'Resistance': We have written the word Resistance with a capital 'R' when referring to the movement itself, but have used a lower-case 'r' when using the word as an adjective.

Commemoration: Some of the people in the preceding chapters have been honoured by their local or adopted communities, and/or decorated by the British, French and American governments. In 2014, a plaque to honour all the Irish who took part in the Resistance was unveiled at the Irish College in Paris. To date, there is no such memorial in Ireland.

Chapter 1: Janie McCarthy's Indomitable Spirit

A special thank you to Killarney guide Mary G. O'Sullivan for her thesis on Janie McCarthy. Thank you, too, to Dr Clodagh Tait, Breda Joy, Michelle Crean and Marie Moloney.

Information on Janie McCarthy's participation in at least five resistance networks comes from her own post-war military files and those of fellow resistance members and Allied servicemen. They include:

Archive Report US Forces 1941–5, Aircrew Remembered: https://aircrewremembered.com/flickinger-paul.html.

Dissertation on Janie McCarthy by Mary G. O'Sullivan, UCC, 2021.

Elisabeth Barbier's testimony from the National Archives France: https://www.siv.archives-nationales.culture.gouv.fr/siv/media/FRAN_IR_053870/cuoodirfwba-1ou85r5xlhkpm/FRAN_0086_038286_L.

Escape and Evasion Reports, Iva Lee Fegette, E & E 31, 32, NARA: https://catalog.archives.gov/id/5554673?objectPage=9.

Escape and Evasion Reports, Sidney Casden, E & E 335, NARA https://catalog.archives.gov/id/5554995.

Evasion report SPG 3317/1665 from Clarence Witheridge: https://www.evasioncomete.be/fwitherch.html.

File on Janie McCarthy at the Service Historique de la Défense, Vincennes, 16 P 381551. (Janie is referred to as a man in this file and her first name is given as Janíl. It is most likely a transcription error. There is no evidence that she was ever called that.)

File on St Jacques network at the Service Historique de la Défense, Vincennes, 17P 210.

File on Comet network at the Service Historique de la Défense, Vincennes, 17P 214.

Janie McCarthy's file at the National Archives and Records Administration (NARA), United States, courtesy of Michael Moores LeBlanc.

References to Jean and Lucienne Bodin, Box 935, NARA, Washington DC, and Frank Bulfield, Box 949, NARA, Washington DC, both quoted in *No Way Out*, Isadore Ryan (Mercier Press, 2017), p. 223.

Other works cited:

Census, 1901: https://www.census.nationalarchives.ie/pages /1901/Kerry/Killarney/New_Street__Lower_/1414679/.

Joy, Breda, *Hidden Kerry: The Keys to the Kingdom* (Mercier Press, 2016), pp. 230–1.

Lucey, Anne, 'Killarney recognises woman who saved hundreds of lives in WWII', *Irish Examiner*, 27 June 2022: https://www .irishexaminer.com/news/munster/arid-40904855.html.

Mellor, Gordon, *ETA: A Bomber Command Navigator Shot Down and on the Run* (Fighting High Publishing, 2016).

List of people who 'left Kerry and achieved distinction': *The Kerryman*, 11 December 1954.

News of her teaching award: *Cork Examiner*, 11 February 1920, p. 3. Photo is attributed to Fitzgerald, Killarney.

References to Paris during the mass exodus from Janie's fellow resistance member Drue Tartière's memoir, Tartière, Drue, *The House Near Paris: An American Woman's Story of Traffic in Patriots* (Simon and Schuster, 1946).

Chapter 2: Cat and Mouse Games

The description of Samuel Beckett's resistance work in Paris is based on his resistance file at the Service Historique de la Défense, Vincennes, 16P 42711, also on the file on the Gloria SMH network, 17P 135.

Beckett's post-war interview with British security officials is outlined in Gabrielle Cecile Martinez Picabia's file. National Archives, Kew. File KV2/1313. Original reference: PF 601, 715.

His biographical details and interviews about his resistance work are from Knowlson, James, *Damned to Fame: The Life of Samuel Beckett* (Bloomsbury, 1996), pp. 297–340.

Other works cited:

Alfred Péron, biography, memorial of the deceased of Mauthausen concentration camp: https://raumdernamen.mauthausen -memorial.org/index.php?id=4&p=104179&L=1.

'I was fighting against the Germans who were making life hell for my friends, and not for the French nation' quote from Simpson, Alan, *Beckett and Behan* (Routledge and Kegan Paul, 1962), pp. 64–5.

Ivry, Benjamin, 'Samuel Beckett's Letters Reveal Roots of Resistance', *Forward.com*, 27 October 2011: https://forward.com/culture /144905/samuel-becketts-letters-reveal-roots-of-resistance/.

Knowlson, James, 'Samuel Beckett's biographer reveals secrets of the writer's time as a French Resistance spy', *Independent*, 23 July 2014.

Nixon, Mark, *Samuel Beckett's German Diaries 1936–1937*, (Continuum International Publishing Group, 2011), p. 87.

O'Brien, Eoin, 'Saint-Lô: Humanity in Ruins' in *The House of Industry Hospitals: The Richmond, Whitworth and Hardwicke (St Laurence's Hospital), A Closing Memoir*, compiled and edited by O'Brien, Eoin, Browne, Lorna and O'Malley, Kevin (The Anniversary Press, 1988), p. 269.

Paul Léon's letters to his wife Mania from *James Joyce and Paul L. Léon: The Story of a Friendship Revisited*. Edited by Léon,

Alexia, Léon, Anna Maria & Crispi, Luca (Bloomsbury, 2002), pp. 199–200.

Shenker, Israel, 'Moody Man of Letters: A Portrait of Samuel Beckett, Author of the Puzzling "Waiting For Godot"', *The New York Times*, 6 May 1956.

Tibère, Clément, 'Boîte aux lettres', Hugues Moutouh (éd.), *Dictionnaire du renseignement* (Perrin, 2018), pp. 108–9.

Comments on being expected to live on his *patrimoine*, and being disbelieved that he could be called Samuel and not be a Jew, come from Paris legation files, P49/4, NAI.

Comments on interference by the authorities at Roussillon and the legation's response are from Paris legation files, P49/17, NAI. NAI DFA Paris Embassy 49/17.

His financial affairs were referenced in a letter from Count Gerald O'Kelly de Gallagh to Seán Murphy (Vichy) Paris, 20 September 1940, NAI DFA Paris Embassy P33/13.

The letter suggesting Beckett was trying to leave France for Ireland in 1940 comes from Letter from Patrick J. O'Byrne to Seán Murphy (Vichy) (M.10/11) Madrid, 8 August 1940. NAI DFA Madrid Embassy 34/1A. https://www.difp.ie/volume-6/1940/samuel-beckett/3255/#section-documentpage.

Chapter 3: A Kit Kat, a Mars Bar and an Orange

The account of Sgt Bill Magrath and Sgt Ollie James's escape is based on their own escape reports, NAK WO 208/3308 (National Archives, Kew), and also several interviews Sgt Magrath gave after the war. Among them:

Flight to Freedom, BBC Northern Ireland documentary (2005).

'Back from the Dead,' *Belfast Telegraph*, 20 June 2005: https://www .belfasttelegraph.co.uk/news/back-from-the-dead/28240689.html.

Other works consulted or cited:
'A Remarkable Career: Banker, Soldier And Now Passionist',
    The Catholic Standard, 15 April 1933.
National Archives, Kew file on St Joseph's Church, FO 561/123.
Quinn, Joseph, 'Irish Volunteers in the Royal Air Force during
    the Battle of France', *Nacelles* journal, Issue 10, 2021: Irish
    Volunteers in the Royal Air Force during the Battle of France –
    Nacelles (univ-tlse2.fr).
Travers, Patrick, 'Some Experiences During the War Years: The
    Irish College in Paris 1939–1945', Colloque, No. 18, Autumn
    1988, pp. 440–57. http://www.diskon.ie/assets/Colloque%20
    Volume%2018.pdf.

Agnes Hannigan's comments to author David O'Donoghue
in 1993 that Fr Kenneth Monaghan was sent to Paris by British
intelligence to establish links with the Resistance appear in *Hitler's
Irish Voices* (Beyond the Pale Publications, 1998), p. 196.

Agnes's letters to the Irish legation on the deprivations faced by
the Irish community in Paris during the war years: Paris Legation
files, P49/12 (16) – 49/13 (17), NAI.

Details about Judith Winifred 'Pat' Fitzpatrick in Nelson, June,
Auntie Pat's War (Independently published, 2023).

Insight into making false identity papers from French Resistance
forger, Adolfo Kaminsky are from 'How a WWII-era forger saved
lives, one fake document at a time', CBS News, 29 October: https://
www.cbsnews.com/news/how-a-wwii-era-forger-saved-lives-one
-fake-document-at-a-time/.

Insights from Fr Kenneth's nephew are from Monaghan,
Michael Joseph, *My uncle's army history*: https://www.europeana
.eu/item/2020601/https___1914_1918_europeana_eu_contributions
_3549.

Keith Janes on the two men who escaped with Magrath and
James: 'I suspect that Sgt Patterson was Sgt G Patterson (LIB/186
– missing) from 57 Sqn Wellington T2970 which FTR 14 Mar '41,

and that Sgt Maderson was Sgt A A Maderson from 12 Sqn Battle L5190 which FTR 10 May '40. Maderson is reported as wounded, and repatriated in Oct '43. He was recaptured.' https://www. conscript-heroes.com/Art52-Heilag-at-Rouen.html.

Notes on the Resistance and keeping silent under torture are from https://adst.org/2013/07/an-american-diplomat-in-vichy-france/: by diplomat Douglas MacArthur II (and nephew of US military leader, General Douglas MacArthur).

Quotes from the newspaper articles on Fr Monaghan's military career come from:

Irish Independent interview with Lily Hannigan, 'An Irish Club in Paris', 6 October 1956.

'Priest's thrilling career', *Frontier Sentinel*, 19 January 1929.

'The ex-soldier priest; Irishman who escaped Trotsky's vengeance', *Nottingham and Midland Catholic News*, 19 January 1929.

Chapter 4: 'I Risked My Neck'

The account of Delia's years in Rome is based on newspaper reports, as well as transcripts and conversations quoted in Aidan O'Hara's biography, *I'll Live Till I Die* (Drumlin Publications, 1997). Thank you too to her nephew, Leo Cullen, for recounting memories of his aunt. Many thanks also to Leo and Carole Cullen for photographs.

Other works consulted or cited:

'Delia is dead', *Sunday Independent*, 14 February, 1971.

'Delia Murphy Sings During Raid', *The Irish Weekly and Ulster Examiner*, 26 April 1941.

Derry, Sam, *The Rome Escape Line* (Franklin Classics Trade Press, 2018).

Derry, speaking on the numbers in hiding, Derry, S., op. cit., pp. 53–4.

'Dublin Presentation to Delia Murphy', *The Irish Weekly and Ulster Examiner*, 4 October 1941.

Fleming, Brian, *The Vatican Pimpernel: The Wartime Exploits of Monsignor Hugh O'Flaherty* (Collins Press, 2008).

Kennedy, Michael, 'Kiernan, Thomas Joseph ('Tommy'; 'T.J.')', *Dictionary of Irish Biography*: https://www.dib.ie/biography/kiernan-thomas-joseph-tommy-t-j-a4539.

Letter on fake passport from December 1942 is in the MacWhite archives, quoted in Fleming, B., op. cit., p. 25.

'New Irish Envoy to the Vatican Leaves', *The Irish Weekly and Ulster Examiner*, 18 October 1941.

Piondar, Sean, 'Eire's Legation Hostess at the Vatican', *Waterford Standard*, 20 December 1941.

Br Humilis's comments are quoted in O'Hara, A., op. cit., p. 118.

Conditions in Rome are outlined in 'Extract from a letter from Michael MacWhite to Joseph P. Walshe (Dublin)', 28 February 1942, No. 191 NAI DFA 219/6.

Delia's first impression of Rome is described in a letter from Delia Kiernan (Murphy) to Kathleen O'Connell (Dublin), 16 November 1941, No. 148 NAI DFA Secretary's Files P15.

Instructions to diplomatic staff: Personal code telegram from Joseph P. Walshe to William Warnock (Berlin) No. 96 NAI DFA Secretary's Files P3, 4 June 1941.

The official death toll for the raid on Belfast on 15/16 April was 745, according to the Imperial War Museum: https://www.iwm.org.uk/history/the-blitz-around-britain.

T.J. Kiernan's description of the fall of Mussolini is from his book, *Pope Pius XII* (Clonmore & Reynolds, 1958), p. 41. Quoted in Fleming, B. op. cit., p. 34.

Chapter 5: Callers at Dawn

The account of Bluebell's war years is based on her own words, as spoken to her biographer, George Perry, in *Bluebell: the Authorized*

Biography of Margaret Kelly, Founder of the Legendary Bluebell Girls (Pavilion, Michael Joseph, 1986).

Other work cited or consulted:

'Founder of Bluebell Girls dies at 94', *The Guardian*, 16 September 2004.

Gillespie, Elgy, 'Belles who don't get too blue', *The Irish Times,* 14 June 1980.

Insdorf, Annette, 'How Truffaut's *The Last Metro* Reflects Occupied Paris', *The New York Times*, 8 February 1981.

'Josephine Baker: From Creole Goddess to Siren of the Resistance,' the National WW2 Museum, March 2023. https://www.nationalww2museum.org/programs/ josephine-baker-creole-goddess-siren-resistance.

Margaret Kelly obituary, *Sunday Tribune*, 19 September 2004.

Marlowe, Lara, 'Remarkable life of Miss Bluebell', *The Irish Times*, 11 October 2000.

'Miss Bluebell, *La véritable histoire de l'héroïne du dernier métro*' (Miss Bluebell, the true story of the heroine of *The Last Metro*), *Mollat*: https://www.mollat.com/livres/346794/george-perry -miss-bluebell-margaret-kelly-la-veritable-histoire-de-l-heroine -du-dernier-metro.

Morgan, Andrew, 'Legend who leads the Bluebell girls', *Liverpool Echo*, 10 January 1986.

The Deportation of the Jews from France, Yad Vashem: https://www .yadvashem.org/holocaust/france/deportation-from-france.html.

United States Holocaust Memorial Museum, Holocaust Encyclopedia, Gurs: https://encyclopedia.ushmm.org/content/en /article/gurs.

White, Lawrence William, 'Kelly, Margaret ("Miss Bluebell")', *Dictionary of Irish Biography*: https://www.dib.ie/biography /kelly-margaret-miss-bluebell-a9377.

Chapter 6: 'This is Vicky with Three Kisses for You'

This chapter is based on Agnes Bernelle's own account of her life and on the research carried out by Agnes Bernelle's son, Mark Leslie, and her granddaughter Leah Leslie, who very kindly shared their findings and spoke to us at length. We are very grateful for their invaluable help.

Books and articles cited:

Bernelle, Agnes, *The Fun Palace* (Lilliput Press, 1996).

Castle Leslie, Between Two Worlds exhibition catalogue: Arts, Heritage and the Gaeltacht and Monaghan County Council, 1983.

Leslie, Leah, 'Flight of the Rooks' (University project).

Rozell, Matthew, 'A Train near Magdeburg', Friends of the National World War II Memorial, Monthly Conference Series, 2021: https://www.youtube.com/watch?v=PWLTa1ZIFzQ&t=4s.

Chapter 7: The Intelligence Factory

We are very grateful to Shane Ross for recalling his mother and what little she said about her time at Bletchley Park. Special thanks to Issy Ross, too, for her project on codebreakers.

Works cited:

McQuinn, Cormac, 'Minister pays tribute to mother who worked as WWII codebreaker', *Irish Independent*, 22 October 2016: https://www.independent.ie/irish-news/minister-pays-tribute-to -mother-who-worked-as-wwii-code-cracker/35151998.html.

O'Reilly, Ronan, 'My mother the wartime codebreaker', *Irish Mail on Sunday*, 13 November 2016.

Rubel Ross's words come from her only public interview, *Miriam Meets*, RTÉ Radio 1, 15 August 2010.

Rubel's Service Certificate at Bletchley Park: https://bletchleypark .org.uk/roll-of-honour/certificate/1684/.

Russell-Jones, Mair, *My Secret Life in Hut Six: One Woman's Experiences At Bletchley Park* (Lion Book, 2014).

Uí Chionna, Jackie, *Queen of Codes: the Secret Life of Emily Anderson, Britain's Greatest Female Code Breaker* (Headline, 2023).

Details of 'My bonnie is stationed at uh-uh' are from 'Obituary
of Patricia Brown, Bletchley Park codebreaker', *The Times*, 18 May
2021: https://www.thetimes.co.uk/article/patricia-brown-obituary
-sf9w2ffkz?t=ie.

Chapter 8: 'A Cool and Lonely Courage'

We are particularly indebted to John Alvey for sharing memories of
his mother and also many photographs.

This chapter draws on his memories and the content of Maureen
Patricia O'Sullivan's personnel file at the National Archives in Kew,
HS 9/1427/1.

Other works cited or consulted:

Meagher, John and Mulqueen, Michael, 'Why a war hero turned
her back on Ireland', *Irish Independent*, 29 March 2002.

Meagher, John and Mulqueen, Michael, 'The Mystery of Ireland's
Seductive Spy', *Irish Independent*, 21 March 2002.

Pattinson, Juliette. S., 'Playing the daft lassie with them: gender,
captivity and the Special Operations Executive during the
second world war', *European Review of History*, 13(2), 2006,
pp. 271–92. https://doi.org/10.1080/13507480600785955.

Stevenson, William, *Spymistress: The Life of Vera Atkins, the
Greatest Female Secret Agent of World War II* (Arcade
Publishing, 2011).

'Women in a Man's War: The Employment of Female Agents in
the Special Operations Executive, 1940–1946', A thesis by
Cameron Davis Carlomagno Chapman, University Orange,
California, Wilkinson College of Arts, Humanities, and Social
Sciences submitted in partial fulfilment of the requirements for
the degree of Masters of Arts in War and Society, May 2019.

Insights into dressing agents from: Sears, Jocelyn, 'Clothing Britain's Spies during World War II', JSTOR, August 2018.

Major Aonghais Fyffe's comments on SOE agent training for men and women, are quoted in Vigus, Kate, *Mission France: The True History of the Women of SOE* (Yale University Press, 2021), p. 30.

Methods of hiding codes are from Berg, Sanchia, 'Phyllis Latour: The secret life of a WW2 heroine revealed', BBC *News*, 14 October 2023: https://www.bbc.com/news/uk-67100792.

Chapter 9: The Moonlight Hours

This chapter is based on Brian Dominic Rafferty's SOE file at the National Archives, Kew, HS 9/1225/2.

Other works cited:

List of SOE agents, their codenames and their fates: http://soe
_french.tripod.com/.

Rafferty biography at Christ Church, University of Oxford: Captain
Brian Dominic Rafferty | Christ Church, University of Oxford.

Sacquety, Troy J., 'Supplying the Resistance', *Veritas*, Vol. 3, No. 1,
2007: https://arsof-history.org/articles/v3n1_supplying_
resistance_page_1.html.

Vigus, Kate, *Mission France: The True History of the Women of
SOE* (Yale University Press, 2021).

Chapter 10: Passing the Baby

Details of Mary Herbert's career in the field are from her SOE file at National Archives, Kew, HS9/77/2.

Other works cited:

Balu, Raphaële, 'The French maquis and the Allies during the
Second World War', in *France in an Era of Global War,
1914–1945, Occupation, Politics, Empire and Entanglements*
(Palgrave Macmillan, 2014), pp. 192–209.

Churchill, Peter, *Duel of Wits* (G.P. Putnam's Son, 1995).

Escott, E. Beryl, *The Heroines of SOE, Britain's Secret Women in France F Section* (The History Press, 2010), p. 61.

Hemmings, Jay, 'Cockleshell Heroes Raid ruined another Unit's plans which would have caused more damage, *War History Online*, 8 February 2019.

Jones, Liane, *A Quiet Courage* (Corgi, 1991), p. 208.

Vigus, Kate, *Mission France: The True History of the Women of SOE* (Yale University Press, 2021).

Chapter 11: Two Pairs of Silk Pyjamas

This chapter is based on Capt. John Keany's SOE file at the National Archives, Kew, HS 9/824/4.

Other works cited:

'Left secretary of war £20 in will', *Leicester Daily Mercury*, 22 June 1946.

Details of Operation Chariton are taken from Pickering, William with Hart, Alan, *The Bandits of Cisterna* (Leo Cooper, 1991).

The account of the shooting dead of Capt. John Keany's father, *Irish Examiner*, 13 February 1921.

Chapter 12: From the Ritz to a Prison Cell

A very big thank you to Christopher Massy-Beresford who has helped us enormously with this chapter, sharing his own research and taking the time to meticulously check details. Thank you, too, to Nic Paton for putting us in touch.

Other works cited or consulted:

Freedom Museum Archives: https://modstand.natmus.dk/Person .aspx?10572.

Muus, Fleming, *The Spark and the Flame* (Museum Press Ltd, 1956).

Straede, Therkel, 'The Lesson of Denmark's Unparalleled
    Effort to Save Its Jewish Population During World War II,'
    Time, 8 November 2023: https://time.com/6332953/
    denmarks-effort-to-save-jewish-population-world-war-ii/.

Sutherland, Christine, *Monica: Heroine of the Danish Resistance*
    (Farrar Straus Giroux, 1990).

'The Letter of Eve,' *The Tatler*, No. 1695, 20 December 1933.

Vargo, Mark E., *Women of the Resistance: Eight Who Defied the
    Third Reich* (McFarland & Company, 2012), p. 67.

Chapter 13: Carve his Name with Pride

A special thank you to writer Ronan McGreevy and historian
Michael Moores LeBlanc for their help with this chapter.

Other sources include:

ROBERT ARMSTRONG

DeAngelis, Caitlin Galante, *The Caretakers: War Graves Gardeners
    and the Secret Battle to Rescue Allied Airmen in World War II*
    (Prometheus, 2024).

Escape and Evasion Reports E & E 47, Cox, Arthur B., National
    Archives and Records Administration (NARA), Washington.

McGreevy, R., 'A Natural Rebel', 2015: 'A Natural Rebel' –
    Robert Armstrong, the Irish gardener killed by the Nazis
    (youtube.com).

Robert Armstrong's file at SHD, Vincennes, 16P 17321.

Robert Armstrong's NARA file, courtesy of historian Michael LeBlanc.

Ronan McGreevy's interview with Harry Lindsay from McGreevy,
    R., *Wherever the Firing Line Extends: Ireland and the Western
    Front* (The History Press Ireland, 2016), pp. 319–20.

Teacher Marie-Thérèse Debrabant's name appears on a
    consolidated list of French helpers who were proposed for a US
    award. NND 913529.

WILLIAM O'CONNOR

Capt. Gaston Lepine's comments are quoted in DeAngelis, op. cit. p. 105, Kindle edition.

Emilie Nisse comment about William O'Connor, DeAngelis, op. cit. p. 183.

Halifax bomber Brian Desmond Barker's evasion report: fiche D370 (cometeline.org).

Letter from Dutchman to Madame Debrabant in Robert Armstrong, AC 27 P8898, BAVCC, Caen.

Murphy, David, *'Paddy fait la Résistance, Les Irlandais dans la Résistance française et la section F du SOE, 1940–1945'*, Revue historiques des armées, pp. 86–98, 2008, Dossier France-Irlande.

SHD, Vincennes, Voix du Nord 18P44.

William O'Connor, 18P 44 8836, SHD, Vincennes, referenced in Murphy, D., '"I was terribly frightened at times": Irish men and women in the French Resistance and F Section of SOE, 1940–5', in Genet-Rouffiac, N. and Murphy, D. (eds), *Franco-Irish Military Connections, 1590–1945* (Four Courts Press, 2009).

Chapter 14: A Friend to Comb My Hair

Catherine Crean's war file is courtesy of the Belgian State Archives. Service Archives des Victimes de la Guerre Bruxelles (Archives de l'Etat en Belgique), dossier personnel établi au nom de CREAN Catherine, née le 11/12/1879 (AOS-AVG-d050464).

Other works cited:

Bernard 'Bobby' Conville's escape file: Dossier d'évasion SPG 658: http://www.cometeline.org/fiche002.html.

Boyle, Hal, *Help, Help! Another Day! The World of Hal Boyle* (Associated Press, 1969).

Boyle, Hal, 'The Door of Madame Duchene', *The Daily Reporter*, Ohio, 18 November 1954.

Dumon, Andrée (Code name 'Nadine'), *I Haven't Forgotten You, Freedom 1945* (Independently published, 2022).

Van der Vat, Obituary of Countess Andrée de Jongh, *The Guardian*, 22 October 2007: https://www.theguardian.com/news/2007 /oct/22/guardianobituaries.obituaries.

Vecsey, George, 'Cosmic Questions on a Journey of Discovery', *The New York Times*, 9 June 2006.

Pilot Larry Birk's comment on his life depending on a schoolgirl is from Shuff, Derek, *Evader: The Epic Story of the First British Airman to be Rescued by the Comète Escape Line in World War II*, (Spellmount, 2010), p. 1548, Kindle edition.

Thank you Claire Bradley for Catherine Crean's birth certificate: 2057557.pdf (irishgenealogy.ie).

Chapter 15: The Extraordinary Resilience of Two Marys

A special thank you to Dorothy Seagrave for talking to us about her grand-aunt Mary Cummins and for providing photographs. We are very much indebted to Jamie O'Shaughnessy for sharing his research on his great-aunt Mary O'Shaughnessy. A very special thank you, too, to Barbara Hennessy for many insights and discoveries from her research on the life of Mary O'Shaughnessy.

Other works cited or consulted:

MARY CUMMINS

Background notes on the Resistance from: De Wever, Bruno and Nico, Wouters, translated by Asbury, Anna, 'Why the Belgian Resistance deserves more attention,' *thelowcountries.com*, 6 May 2020. https://www.the-low-countries.com/article/why -the-belgian-resistance-deserves-more-attention.

Details of diplomat Con Cremin's efforts to have Mary Cummins released from Keogh, Dr Niall, *Con Cremin: Ireland's Wartime Diplomat* (Mercier Press, 2006), pp. 84–5.

'Doughty survivor of a Nazi death decree,' Obituary, *The Irish Times*, 3 July 1999: https://www.irishtimes.com/news/doughty -survivor-of-a-nazi-death-decree-1.202637.

Helm, Sarah, *If This Is A Woman: Inside Ravensbrück: Hitler's Concentration Camp for Women* (Abacus, 2016).

'In the Shadow of Death', documentary presented and produced by Padraic Dolan for the *Documentary on One*, RTÉ Radio, broadcast, January 1993.

Murphy, David, 'O'Kelly, Countess Mary de Galway (1905–99)', *Dictionary of Irish Biography*: https://www.dib.ie/biography /okelly-countess-mary-de-galway-a6853.

MARY O'SHAUGHNESSY

Details of Cecily Lefort and her husband's request for a divorce: National Archives Kew, HS 9/908/1.

'Discovery Meant Death', *The Courier and Advertiser*, 12 December 1946.

Escapers' report of Sergeant Hillyard. National Archives Kew, WO 203/3302.

Heminway, John, *In Full Flight: A Story of Africa and Atonement* (Listening Library, 2018).

'Irish Girl's Brutal Treatment at Ravensbrück', *The Londonderry Sentinel*, 12 December 1946.

'Irish Governess Gives Evidence', *Cork Examiner*, 12 December 1946.

Mary O'Shaughnessy's sworn affidavit: RW2/7/17, courtesy of Jamie O'Shaughnessy.

'Miss Mary's Appeal', *The Journal*, December 1945.

'Miss Mary (late of gas camp) has her say now', *Liverpool Evening Express*, 20 December 1946.

Pritchard, Holly, 'Memorial tribute unveiled in honour of Wigan war heroine', *Wigan Today*, 25 September 2022: https://www .wigantoday.net/news/people/memorial-tribute-unveiled-in -honour-of-wigan-war-heroine-3852436.

'Woman's story of Nazi torture', *The Journal*, 12 October 1945.

Chapter 16: Pugna Quin Percutias

Millar, George, *Horned Pigeon* (Time Life Books, 1989),
pp. 413–14.
Quote from Eric McGrath from *Unspoken: A Father's Wartime
Escape. A Son's Family Discovered* (Gill Books, 2022), p. 302.

Comet Line escape notes:
Alfred Martin: http://www.cometeline.org/fiche111.html.
Edward Kinsella: http://www.cometeline.org/fiche138.html.
John Finn: https://www.evasioncomete.be/ffinnjp.html.
Richard Irwin: http://www.cometeline.org/ficheD120.html.
Robert 'Bob' Clarke: http://www.cometeline.org/fiche128.html.

ROLL OF HONOUR

Helping Allied Soldiers
BRIDGET BOLGER
With special thanks to Thomas Bolger, Emeritus Professor of Zoology at University College Dublin, who spent a number of years tracing his grand-aunt and her involvement in the French Resistance.

Bridget's work helping a British airman is outlined in her application for a pension and the subsequent award of compensation, which are detailed in a US National Archives and Records Administration dossier, RG 498 Entry 193 Box 963 Chevallier.

She is also mentioned in Janes, Keith, *Express Delivery, The Men Brought Back by the Shelburn Escape Line, and the People who Made it Possible* (Matador, 2019).

OLGA BAUDOT DE ROUVILLE
Olga Baudot de Rouville's papers are held in the Cumbria Archive: https://www.bbc.com/news/uk-england-cumbria-34845086.amp.

Her Tipperary connections are mentioned in 'Appeal for Information', a letter from Miss J. Moore, Cumbria, published in the *Tipperary Star*, 30 June 2011.

'A Most Remarkable Woman', Sister Olga Baudot de Rouville (1891–1979), World War 2 Escape Lines Memorial Society: https://ww2escapelines.co.uk/1300-2/.

Letter showing she was in Ireland in 1951: Legal Notices, *Irish Press*, 28 May 1951.

AGNES FLANAGAN

State Archives Belgium:

Agnes Flanagan's file requesting recognition of the status of Foreign Political Prisoner: 24881/PPE2178.

Agnes Flanagan's file requesting recognition of Civil Resistant status: 777073/41551.

Ryan, Isadore, 'Agnes Flanagan from Birr – A Lonely *Résistante*', *History Ireland*, September/October 2023.

UNA GIONCADA (NÉE HALDENE)

A special thank you to Lynsey Gillespie, Public Record Office of Northern Ireland.

Researcher: Bronagh McAtasney, Makingthefuture.eu.

Una Gioncada (née Haldene)'s diaries: PRONI T2678/6.

FR PATRICK KELLY

Goodall, Scott, *The Freedom Trail: Following one of the hardest wartime escape routes across the central Pyrenees into Northern Spain* (Inchmere Design, 2005).

'"I thought it was time to get out", The escape tale of Lt. Harry E Roach, Jr. 427th Bomb Squadron, 303rd Bomb Group, 8th Air Force', 303rd Bomb Group (H) Association, Inc. Newsletter, Vol. VII, No. 3, July 1983: https://www.303rdbg.com/hanl/1983-07.pdf.

Roach III, Harry E., Flak City: *The Life and Death of a Bomber Crew* (Privately published).

SR KATHERINE ANNE McCARTHY

Cronin, Siobhan, 'Sr Kate's family makes contact with escapee', *Southern Star*, 23 February 2022: https://www.southernstar.ie /news/sr-kates-family-makes-contact-with-escapee-4238894.

Fleming, Catherine, 'An Irish nun, the French Resistance, the Gestapo and Nazi death camps', *RTÉ Brainstorm*, 6 May 2020.

Finn, Clodagh, 'Ten women who should be celebrated with statues', *Irish Independent*, 11 July 2020: https://www.independent.ie /irish-news/from-gormlaith-to-nan-joyce-10-women-who-should -be-celebrated-with-statues/39355451.html.

Horgan, Jennifer, 'Cork nun Sr Kate deserves better', *Irish Examiner*, 19 January 2024: https://www.irishexaminer.com /opinion/columnists/arid-41310856.html.

Katherine Anne McCarthy, Service Historique de la Défense (SHD) Vincennes, 17P 173.

Prévost, Jean, *L'odyssée de Soeur Marie-Laurence et de ses Compagnes déportées* (Beuvry, 1946).

'Sister Kate McCarthy', *The History Show*, 26 April 2020.

ROME ESCAPE LINE

The names of the Irish priests involved in Monsignor Hugh O'Flaherty's escape line from Fleming, Brian, *The Vatican Pimpernel* (The Collins Press, 2008).

Sr Noreen Dennehy spoke about her work on *Irish Life & Lore*, the podcast run by Maurice and Jane O'Keeffe, April 2024.

Helping Jews

HUBERT BUTLER

Erwin Strunz's comments are recounted in 'Austrian Refugees, Ardmore Journal in 1989', Waterford County Museum exhibit.

'Hubert Butler – Ireland's forgotten World War II hero', Irish History podcast.

'Not welcome at the Unicorn', letter from D.K. Henderson, Castle

Ave, Dublin 3, *The Irish Times*, 24 May 2007: https://www.irishtimes.com/opinion/letters/not-welcome-at-the-unicorn-1.1207340.

O'Toole, Fintan, 'In saving Jews from the Nazis, Hubert Butler saved Ireland from shame', *Irish Times*, 24 January 2015.

MARY ELMES

Letters discussing the 'liberation' of children from Rivesaltes camp between the Quakers' office in London, Una Mortished and Mary Elmes, American Friends Service Committee archive: b11, f29, p. 63 and p. 66.

Lindsley Noble's wire from the US embassy in Vichy to Clarence Pickett, executive secretary, American Friends Service Committee, August 1942, is in the personal archive of Ronald Friend.

MARGARET KEARNEY TAYLOR

Fitzpatrick, Richard and Desmond, Tim, 'Tearoom, Taylor, Saviour, Spy', *RTÉ Documentary on One*, RTÉ 1, July 2016.

Fitzpatrick, Richard, 'The Irish woman who led a double life smuggling Jewish refugees', *The Irish Times*, 8 July 2016.

Martínez de Vicente, Patricia, 'The Secret Spanish Evasion Routes to Save Refugee Jews from the Holocaust', International Raoul Wallenberg Foundation, 28 June 2005: https://www.raoulwallenberg.net/saviors/others/secret-spanish-evasion-routes/.

SR AGNES WALSH

'City honours sister who saved Jews from Nazis', *Catholic Herald*, 2 February 2017.

Yad Vashem, File 4590 on Clara (Agnes) Walsh.

Special Agents
WILLIAM CUNNINGHAM

HS6/353 File on sabotage operation, Dressmaker, National Archives Kew.

Murphy, D., '"I was terribly frightened at times": Irish men and
women in the French Resistance and F Section of SOE, 1940–5',
Genet-Rouffiac, N. and Murphy, D. (eds), *Franco-Irish Military
Connections, 1590–1945* (Four Courts Press, 2009).

CAPT. CONAL O'DONNELL

We are indebted to Conal O'Donnell for this account of his father's
experience as an SOE agent in Greece. Many thanks, too, for permission to use the photograph of his father and uncle. Other sources
include:

O'Donnell, Conal, 'WW2 People's War: SOE, the Irish Agent and
the Greek Massacre', BBC, 31 October 2004: BBC – WW2
People's War – SOE, the Irish Agent and the Greek Massacre.
Information on O'Donnell's signal to SOE HQ Cairo Dec 1943,
PRO HS5 620.
Reference to Capt. O'Donnell's debriefing notes from Public
Records Office (PRO) H55 699.

In an updated edition of *Irish Men and Women in the Second
World War* (Four Courts Press, 2021), historian Richard Doherty's
study of new sources revised upwards the numbers of Irish in the
UK forces. An estimated 133,000 people – at least 66,000 from
the Republic of Ireland and some 64,000 from Northern Ireland –
volunteered for service with the British armed service during World
War II.

ERICA O'DONNELL

Erica O'Donnell, personnel file, National Archives in Kew, HS 9/442/4.
Murphy, David, 'O'Donnell, Erica Marie-Josèphe', *Dictionary
of Irish Biography*: https://www.dib.ie/biography/odonnell
-erica-marie-josephe-a6689.

MICHAEL TROTOBAS

Kent, Stewart and Nicholas, Nick, *Agent Michael Trotobas and SOE in Northern France* (Pen & Sword, 2016).

Radio operator
ROBERT VERNON

Dublin city council electoral roll, 1908–15: https://databases .dublincity.ie/burgesses/viewdoc.php?searchid=335303&source =integration.

Keogh, Niall, *Con Cremin: Ireland's Wartime Diplomat* (Mercier Press, 2006), pp. 85–6.

Robert Vernon file at the SHD, Vincennes, 16P 590803.

Codebreakers
(CONEL) HUGH (O'DONEL) ALEXANDER

Bletchley Park Roll of Honour: https://bletchleypark.org.uk/roll-of -honour/75/.

Dolan, Anne, 'Alexander, (Conel) Hugh (O'Donel)', *Dictionary of Irish Biography*: https://www.dib.ie/biography/alexander-conel -hugh-odonel-a0094.

SHEILA DUNLOP/LADY KILLANIN

Bletchley Park Roll of honour: https://bletchleypark.org.uk/ roll-of-honour/2700/.

'Calm contributor to war effort and charitable causes', *The Irish Times*, 17 March 2007: https://www.irishtimes.com/news/calm -contributor-to-war-effort-and-charitable-causes-1.1293001.

KATHLEEN FERGUSON (CUTHBERT)

Black, Rebecca, 'Modest heroine who was part of code-breaking team that helped defeat the Nazis', *Belfast Telegraph*, 25 November 2016: https://www.belfasttelegraph.co.uk/news /obituaries/kathleen-cuthbert-modest-heroine-who-was-part-of -code-breaking-team-that-helped-defeat-the-nazis/35243287.html.

Bletchley Park Roll of Honour, https://bletchleypark.org.uk
/roll-of-honour/9257/.
Kathleen Cuthbert, Wartime NI, https://archives.wartimeni.com
/person/kathleen-cuthbert/.
Obituary and family appreciations, Queen's University Belfast:
https://daro.qub.ac.uk/document.doc?id=556.

EILEEN LESLIE GREER
Bletchley Park Roll of Honour: https://bletchleypark.org.uk/roll-of
-honour/9257/.
Murtagh, Peter, 'Irish woman honoured for wartime work at
Bletchley Park,' *The Irish Times*, 19 January 2016: https://www
.irishtimes.com/news/ireland/irish-news/irish-woman-honoured
-for-wartime-work-at-bletchley-park-1.2501486.
Obituary, 'Leslie Greer: natural linguist who used her talents at
Bletchley Park,' *The Irish Times*, 16 July 2016: https://www
.irishtimes.com/life-and-style/people/leslie-greer-natural-linguist
-who-used-her-talents-at-bletchley-park-1.2723713.

RICHARD HAYES
McMenamin, Marc, *Code Breaker: The untold story of Richard
Hayes, the Dublin librarian who helped turn the tide of* WWII
(Gill Books, 2018).
McMenamin, Marc and Hayes, Richard, 'Nazi Codebreaker',
Documentary on One, RTÉ Radio, 3 October 2017.

JOHN HERIVEL
Bletchley Park Roll of Honour: https://bletchleypark.org.uk/
roll-of-honour/4258/.
Cousins, Graeme, 'Plaque unveiled for codebreaker John Herivel',
Belfast *Newsletter*, 11 November 2022.
Smith, Michael, 'John Herivel obituary: One of Bletchley Park's
most brilliant wartime codebreakers', *The Guardian*,
13 Feb 2011: www.theguardian.com/world/2011/feb/13
/john-herivel-obituary.

Counterfeiter

ELIZABETH FRIEDLANDER

Elizabeth Friedlander Collection, University College Cork: https://libguides.ucc.ie/ElizabethFriedlanderCollection.

Muraben, Billie, 'Elizabeth Friedlander: one of the first women to design a typeface', *It's Nice That*, 8 March 2018.

Steven, Rachael, 'Ditchling exhibition celebrates book cover artist Elizabeth Friedlander', *Creative Review*, 22 January 2018.

Courier

MARY GIORGI (NÉE DEWAN)

With special thanks to historian David Murphy for the details of Mary Dewan, which are also published in '"I was terribly frightened at times": Irish men and women in the French Resistance and F Section of SOE, 1940–5' in Genet-Rouffiac, N. and Murphy, D. (eds), *Franco-Irish Military Connections, 1590–1945* (Four Courts Press, 2009).

Intelligence-gathering

DANIEL O'CONNELL'S DESCENDANTS

Murphy, D., '"I was terribly frightened at times": Irish men and women in the French Resistance and F Section of SOE, 1940–5', in Genet-Rouffiac, N. and Murphy, D. (eds), *Franco-Irish Military Connections, 1590–1945* (Four Courts Press, 2009).

O'Connell à Tây-Ninh, Marie-Madeleine, 'une planteuse résistante face aux Japonais et aux caodaïstes', *Entreprises Coloniales*, April 2015: https://entreprises-coloniales.fr/inde-indochine/O'Connell_resistance.pdf.

JOHN PILKINGTON

Murphy, D., '"I was terribly frightened at times": Irish men and women in the French Resistance and F Section of SOE, 1940–5', in Genet-Rouffiac, N. and Murphy, D. (eds), *Franco-Irish Military Connections, 1590–1945* (Four Courts Press, 2009).

Maquis (underground fighters)

SAM MURPHY

Murphy, D., '"I was terribly frightened at times": Irish men and women in the French Resistance and F Section of SOE, 1940–5', in Genet-Rouffiac, N. and Murphy, D. (eds), *Franco-Irish Military Connections, 1590–1945* (Four Courts Press, 2009).

Select Bibliography

Bacca Dowden, Mavis, *Spy-jacked!* (SMH Books, 1991)

Bailey, Rosemary, *Love And War In The Pyrenees: A Story Of Courage, Fear And Hope*, 1939–1944 (Weidenfeld & Nicolson, 2009)

Bles, Mark, *A Child at War: The True Story of Hortense Daman* (Warner, 1990)

Bowden, Ray, *The Flight of Eagles: USAAF Evasion in Occupied Europe: December 1943* (Independently published, 2020)

Bowman, Martin W., *RAF Escapers and Evaders in WWII: Voices in Flight* (Pen & Sword Aviation, 2015)

Braddon, Russell and Wake, Nancy, *World War Two's Most Rebellious Spy* (Little A, 2019)

Bradford-White, Francelle, *Andrée's War: How One Young Woman Outwitted the Nazis* (Elliott & Thompson Limited, 2014)

Buckmaster, Maurice, *They Fought Alone: The True Story of SOE's Agents in Wartime France* (Biteback Publishing, 2014)

Burns, Jimmy, *Papa Spy: Love, Faith, and Betrayal in Wartime Spain* (Bloomsbury Paperbacks, 2010)

Carr, Matthew, *Savage Frontier: The Pyrenees in History* (C Hurst & Co Publishers Ltd, 2018)

Christenson Janiszewski, Kathryn A., *Only One Returned* (Kathryn A. Janiszewski, 2008)

Clark, Alan and Foster, Steve, *The Soldier Who Came Back* (Mirror Books, 2019)

Clutton-Brock, Oliver, *RAF Evaders: The Complete Story of RAF Escapees and their Escape Lines, Western Europe, 1940–1945* (Grub Street Publishing, 2009)

Cobb, Matthew, *The Resistance: The French Fight Against the Nazis* (Simon & Schuster UK, 2010)

Cohen, Marthe and Holden, Wendy, *Behind Enemy Lines: The True Story of a French Jewish Spy in Nazi Germany* (Three Rivers Press, 2006)

Cooper, Alan W., *Free to Fight Again: RAF Escapes & Evasions, 1940–1945* (Pen & Sword Aviation, 2009)

Cosgrove, Edmund, *The Evaders* (Clarke, Irwin, 1970)

DeAngelis, Caitlin Galante, *The Caretakers: War Graves Gardeners and the Secret Battle to Rescue Allied Airmen in World War II* (Prometheus, 2024)

Derry, Sam, *The Rome Escape Line: The Story of the British Organization in Rome Assisting Escaped Prisoners-of-War in 1943–44* (Ironmonger Publishing, 2023)

Doherty, Richard, *Irish Men and Women in the Second World War* (Four Courts Press Ltd, 1999)

Doherty, Richard, *Irish Volunteers in the Second World War* (Four Courts Press Ltd, 2000)

Dormer, Hugh, *Hugh Dormer's Diaries* (Kessinger Publishing, 2010)

Dowding, Peter, *Secret Agent, Unsung Hero: The Valour of Bruce Dowding* (Pen & Sword Military, 2023)

Dumon, Andrée, *I Haven't Forgotten You, Freedom 1945* (Independently published, 2022)

Escott, Beryl E., *Mission Improbable: A Salute to the Royal Air Force Women of Special Operations Executive in Wartime France* (Patrick Stephens Ltd., 1991)

Escott, Beryl E., *The Heroines of SOE, Britain's Secret Women in France F Section* (The History Press, 2010)

Eisner, Peter, *The Freedom Line: The Brave Men and Women Who Rescued Allied Airmen from the Nazis During World War II* (Harper Perennial, 2013)

Etherington, William, *A Quiet Woman's War: The Story of Elsie Bell* (Mousehold Press, 2002)

Felton, Mark, *Zero Night: The Untold Story of World War Two's Greatest Escape* (SMP Trade, 2015)

Felton, Mark, *Castle of the Eagles: Escape from Mussolini's Colditz* (Icon Books, 2017)

Fleming, Brian, *The Vatican Pimpernel: The World War II Exploits of the Monsignor Who Saved Over 6,500 Lives* (Skyhorse, 2012)

Fleming, Brian, *Heroes in the Shadows: Humanitarian Action and Courage in the Second World War* (Amberley Publishing, 2019)

Fry, Helen, *MI9: A History of the Secret Service for Escape and Evasion in World War Two* (Yale University Press, 2020)

Gaffney, Phyllis, *Healing Amid the Ruins: The Irish Hospital at Saint-Lô, 1945–46* (A & A Farmar, 1999)

Garlinski, Jozef, *The Survival Of Love: Memoirs of a Resistance Officer* (Wiley Blackwell, 1991)

Genet-Rouffiac, Nathalie and Murphy, David (eds), *Franco-Irish Military Connections, 1590–1945* (Four Courts Press, 2009)

Gildea, Robert, *Fighters in the Shadows: A New History of the French Resistance* (Faber & Faber, 2015)

Goodall, Scott, *The Freedom Trail: Following One of the Hardest Wartime Escape Routes across the Central Pyrenees into Northern Spain* (Inchmere Design, 2005)

Grady, Stephen and Wright, Michael, *Gardens of Stone: My Boyhood in the French Resistance* (Hodder & Stoughton, 2013)

Greene Ottis, Sherri, *Silent Heroes: Downed Airmen and the French Underground* (The University Press of Kentucky, 2021)

Grunwald-Spier, Agnes, *The Other Schindlers: Why Some People Chose to Save Jews in the Holocaust* (The History Press, 2010)

Hackett, General Sir John, *I was a Stranger* (Pimlico, 1999)

Hall, Monty, *Escaping Hitler: Stories Of Courage And Endurance On The Freedom Trails* (Sidgwick & Jackson, 2017)

Harding, Stephen, *Escape from Paris: A True Story of Love and Resistance in Wartime France* (Hachette Books, 2021)

Harvey, Dan, *A Bloody Dawn: The Irish at D-Day* (Merrion Press, 2019)

Helm, Sarah, *A Life in Secrets: Vera Atkins and the Missing Agents of SOE* (Abacus, 2006)

Helm, Sarah, *If This Is A Woman: Inside Ravensbrück: Hitler's Concentration Camp for Women* (Abacus, 2016)

Hemingway-Douglass, Réanne and Douglass, Don, *The Shelburne Escape Line: Secret Rescues of Allied Aviators by the French Underground, the British Royal Navy & London's MI-9* (Pen & Sword Military, 2015)

Heminway, John, *In Full Flight: A story of Africa and Atonement* (Listening Library, 2018)

Hewitt, John, *Ireland's Aviator Heroes of World War II: Vol II* (Mercier Press, 2016)

Howarth, David, *We Die Alone* (Canongate, 2010)

Janes, Keith, *They came from Burgundy: A study of the Bourgogne Escape Line* (Troubador Publishing Ltd, 2017)

Janes, Keith, *Express Delivery: The Men Brought Back by the Shelburn Escape Line, and the People who Made it Possible* (Matador, 2019)

Jouan, Cecile, *Comète* (éditions du Beffroi, 1948)

Joy, Breda, *Hidden Kerry: The Keys to the Kingdom* (Mercier Press., 2016)

Kent, Stewart and Nicholas, Nick, *Agent Michael Trotobas and SOE in Northern France* (Pen & Sword Military, 2015)

Keogh, Niall, *Con Cremin: Ireland's Wartime Diplomat* (Mercier Press, 2006)

Knowlson, James, *Damned to Fame: The Life of Samuel Beckett* (Bloomsbury, 1996)

Koreman, Megan, *The Escape Line: How the Ordinary Heroes of Dutch-Paris Resisted the Nazi Occupation of Western Europe* (Oxford University Press, 2018)

Laxalt, Robert, *The Land of My Fathers: A Son's Return to the Basque Country* (University of Nevada Press, 2012)

Le Febvre, Marie, *Risking and Resisting: Discovering the Untold Story of My Family's Fight for Freedom in World War II* (Marie Le Febvre, 2015)

Léon, Alexia, Léon, Anna Maria & Crispi, Luca (eds), *James Joyce and Paul L. Léon: The Story of a Friendship Revisited* (Bloomsbury, 2022)

Lett, Gordon, *Rossano: Valley in Flames – An Adventure of the Italian Resistance* (Frontline Books, 2011)

Lewis, Damien, *The Flame of Resistance: American Beauty. French Hero. British Spy* (Quercus, 2022)

Long, Helen, *Safe Houses Are Dangerous* (HarperCollins Publishers, 1985)

Lougarot, Gisèle, *Dans l'ombre des passeurs* (ELKAR, 2004)

Lucas Harrison, Elizabeth, *Receipt For A Dead Canary* (Independently published, 2013)

Marks, Leo, *Between Silk and Cyanide: A Codemaker's War, 1941–1945* (Free Press, 1998)

Marnham, Patrick, *War in the Shadows: Resistance, Deception and Betrayal in Occupied France* (Oneworld Publications, 2020)

Marino, Andrew, *A Quiet American: The Secret War of Varian Fry* (St Martin's Press, 1999)

Martin, Gwyn, *Up and Under* (David Martin, 2013)

McConnon, Aili and McConnon, Andres, *Road to Valour: Gino Bartali: Tour de France Legend and Italy's Secret World War Two Hero* (Weidenfeld & Nicolson, 2013)

McGrath, Tom, *Unspoken: A Father's Wartime Escape. A Son's Family Discovered* (Gill Books, 2022)

McMenamin, Marc, *Codebreaker: The Untold Story of Richard Hayes, the Dublin Librarian who helped Turn the Tide of World War II* (Gill Books, 2018)

McMenamin, Marc, *Ireland's Secret War: Dan Bryan, G2 and the Lost Tapes that Reveal the Hunt for Ireland's Nazi Spies* (Gill Books, 2022)

Mellor, Gordon, *ETA: A Bomber Command Navigator Shot Down and on the Run* (Fighting High Publishing, 2016)

Miller, Donald L., *Masters of the Air: America's Bomber Boys Who Fought the Air War Against Nazi Germany* (Ebury Press, 2024)

Mulley, Clare, *The Spy Who Loved: the Secrets and Lives of one of Britain's Bravest Wartime Heroines* (Pan, 2013)

Muss, Fleming B., *The Spark and the Flame: The Saga of Wartime Sabotage in Denmark* (Museum Press Limited, 1953)

Nelson, June, *Auntie Pat's War* (Independently published, 2023)

Newby, Eric, *Love and War in the Appenines* (William Collins, 2010)

O'Donoghue, David, *Hitler's Irish Voices: The Story of German Radio's Wartime Irish Service* (Beyond the Pale Publications, 1998)

O'Hara, Aidan, *'I'll Live till I Die': The Story of Delia Murphy* (Drumlin Publications, 1997)

Ott, Sandra, *War, Judgment, And Memory In The Basque Borderlands, 1914–1945* (University of Nevada Press, 2008)

Ott, Sandra, *Living with the Enemy: German Occupation, Collaboration and Justice in the Western Pyrenees, 1940–1948* (Cambridge University Press, 2017)

Pape, Richard, *Boldness be my Friend* (Headline Review, 2008)

Pelly-Fry, James, *Heavenly Days: The Recollections of a Contented Airman* (Crecy Publishing, 1993)

Perrin, Nigel, *Spirit of Resistance: The Life of SOE Agent Harry Peuleve DSO MC* (Pen & Sword Military, 2014)

Pickering, William with Hart, Alan, *The Bandits of Cisterna* (Leo Cooper, 1991)

Portela, Edurne, *Maddi y las fronteras* (Galaxia Gutenberg, 2023)

Purnell, Sonia, *A Woman of No Importance: The Untold Story of Virginia Hall, WWII's Most Dangerous Spy* (Virago, 2020)

Resch, Synnestvedt, Alice, *Over The Highest Mountains: A Memoir*

Of Unexpected Heroism In France During World War II (Intentional Productions, 2005)

Ryan, Isadore, *No Way Out: The Irish in Wartime France, 1939–1945* (Mercier Press, 2017)

Sebba, Anne, *Les Parisiennes: Resistance, Collaboration, and the Women of Paris Under Nazi Occupation* (St Martin's Griffin, 2017)

Seymour-Jones, Carole, *She Landed By Moonlight: The Story of Secret Agent Pearl Witherington: the 'real Charlotte Gray'* (Hodder & Stoughton Ltd, 2013)

Shuff, Derek, *Evader: The Epic Story of the First British Airman to be Rescued by the Comète Escape Line in World War II* (Spellmount, 2010)

Simmons, Mark, *Ian Fleming and Operation Golden Eye: Keeping Spain out of World War II* (Casemate, 2018)

Smith, David Scott and Smith, Sydney Percival, *Lifting the Silence: A World War II RCAF Bomber Pilot Reunites with his Past* (Dundurn Press, 2010)

Smith, Michael, Foley: *The Spy Who Saved 10,000 Jews* (Biteback Publishing, 2016)

Spiller, H.J., *Ticket to Freedom* (William Kimber & Co Ltd, 1988)

Stokes, Peter, *No Ordinary Life* (FeedARead.com, 2013)

Stourton, Edward, *Cruel Crossing: Escaping Hitler Across the Pyrenees* (Doubleday, 2013)

Strauss, Gwen, *The Nine: How a Band of Daring Resistance Women Escaped from Nazi Germany* (Manilla Press, 2022)

Tartière, Drue, *The House Near Paris: An American Woman's Story of Traffic in Patriots* (Simon and Schuster, 1946)

Téllez Solá, Antonio, *The Anarchist Pimpernel: Francisco Ponzan Vidal (1936–1944): The Anarchists in the Spanish Civil War and the Escape Networks in World War II* (Christie Books, 2012)

Travers, Patrick, 'Some Experiences during the War Years: the Irish College in Paris 1939–1945', *Colloque*, No. 18, Autumn 1988, pp. 440–57.

Turner, Dennis J., *What Did You Do In The War, Sister?: Catholic Sisters in the WWII Nazi Resistance* (Dennis J. Turner, 2020)

Ui Chionna, Jackie, *Queen of Codes, The Secret Life of Emily Anderson, Britain's Greatest Female Code Breaker* (Headline, 2023)

Vanderstok, Bram, *Escape from Stalag Luft III: The True Story of My Successful Great Escape: The Memoir of Bob Vanderstok* (Greenhill Books, 2019)

Vigurs, Kate, *Mission France: The True History of the Women of SOE* (Yale University Press, 2021)

Watt, George, *The Comet Connection: Escape from Hitler's Europe* (University Press of Kentucky, 2014)

Walters, Anne-Marie, *Moondrop to Gascony* (Moho Books, 2009)

Walters, Guy, *Real Great Escape* (Bantam, 2014)

Weber, Ronald, *The Lisbon Route: Entry and Escape in Nazi Europe* (Ivan R. Dee, Inc., 2011)

White, Rowland, *Mosquito: The RAF's Legendary Wooden Wonder and its Most Extraordinary Mission* (Bantam, 2023)

Acknowledgements

Resistance work is, by its very nature, secret. The Irish people who sent intelligence to the Allies, parachuted behind enemy lines or harboured fugitives during World War II covered their tracks. Their lives depended on it. They worked in the shadows and very often they wanted to stay there. Writing about such people, then, poses an obvious difficulty: how do you coax them out of hiding?

Dr David Murphy, a military historian at Maynooth University, began that slow, methodical work two decades ago. He published his findings in a seminal chapter in *Franco-Irish Military Connections, 1590–1945* (Four Courts Press, 2009). It was a ground-breaking piece of research that revealed the names of some 50 Irish people who had contributed to the Resistance in France in some form or another.

We are deeply indebted to David for his help with this book and his pioneering work in helping to bring Irish *résistants* out of the shadows.

In recent years, the war experiences of more Irish people have come to light with the release of unclassified documents in archives, the discovery of new material and the publication of family memoirs.

We have drawn on all of these sources, along with witness statements, interviews, letters, newspaper articles and servicemen's escape reports to piece together a narrative of the Irish people who took action all over occupied Europe, and beyond, to try to defeat the Nazis. Undoubtedly, there were many others, and we hope this book will help to unearth more forgotten Irish *résistants*.

None of it would have been possible without Gill Books and the patient support of Teresa Daly, Isabelle Hanrahan, Iollann Ó Murchú, Kristin Olson and Noel O'Regan.

Many family members, historians and experts in their field gave us invaluable help. We are deeply indebted to all of them and each one is acknowledged in the endnotes for each chapter.

Thank you to the Escape Lines Memorial Society and particularly to the Basque Pyrenees Freedom Trails' Association for their support. Our special thanks also to the inestimable Andrée 'Nadine' Dumon, who sheltered the memory of her friend, Catherine Crean, and which in many ways was the springboard for this book.

We are indebted to several family members who gave us access to their personal archives of documents and photographs. They include Mark and Leah Leslie, Christopher Massy-Beresford, Shane Ross, John Alvey, Jamie O'Shaughnessy, Doug Armstrong, Dorothy Seagrave, Thomas Bolger and Conal O'Donnell.

A special thank you to Mary G. O'Sullivan, and to Ronan McGreevy for his research on Robert Armstrong. Thank you, too, to Dr Jackie Uí Chionna, Leo and Carole Cullen, Michael LeBlanc, Tom McGrath, Keith Janes, Isadore Ryan, John Clinch, Ronald Friend, Tony McGrath and Roger Stanton for their help with documents, books, photographs and/or insights. A very big thank you is also due to the archivists whose work safeguarding and cataloguing the collections we consulted is invaluable.

One of the best pieces of writing advice we received was 'keep going', and there were so many people who helped us to do that.

A huge thank you to all the Finns: Nuala and Ciara, and to Claire and Brendan for the writing bolthole. A special shout-out to all the Finnolans too, and those who read drafts, checked details and provided endless support. A very big thank you to Mary Quirke, Deirdre Trant, Angela Crowley, Karine Bigand, Vickie Maye, Maurice Maye, Rowena Walsh, Ciaran Walsh, Walt Kilroy, Margaret Doody, Sarah Ranouf, Niamh and Cliona Graham, Aideen Sherry, Conal Sherry, Grainne Cunningham, Margaret Jennings, Bob and Dorothy Smith, Marguerite Moran, Anne O'Connell, Medbh Boyle, Michelle Byrne, Siofra Pierse, Emer O'Beirne, Claire Kerr, Kay Gilliland, Irene Feighan and Eibhlís and Jay Carcione. And a special thank you to Douglas Smith.

A huge thanks to the Morgan and O'Reilly families for much more than can be recorded here: Eileen, Eamonn, Joseph, Ann, Myles, Ciaran, Brendan, Eamonn Jnr, Francine, Seamus, Dermot and Dympna. In special memory of the late Peter Morgan. Thank you also to Joseph, Cristina and Sinead Linehan, Alan and Rosie Traynor, Colin Babe, Kim Clark, Seamus and Sile Fitzpatrick, Declan Martin, Majella Fitzpatrick, Stuart Brady, Andrew Clarke, Robert Browne, Hugh Donovan and Jeremy Pearcy.